Joseph Wore Tennis Shoes: Stories From Small Town Journalism

Dale Kovar

ISBN 979-8-9923274-0-3 (paperback)

First publication: January 2025

Material from various newspapers and associated titles reprinted with
permission from Herald Journal Publishing, Inc.
Material from Redwood Gazette reprinted with permission from
CherryRoad Media.

Dedication

This book is dedicated to the following, not necessarily in order of importance:

• my wife, Linda, who kept her vows of "for better or worse."

• my business partner, Chris Schultz, who did the heavy lifting while letting me keep a hand on the steering wheel.

• Jesus Christ, who took the nails for me.

Contents

Foreword

By Tim Lammers

DirectConversations.com

former editor of the Howard Lake Herald

I was honored when Dale Kovar asked me to write the foreword for *Joseph Wore Tennis Shoes*. Simply put, had Dale not had the foresight to give this dopey writer from Waverly, Minn., a chance to write for the Howard Lake Herald about 35 years ago, my life would be dramatically different.

I was working at the U.S. Bankruptcy Court in Minneapolis out of college in the late 1980s and writing two-line movie reviews for a court newsletter when a co-worker of mine suggested that I check with my local newspaper about publishing reviews there. As such, I popped a letter in the mail (remember when we used to write letters?) with some clips and Dale – the general manager at Winsted Publishing – replied that the work was impressive as something you'd see in a daily newspaper and offered me $5 per column. Though I've never had a million dollars in my life, I can tell you with certainty that getting paid $5 to write about movies made me feel like a millionaire.

Before too long, the Herald's editor, Mikkel Kelly, took on a job at another newspaper and Dale offered me the chance to replace him. Naturally, I leaped at the opportunity and thus my baptism by fire as a newspaper editor began. Luckily, Dale's expert guidance helped me foster my talents as a writer and learn about the layout and design of the newspaper. He also taught me how to use the darkroom to develop photos – something that's become somewhat of a lost art in the digital age.

Over the years I've been fortunate to work with some of the greatest talents in Minnesota's media history in radio and television like Bill Carlson, Tom Barnard, Paul Douglas, Jordana Green, Adam Carter, and Diana Pierce, but when it comes to newspaper, Dale is the guy.

For someone working at a newspaper for the first time, Dale was very patient with me as I learned the ropes. Since I was still in my 20s, I was no doubt a pain in the ass at times, but it didn't deter Dale from bringing out the best in me. Today, I'm a Forbes.com contributor and without question, Dale's guidance at the Herald laid the foundation for what would become an amazing career.

If there's anything that sticks in my mind about working with Dale, it is his simple philosophy that he'd impart every time I would get writer's block. Dale would simply say, "Tell the truth." That ideal – an ideal that's simply become lost in journalism in recent years – would immediately loosen the logjam and help me finish the writing task at hand.

So, I can tell you with certainty that what you're about to read in *Joseph Wore Tennis Shoes* is the truth. Dale is and has always been an honest Joe, and you can't ask for a better person to be a mentor in the crazy, ever-changing world of journalism.

As such, please know what you're about to read is the truth … mostly. After all, Dale has been known to embellish things a wee bit when pulling his April Fools' Day pranks, which you'll be delighted to read about in this book.

This page is NOT intentionally left blank.

Page 1 over there needs to be on a right-hand page to be placed correctly in a book layout, so this is just to keep you entertained until we get to the beginning . . . Hang on, we're almost there . . . okay . . . NOW! Go to the next page.

Introduction

First, I'd like to tell you what this book is not.

• It is not meant to be a full life story of an autobiography. There is a lot of personal stuff, but it's primarily about my work and writing. I hope you'll enjoy the articles about other people and topics that are included.

• it is not a documentary or comprehensive historical record.

• it is not a "how-to." I'll touch on some lessons learned, and someone interested in journalism – or what's left of it – may pick up some pointers, but this is not a textbook.

Instead, think of it as a newspaper itself. There is a mix of news articles, feature stories, and opinion pieces reprinted from throughout my weekly newspaper career. They are included because it's my book and I thought they were interesting or important. Everything is my writing unless noted.

I'll let the original articles tell their own stories, and fill in some background before or after. Some are slightly shortened where it doesn't affect the story, and what is reprinted remains intact with only negligible editing. The book is generally chronological but certain articles are grouped by topic so the timeline does jump around a bit.

To help keep things straight, reprinted newspaper items are in a different font and narrower columns than the main text.

Joseph

One time while taking pictures at a Holy Trinity Grade School Christmas program in Winsted, it hit me. There was both the simplicity and routineness of it, and at the same time, the scene signified the spirit and values of small-town life.

Students were portraying the night of Jesus's birth in the manger. There weren't elaborate props. The kids had makeshift costumes over their regular clothes, while reciting the greatest story ever told.

I had the fleeting thought: "If I ever write a book about newspaper work, I'll have to call it *Joseph Wore Tennis Shoes.*"

More than 40 years later, one morning before getting out of bed, it popped into my head: what if I write a book? My mom had done a book about stories of her youth. My uncle had put together several books with collections of his newspaper column writings. Am I that old that I should do one too while there's time left? I guess the answer was yes.

And what should it be titled? At first, I was going with *I Couldn't Think of Anything Else To Do* which was how I sometimes answered the question "How did you get into journalism?"

Then I recalled that Christmas program of 1981 and there was no doubt. So here is: *Joseph Wore Tennis Shoes.*

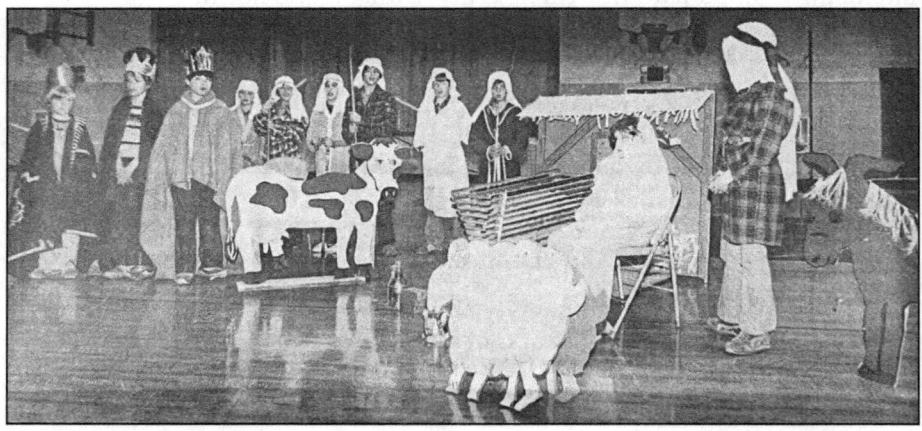

Dec. 17, 1981 • Winsted Journal
Holy Trinity Grade School Christmas program: Wise men are Matt Littfin, Guy Pariseau, and Bruce Koch; shepherds are Mike Henkel, Matt Hertel, Gerald Fasching, Roger Knott, Bill Guggemos, and Paul Karels; Mary and Joseph are played by Holly Holets and James Hausladen.

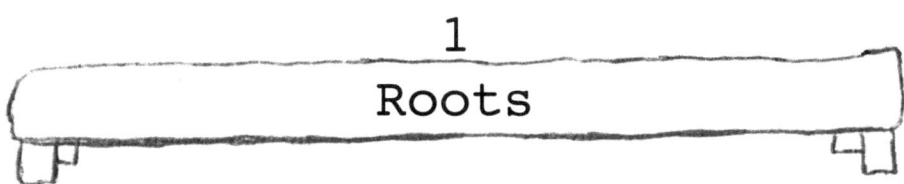

1
Roots

To tell a good story, let's start near the end. This column from when Herald Journal Publishing took over the Glencoe and Arlington papers tells a lot of local newspaper background.

McLeod County newspaper history: roots start in Lester Prairie
Nov. 3, 2023 • Herald Journal/McLeod County Chronicle/Senior Connections

As Herald Journal Publishing recently acquired the McLeod County Chronicle and Arlington Enterprise, here's a look back at tracing the roots of local newspaper history.

Interestingly, all roads lead back to Lester Prairie.

A Lester Prairie Journal began in 1895. In January 1901, a competing Lester Prairie News started, and then took over the Journal that summer.

Nearby, the People's Advocate started in Howard Lake in 1878, changing its name to the Howard Lake Herald in 1881.

The Winsted Examiner began in 1910, then becoming the Western Immigrant before going out of business. The Winsted Journal was formed in 1919.

Also in the area, the Glencoe Enterprise began in 1880, the Brownton Bulletin in 1892, Stewart Tribune in 1895, and Silver Lake Leader in 1901.

As the small communities were much more self-contained for decades with locally owned businesses up and down the main streets, the local newspapers carried out their roles independently.

Neighboring newspapers weren't really competitors. It wasn't unusual for them to help each other out if a press broke down or a key employee was out for an extended time.

If anything, their focus was encouraging a shop-at-home mentality rather than having people get in their automobiles and travel to a larger town to save 14 cents on toilet paper.

In the 1960s, a new printing technology known as "offset" came to the area. It involved essentially creating each page on a type of paper, then reproducing it onto a negative and plate to be printed on a large high-speed press.

Rather than each publisher operating his own small printing press, a "central plant" – Crow River Press in Hutchinson – was formed, with a large capacity press that could serve newspapers from several counties around.

In 1980, the local newspaper landscape began to change significantly.

In December, William McGarry purchased the Lester Prairie News from

Lew Buss, moved it to Glencoe, and re-named it the McLeod County Chronicle. Rather than starting new, this allowed it to maintain status as a publication quali-fied to print public notices and compete with the Glencoe Enterprise.

At the same time, Winsted Journal owners Floyd and JoAnn Sneer began a newspaper titled the Lester Prairie Jour-nal. I was part of their six-person staff for that undertaking.

Also at the same time, Buss began a free-distribution paper named the Prairie Ad-News.

This series of moves established com-peting publications in both Glencoe and Lester Prairie.

Local newspapering was at its prime then. Slowly, more consolidation and technology advancements began to change the industry.

In 1983, the Sneers purchased the Howard Lake Herald to add to their business, then selling the group to Bill Ramige in 1986 who had taken over the Chronicle from McGarry.

The Winsted and Lester Prairie pa-pers were merged in 1991, unfortunately timed that the first combined issue was done during the Halloween Blizzard.

That week, we left the office Thurs-day after work, took the kids trick-or-treating in several inches of snow, and didn't make it back to put the paper to-gether until Sunday afternoon.

In 2001, Lester Prairie native Chris Schultz and I purchased the W-LP-HL group from Ramige, choosing the obvi-ous name of Herald Journal Publishing.

In 2002, we acquired the Ad-News and merged it into the Winsted-Lester Prairie Journal.

Those papers went through a few more name changes such as the Winst-ed-Lester Prairie-New Germany Journal, and later the Winsted-Lester Prairie-New Germany Herald Journal. Quite a mouth-ful, huh?

The culture of our local communities was shifting fast and this thing called the Internet really changed the game. People no longer lived, worked, worshiped, at-tended school, and shopped primarily in one town. It was a transportation free-for-all.

Schools were going through various consolidations as were many other lines of business. In many cases, businesses were no longer locally owned, if they existed at all.

Recognizing that many readers knew and were interested in people from other nearby towns, the Winsted-Lester Prai-rie-New Germany Herald Journal and the Howard Lake-Waverly-Montrose Herald Journal were combined in 2005 to simply become Herald Journal.

Having now combined three news-papers into one, HJ went on to buy the Dassel-Cokato Enterprise Dispatch lat-er in 2005 and start the Delano Herald Journal from scratch in 2006 – back to three newspapers.

Meanwhile, the consolidation trends continued among our neighbors as well.

The Brownton Bulletin and Stewart Tribune became one paper, which was later merged into the McLeod County Chronicle as were the Silver Lake Lead-er and the Glencoe Enterprise.

Now we take another step, not in con-solidating publications, but in common ownership as Herald Journal Publishing expands to Glencoe and Arlington.

For the record, Chris Schultz took over my ownership interests a couple years ago. We remain committed to local news, both online and in traditional print, and carrying on the newspapers' vital functions of recording and preserving history through news coverage, public notices, and preserving bound volumes of past issues.

Personal connections

My newspaper ties go back to writ-ing a sports column for the Silver Lake Leader while in high school. At the end of the year, Wilbert Merrill gave me a

$20 bill, which seemed like an outrageous windfall.

My mother, Mildred Kovar, also did some submissions for the Leader, and then transitioned from factory work to a reporter job at the Hutchinson Leader where she was known as "The Country Girl."

Also, there may not be too many readers left who remember that my uncle Milton Hakel owned and operated the Brownton Bulletin in the 1940s. Another uncle, Milt's brother Art, also wrote some columns for the Bulletin.

And not to be outdone, my son, Kip, is the sports editor for Herald Journal.

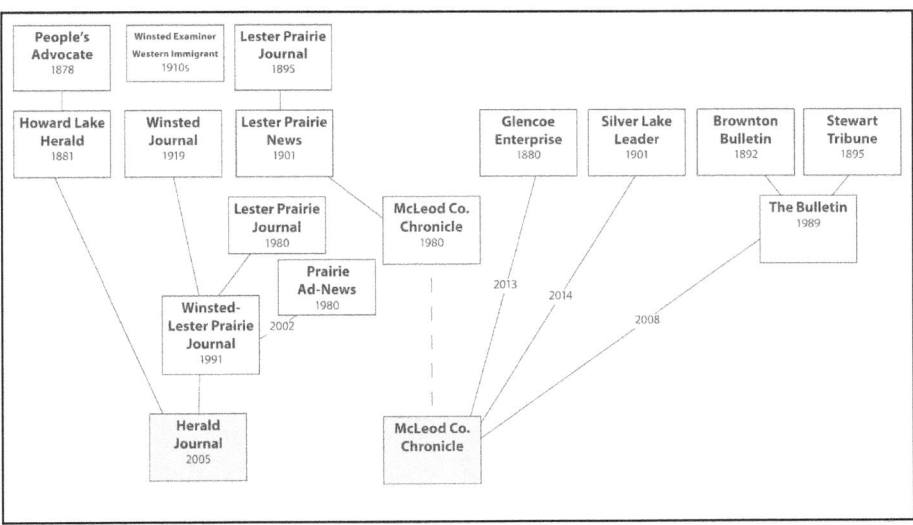

2
My Backstory

Fall of 1974: it was my senior year at Silver Lake High School. We had just finished a successful football season with an 8-1 record.

My father, Edwin, was a World War II veteran. He had been in poor health from malaria and the trauma of war during my entire life. In July, while I pitched a rare victory for our Legion baseball team, he suffered a stroke and was taken to the hospital. He never returned home.

Dad passed away Nov. 6, a day after his 65th birthday. That same day, I received a letter in the mail announcing my acceptance at Willmar Community College. That weekend was the high school play, in which I had one of the lead roles.

So within that week, my dad died on Wednesday, the play was on Friday, the funeral on Sunday, and I had a speaking part at the Veterans Day program on Monday.

Shortly after that, it was time for basketball season to begin, and as an immature 17-year-old in turmoil, I told Coach Larry Starks I wouldn't be playing because I refused to get my hair cut.

Advice to young people: don't give up your seasons of eligibility for foolish reasons. You'll never get that chance back again.

When things settled down, I was looking for something to do. I wrote a letter (because I was too shy to ask) to Wilbert Merrill asking if I could write a weekly sports column in the Silver Lake Leader. I don't know why, but I also asked if I could use a pen name. He said yes to both requests.

In January, the first "Off The Bench" by R. T. Johnson appeared in the Leader, and here it is:

Off the Bench

Jan. 9, 1975 • Silver Lake Leader

Greetings, everyone! This is the first of what I hope will become a weekly feature of this newspaper.

I will try to concern myself with athletics in general, Silver Lake in particular. And, of course, you will find several predictions each week telling you exactly how upcoming games will result.

Silver Lake's basketball team is off to its best start since the 1969-70 season with a 3-4 record at the holiday break. 3 and 4 may not sound too impressive but for a team that won only four games in the last three years, it's a good start for a respectable season.

Looking at those four losses, one cannot complain about losing to Renville. And losing to the hustling Bird Island team is something many teams will do this year. (However, I'm sure I'm not alone in feeling that Bird Island would never have beaten the Lakeites in a football playoff, right?)

A while ago, the Lakeites dropped a close one to Arlington – a game which they should have won handily. Silver Lake is an improved team which still has a long way to go. As I see it, this may be a parallel to the football team. Last year's football team won four games after several poor seasons, followed by a conference championship this year.

This may be the mediocre year in basketball which separates the bad and good years. It's just a matter of getting in the winning habit. Certainly with all the experienced underclassmen (mostly juniors) and a "B" team full of potential, next year's squad will surpass this year's record by several victories.

In effect, what I'm saying is that Silver Lake basketball is on the rise now but won't peak until next year.

Meanwhile on the wrestling mats, the Lakeites have a 1-3 dual meet record. Lack of numbers seems to be the big problem. It's tough to win working against a forfeit or two, and having some wrestlers in a weight class other than their best just to fill out the lineup. Without a balanced set of grapplers, a winning season is not too likely.

The Lakeites do have some fine matmen and I'm not knocking them – just pointing out that winning three or four matches does not win a meet.

HOT SHOTS: Like 'em or not, here are my predictions:

WRESTLING: Thursday: Silver Lake is good enough to edge Stewart. Lester Prairie is no match for the tough Cosmos team. Brownton at Buffalo Lake is a toss-up – I'll call Buffalo Lake. Maynard's only chance of beating Sacred Heart is right here. Hector can't beat Bird Island at wrestling either. Renville may be one match better than Danube.

Friday: Hutch has a fine team – no trouble with Shakopee. Glencoe will squeak by Buffalo. Monday: Brownton's returning lettermen are too much for Silver Lake to handle. Tuesday: Hutch wins again, this time over Eden Prairie. Now it's Glencoe's turn to beat up on Shakopee.

BASKETBALL: Friday: Silver Lake is good enough to beat Cosmos by 10. Buffalo Lake does not have to worry about playing Stewart – Lakers by 24. Lester Prairie's hustle gives them 9 points over Brownton. Hector will lose to Renville by a modest 30. Danube can take Maynard by 4. Sacred Heart should stay home – Bird Island by 25. Hutch has the teamwork to drop Shakopee by 12. Buffalo is the cream of the Suburban West crop – over Glencoe by 20.

Tuesday: Silver Lake again by 10, over Stewart. Cosmos's height loses 5 points to Lester quickness. Buffalo Lake remains undefeated downing Brownton by 15. Renville at Danube – can the

Hawks stay within 40? Sacred Heart is 12 points better than Maynard. Hutch and Glencoe over Eden Prairie and Shakopee respectively by a dozen. There is no way Winsted can beat Prinsburg.

NOTE TO READERS: Check all these predictions out. If I don't get at least half of them right, I'll eat my electric typewriter.

R. T. didn't stand for anything. The pseudonym was meant to be unidentifiable in a community filled with Polish and Bohemian names ending with "ski." How about Johnson?

Teacher/coach Buz Rumrill was quick to figure it out – a kid who was going to college for journalism and knew about SLHS sports. It didn't take that much to put the pieces together, and I acknowledged my identity in a column a short time later. After all, it was one of Buz's classes in which I turned in this essay about future plans:

After high school
1974 • class assignment

If it were possible to take a survey of newspapermen, it would be interesting to learn at what point in their lives, each made the decision to be part of that profession. So many small children aspire to become a fireman, a policeman, or a doctor when they grow up, but you seldom hear of any wanting to become an editor or publisher.

Those who do make the decision to become newspapermen usually stay with it their whole adult life. This must mean that they find it a very rewarding profession. At the same time, it must be very frustrating to find your creative masterpieces used in a day to wrap the garbage or to train the puppy.

Why have I chosen the media as my profession and my future? I may have been influenced by the fact that I have two uncles associated with the news media. One started as an apprentice with the Silver Lake Leader, going on to edit and publish the Brownton Bulletin for years. Today he is Director of Research for the Farmers Union and editor of the Minnesota Agriculturist which is the voice of the Farmers Union.

The other got into the news field quite accidentally. After four years at Macalester College in St. Paul, he was unable to find a teaching job and accepted an invitation to go to California where he landed a small position on the staff of the Oakland Tribune. It is a tribute to his intelligence and ability that without any special training in the field, he was able to gain one promotion after another until he became the head of the newspaper's library. In addition, he writes a daily column which appears in the Oakland Tribune and once was seriously considered for national syndication.

I hope someday to have the chance to spend some time on the staff of a small town newspaper and to learn by experience just what it entails. But even before that can happen, I will need some kind of further education in regard to the media. Such training is offered in many areas. Colleges, universities, vocational schools, and some junior colleges offer such courses. If I don't change my mind during the course of my senior year, I plan to attend Willmar Junior College and major in journalism.

While I was writing "Off the Bench" columns in Silver Lake, George Derringer was the sports editor for the Hutchinson Leader. In his column, he would make some predictions of high school sports results in the area, and I took him on with some of my own. That spring, when he covered my high school baseball and track events (it was a small enough school that we could be in both sports during the same season) he got photos of me in action.

Over time, we developed a playful banter between us in our respective columns, and I credit George as being my first highly influential person in working for newspapers.

The journalism program at Willmar CC was so-so. We had a small student newspaper for which I mainly did sports. My girlfriend/future wife, Linda Kosek, drew a column heading for me (see the dedication page), now changed to "On The Bench."

I got actual newspaper experience with a part-time job in the sports department of the daily West Central Tribune. Steve Palmer was the sports editor. On Friday nights, the crew included Bruce Strand, Fritz Busch, Rand Middleton, and me, who would work the phones to get brief summaries of each high school game to run in the next morning's paper. Having come from a 212 Conference school, that became my beat. It was by landline so we had to wait for coaches to get home late from away games to reach them.

In the summer between my college years, the Hutchinson Leader had a vacancy and I was able to fill the hole for about a month. When a permanent replacement was secured, I received a termination notice.

Newspaper Skills Course

As I was graduating from Willmar, the timing was perfect in that the Minnesota Newspaper Association (MNA) was conducting its Newspaper Skills Course to develop more people to work for newspapers. It was an intense program based at the vo-tech school in Anoka.

The instructor was J. Brent Norlem, a professor from St. Cloud State who taught with the fire of a drill sergeant. He was loud and demanding, and knew journalism inside and out. Brent was unrelenting in insisting that everything was not just accurate but perfect. If there was the smallest error of fact in any assignment, it was graded 'F,' no matter how brilliant the rest of it was.

The course lasted four weeks of full-time days, plus homework. Sixteen students, several of whom already worked for local newspapers, made it through and then were turned loose on the world.

Credit to Brent and MNA Manager Bob Shaw as my other big influences. I often said I "blame" them for getting me going.

My first job interview was with the St. Charles Press in southeastern Minnesota. Since it was on press day, it began by having me spend half an hour in the mailroom putting inserts into that week's paper. Despite my having helped get the paper out, a skills course classmate of mine got the job.

1977 MNA Newspaper Skills Course students: front – Sanda Horeis (Delano), Susan Pauls, Joe Twohy; middle – Katherine Cross, Caroline Iammatteo, Debra Rosckes (Watertown), Janet Mildenberg; back – instructor J. Brent Norlem, Ruth Dunn, Rosemary Klein, David Mildenberg, Steve Carlson, Dale Kovar, David Ruble, Lois Anderson, Sandra Churchill, Maxine Gohman (Maple Lake).

3
Redwood Falls

Instead, I was hired as a regional reporter and to cover girls sports at the twice-weekly Redwood Gazette in Redwood Falls, owned by Scott Schoen and John Schneider.

Schoen was a widely respected editorial writer. When I was introduced to him – he was about 70 and I was 19 going on 20 – after a brief greeting, Schoen seemed to take delight in pointing out that I misspelled "Hennipen" on my resume. Brent Norlem would have been disappointed in me.

Schneider was a language expert. I recall him making a point in the newspaper telling people not to go to a certain event because the press release said "there is no admission." Of course, the intended meaning was there was no admission charge. There's a difference.

One of my first assignments was to cover the Seaforth Polka Fest. Following the basic approach of getting as close to your subject as reasonably possible, among my photos was a close-up of the priest conducting a polka mass.

But John taught me a different lesson: "That photo could have been taken in our parking lot," he gruffed. "It doesn't say 'Seaforth.'" Sometimes the context of showing an overall scene is more valuable than a detailed close-up.

Sales rep Lenn "Manny" Zempel took me in for a couple weeks until I secured an apartment of my own. Lee Sundermayer was a master photographer at getting creative, stunning photos at unique angles. Lee advised me in choosing my first single-lens reflex Minolta camera that I wore strapped on my shoulder for many years.

Manny, Lee, and News Editor Barb Ross were in their mid-20s. I constantly teased them, calling them "tottering geeks."

Often, the four of us and perhaps a couple others would go out for lunch on Fridays at Donavon's. On the way back, we'd drive through the city's scenic Ramsey Park making note of the hairpin curve and swayback bridge. This wasn't one of those fluffy team-building exercises. We just hung out as friends.

The regional part of my job took me to the small towns around the area – Belview, Seaforth, Vesta, Lucan, Wanda, Milroy, Wabasso, Walnut Grove, Lamberton, Sanborn, Morgan, Franklin, and Morton. Some of them had small independent papers of their own; the really little ones didn't. I sometimes got a polite greeting but with a skeptical eye from the local publisher when at an event in his town.

Love Story

I got my first ride in a small aircraft when pilot Eugene Swoboda noticed what an area farmer had done and took me up to capture the scene.

A July 1978 hailstorm had destroyed Renville farmer Tom Breitkreutz's bean crop so he plowed large letters into the field "I LOVE LOIS." His wife of two-plus years, the unsuspecting object of affection, didn't even know about it until the newspaper called asking for details. The crop damage was so extensive that "There was nothing else to do with it," Tom said.

It was such a sweet love story that even the Minneapolis Tribune picked it up and ran my aerial photo.

July 1978 • Redwood Gazette

Elroy

The treatment center Project Turnabout at Granite Falls arranged for me to tell Elroy Jones' story, which was done as a first-person account.

For 'higher class' tramp, it started with home brew

Dec. 8, 1977 • Redwood Gazette

By Elroy Jones
as told to Dale Kovar

I applied for a job in St. Louis. They wanted to know my background and I told them I was a "one-time loser." They didn't hire me. I, Elroy Jones, was an alcoholic.

I was born east of Redwood Falls in Paxton Township on Oct. 1, 1914, and started school at about age eight, but I skipped a few grades and by age 13, I had completed eighth grade at District 6 country school of Redwood Falls.

Since I was about 11 years old, I had this idea in my head. I heard about the west coast and wanted to get there. All the snow-capped mountains, trout streams – a land of adventures! This is what I wanted to do and I thought I was a big man already at that age.

I was doing all right in school and probably should have kept it up but I wanted to be out in the country – moving on and seeing things.

My father was killed in World War I. We got a pension because of that so in that way we were lucky, I guess. My mom raised me right but I was the so-called "black sheep" of the family. My mother was a very religious person and we went to church whether I wanted to or not.

When I was 13, I hopped my first freight train to Minneapolis and hitch-hiked back. My mother tried everything to get me back in school. I went for a few more months and then dropped out for good.

I was 14 when I took my first drink. That was some home brew we made out of Pabst Blue Ribbon, potato peelings, rice, and some other stuff.

We made a five-gallon crock of that stuff. We'd let it sit a week and when it stopped settling, we'd bottle it. As I was bottling it, I took some samples.

The next year I got some moonshine. That was real alcohol – the real stuff with brownish color and all. People used to peddle that at night, under the moon, and that's where the name came from. Later, I got beer and that, but I was still too young to drink.

When I was about 24 or 25, I'd go to Fairfax and get four or five quart bottles. Everybody would look at me but I didn't care.

At that time, they couldn't sell beer or liquor to Indians so I had to put up a little bluff. The man asked me if I was Indian and I said, "What the hell do you mean, Indian? I'm no Indian!"

And he said, "Oh, I'm sorry. Sorry." And he gave it to me. I had to bluff like that to get by. But now when I think of it, that was bad. He could have gotten into a lot of trouble.

Around then I was starting to ride the trains. I'd make some "practice trips" from Morton to Pipestone and back. I'd do some field work for farmers around Pipestone.

Well, I knew I was supposed to go someplace so I took off. In Grand Forks, I made $700 doing harvesting and that all went down the hatch. Down the old hatch.

I almost got married once, too. I went with a woman about eight months but we broke up. I wanted to move around, this and that, and finally ended up thinking "the hell with her."

So I got out to the west coast through Idaho, Spokane, and Seattle. I did some pea harvesting in Walla Walla for the Green Giant Company. Then I went down to Mexico and El Paso.

Somehow I always knew where I was gonna go. I'd find an older hobo – one that knew the territory – and he'd tell me where to look for a job. He'd tell me everything and when I got there, I'd know exactly what to do.

That's the way I traveled. I wouldn't hurt nobody, and nobody would hurt me, either.

When I'd want to get on a train, I'd lie flat in the weeds until I'd hear the conductor yell "All aboard!" Then I'd run like hell and clamp on. Once I missed and I just lay there looking at those big wheels. I could have been killed, but I went after the next one anyway.

I went through Los Angeles and Phoenix and Tucson but there was nothing there for me. Never worried if I had a bedroom or not. I'd just sleep in a boxcar. I never did like California for some reason. Too many people, I guess. No matter what I wanted to do, everybody was in the way.

In Tucson, the cops picked a bunch of us up and threw us in jail. Then they made us clean the streets for nothing. We got outta there.

All this time I had been drinking heavily. I went to Little Rock but there wasn't much there, either. Except I sold some of my blood for $10 a pint. I used the money to buy more wine to build the blood back up again.

I was passing out regularly in my 30s. Later, I started having blackouts where I'd walk around, talk to people and get in drunken fights without ever knowing a thing about it.

Eventually, I got back to Minnesota but I was a fool yet. Just as fast as I made any money, I blew it. Mostly on wine, whiskey whenever I could afford it.

In '56, I got drunk with a couple other guys, one of them a juvenile. I passed out in the back of a car between Redwood Falls and Morton. When I woke up, I knew it was a hot car and I thought: "What the heck am I into now?" I got the rap for that and spent about three years in St. Cloud on parole.

Then I went and worked for Goodwill Industries in Minneapolis for awhile. But I was full of self-pity and went on the road again – Spokane, Seattle, Portland, L.A., Phoenix, Tucson, El Paso, San Antonio, Little Rock, Memphis. Yeah, I used to think I knew it all. All I cared about was my freedom and my booze.

Once in Billings, I ran into some tramps like myself and they asked me if I knew what 1,000-mile paper was. Well, I didn't, so one guy showed me. It was a kind of tarpaper with two layers of actual paper and some kind of tar between them. You'd wrap yourself up in that and it could be 15 degrees below and you'd never be cold. I slept all the way to Willmar in that.

Sometimes on the road a few hobos would "jungle up." That meant getting together to gather scraps and making a big meal for all of us. I used to carry a small jar of instant coffee and we'd use a "gunboat" to make that. Gunboat was hobo talk for any old gallon can or whatever we could find that would work.

If it was dirty, we'd hold it upside down over the fire and burn it clean before we used it. We were the clean variety.

There's two types of tramps, you know, and I was the higher class kind. I was a hobo – halfway decent, clean, trying to get a job. Then there were the lobos. They would steal or do anything. They were the real skid-row bums.

Everyone I met was a drinker. Someone always had a bottle. They'd drink anything with alcohol in it – shaving lotion, Listerine, hair oil. I saw guys go blind from drinking the wrong kind of rubbing alcohol. The only thing I tried once was some Canned Heat and that was awful.

The older hobos told me lots of other stuff, too. Like, they said to always find a two-by-four or iron pipe about three feet long. If someone came after me, that was my protection. They said "Kill them or they'll kill you."

I always had it with me, but I never had to use it and I'm glad of that.

In '63, I went to Willmar State Hospital on my own. I stayed there a couple months and then was dry for a month and a half doing odd jobs in the cities. But then I got a job as a spray painter. Seventy-five bucks a week and I drank that all up. Then it was off to the west coast again.

I came back to the Willmar hospital in February of '65. Not 'cause I wanted to quit drinking but I needed a warm place to sleep. After two months, I went back to the west coast again.

Then in '72, I let it all in. I woke up in Willmar State Hospital, and this time I was there by court order. They didn't tell me how long I had to stay and they all kinda laughed at me.

So then I took inventory. I told myself "You're getting too old for this kinda crap. You can't handle it anymore. If you don't stop, it will kill you or put you in the nuthouse."

A fella from Willmar interviewed me and wanted to know if I was really sincere about my thoughts of sobriety. He had a lot of troubles with others before but after he knew I was sincere, he gave me a try.

When they let me out after six months and a half, I got three choices: Minneapolis, Mankato, or Granite Falls. Well, I heard about the different places. Mankato was alright but in order to come back to Morton I would have to go through Minneapolis.

Then I thought about Granite Falls – and that's where I am now at Project Turnabout. It's closer to home and it might be half as good someplace else.

They started me with three days a week, then five days a week. After awhile, they put me on the payroll permanently and this is where I've been ever since as a custodian – working.

This is the longest I ever held a job in my life and I like it. I get along with everybody and feel this is my family. Project Turnabout did a lot of good for me.

I'm part of the staff. I'm not trying to brag myself up. I'm no better than anyone else. But I'm very proud of what I'm doing. I'm very fussy with my job. It's got to be just so, or I'll do it over again. If I have just freshly buffed the hallway, and someone walks over it, I feel like hitting them in the behind.

Since I've been here, I've joined Alcoholics Anonymous and we've met uptown every week for better than three years now. Before, I never planned or counted on anything. Just right now. That's how I used to live.

But I just celebrated my fifth year of sobriety in September.

Three years ago, I got my driver license after I passed the written and road tests. Sometime, when I have enough money saved, I'd like to go on a trip to Wyoming or Idaho. This time I'll drive a car and be sober.

But I haven't licked the habit yet. I'm only one drink away from a good drunk right now, but I hope that never happens. I'll take it one day at a time and it will work out.

I've seen a lot of wonderful things, and I've seen the most filthiest damn things. I wanted to tell this story to be an example to others and give publicity to Project Turnabout.

My hope is to die in my sobriety.

Girl Power

As for the other part of the job, it was a privilege, not a sentence, to cover girls sports in Redwood Falls. During my time there of just more than a year, the Cardinal girls were state runners-up in both volleyball and basketball.

The basketball team was a powerhouse that could compete well against today's top teams. To face the Cardinals, teams had to deal with the pressure from twin guards Jean and Joan Hopfenspirger. The deep starting lineup was also comprised of the smooth-shooting Barb Dording, while Anne Pryor and Dawn Zimmerman dominated rebounding. The twins displayed their athletic ability in other sports as well. Jean was a key member of the volleyball team, while Joan was leader of the pack in numerous cross country races.

In the state championship game, Redwood suffered its only loss of the season to the legendary Janet Karvonen and New York Mills.

Karvonen was a prolific scorer and aided by quality teammates in achieving multiple state titles, but if I were drafting a girls basketball all-star team from the 1970s, my first pick would be Mary Beth Bidinger of Morton. She was highly skilled in every aspect of the game at a time when, frankly, most girls weren't. I was able to get a photo of her shot as Bidinger became the fourth girl in Minnesota history to score her 1,000th point. She accomplished that feat in shorter seasons than current schedules and without three-pointers.

Going into the state tournament, Redwood was 22-0, having won 12 of those games by more than 30 points. Only four games were decided by single-digit margins, three of them against Morton and Mary Beth.

As for volleyball, it was then played two-of-three with teams scoring only on their own serve, which could make for some lengthy battles between evenly matched teams. The Cardinals stumbled by losing opening sets in their first two playoff games but then went on a run all the way to the state championship match where they fell to Sartell.

Fun With Coaches

My sports assignments expanded beyond the girls realm, and it was a highlight when the athletic director and two coaches from the University of Minnesota came to town for a golf tournament and fundraiser. Besides telling about their teams, they cut loose for some good-natured fun.

An evening with the Golden Goofers

June 1, 1978 • Redwood Gazette

When you get some of the U of M's men's athletic staff members together, you're in for some Golden Goofing Around with the Gophers.

At the Williams Fund program Tuesday evening at the golf club, Athletic Director Paul Giel, basketball Coach Jim Dutcher, and football Coach Cal Stoll took their turns adding jokes to otherwise common prognostications about upcoming seasons.

Giel, who shot an 89 in the tournament, started it off needling one of his partners: "The one thing he does best is show up. He gave me some advice on putting: 'Just remember that 90% of the putts that come up short don't go in.'

"The U of M was there before all the professional teams came in and it will be there after they're gone. We aren't so shabby these years either.

"Herb Brooks is still debating his job. I don't believe everything in Sid Hartman's column . . . although I put most of it there. That's why Sid's on vacation.

"I think Cal finally has competition in spots on the team. That gives depth. We're the first school other than Michigan or Ohio State to go to a post-season bowl since 1967."

Dutcher began with: "I'm damn happy to be here. We stopped in Arlington, Gaylord, and Morton selling football tickets at the Legion clubs – and I wasn't even in the army.

"Look at this handout you all got – 'Little known facts about men's intercollegiate athletics at the University of Minnesota.' They got a picture of a swimmer, gymnastics, tennis player, baseball player, and football player. Well, we also play basketball there, too. I asked about it and they said they couldn't find any black pictures. So, you see, I've also got internal problems.

"We just completed the recruiting season and now we're recruiting for next year. In the last two weeks, we sent out 200 letters to will-be seniors asking if they're interested in the U of M. We sent some letters to good juniors, too.

"I think we signed some good basketball players. Basketball Weekly rated our recruiting year number one. As many as three freshmen may be starters. One of the kids from Canada was on a team that was 52-1 last year.

"Kevin Stallings was an outstanding player in Illinois. He had 14 points and 17 assists in an all-star game and said he didn't play well. He's a tremendous passer. Mark Hall from Springfield, Mass., was the player of the year in the east. He scored six dunks from the guard position in one game.

"Michigan will be rated first. They have seven of eight back and have an adequate replacement for the eighth. Indiana will be picked second with 10 lettermen back. Michigan has four starters back and Ohio State has all of them back. It'll be a dogfight, but that's the way we like it. You gotta win at home and hope to be successful on the road.

"We've won 27 Big Ten games in the last two years and that's more than everybody else but it hasn't taken us anywhere – just two seconds. Michigan has won 26. Our goal is to get a post-season bid in some tourney."

Then Stoll took over: "My prime interest is to get the football season over so we can watch basketball.

"Our quarterback situation is so bad that we were trying out everybody. One kid came up and said he used to play quarterback in high school, said he'd like to try. I handed him a football and said 'Can you pass this?' He answered 'Gee, I don't even know if I can swallow it.' That's Dutcher's joke.

"Our first goal is to beat Ohio State. We will do that and you heard it here first. I'm looking forward with cautious optimism. We had a good spring practice and have some returning lettermen who did well for us.

"We'll be big across the front. I don't know if we'll be quick enough to catch anybody, but if we catch 'em, we'll kick the hell out of 'em.

"Only 12 of 95 are seniors – three that play offense and about four or five on defense. Marion Barber will be 18 years old now. Kent Kitzmann had a great spring and will be one of the better backs."

Then it was time for questions and Dutcher revealed his recruiting secret: "We get 'em in before the snow comes."

Continuing on recruiting, he said about one player: "John Wooden was talking to him trying to get him to go to UCLA, but Wooden's not coaching there anymore. That's like me sending Bill Musselman to recruit.

"Also, we led the Big Ten in attendance. We were second in the country to Kentucky in attendance and for that I got a $75 raise.

"Darryl Mitchell of Florida was impressed with our law school. We started calling Mitchell twice a day from March 2 'til the end of May keeping in contact with him. Our basketball telephone bill was $21,000. That's a lot of time on the telephone. But if we play an intrasquad game with freshmen and fill the place up with $2 tickets, we'll pay the phone bill in one scrimmage. Recruiting is an investment. If you get good players, you have good teams and have a good investment."

Cal Stoll's number was drawn for a pair of season tickets to Gopher football games, but he declined the prize, insisting that he could get tickets elsewhere.

Sportswriters Vote Too

In those days it was common for politicians to stop in and visit newspaper offices as the papers were the dominant media they needed to further their careers.

One time, it was made known that secretary of state candidate Joan Growe was coming through on her campaign swing. The office was conspicuously vacant that day and I was tabbed to do the obligatory interview.

Admittedly, I was in over my head, which Growe quickly sensed and was noticeably perturbed at having been given a punk rookie to cover her appearance. When she learned sports was part of my beat, she sarcastically quipped "Maybe I should do something athletic." Neither of us left the meeting with a smile. More later.

By the next fall, the Gazette had been sold to the corporate group Mickelson Media. Staff morale was on the low side, and I was tired of burning up Highways 212 and 19 in my green Chevy Vega on frequent trips home for dating.

I pursued an ad for a reporter position at the Winsted Journal. Floyd Sneer liked my photography portfolio and hired me.

4
Winsted

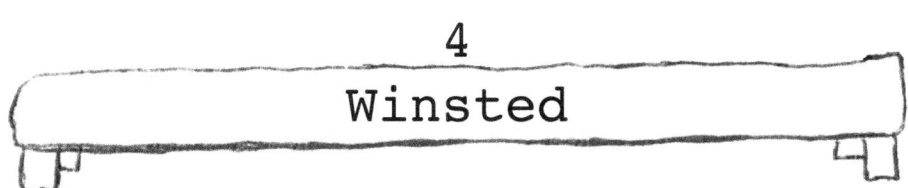

"Winsted! Where's that?" a befuddled John Schneider reacted.

He wasn't so surprised that I was leaving, but he expected I would go some-place bigger and better, like perhaps a daily. It would have been a compliment to the Gazette to have one of its employees advance to a position of higher status.

No, John, this wasn't a daily. It was a literal mom-and-pop operation owned and operated by Floyd and JoAnn Sneer with only a couple other employees. It helped by explaining that Winsted was near enough for free rent at home and closer to my romantic interest.

The tribute column I wrote after Floyd's passing tells about the good ol' days.

'Thoughts on Things:' tribute to Floyd Sneer
July 23, 2021 • Herald Journal

On July 14, 2021, the ashes of Floyd Sneer were interred at the Winsted Public Cemetery. He passed away in November 2019.

Floyd and his wife, JoAnn, were publishers of the Winsted Journal from 1961 to 1986. For the small group gathered at the cemetery that day during a much-needed rain, it was a time of remembrance and acknowledgment.

I arrived in Winsted Oct. 16, 1978, having been hired on-the-spot by Floyd as the Journal's first reporter. I was deemed worthy with a year's experience at the county seat twice-a-week paper in Redwood Falls and being from Silver Lake. "People from Silver Lake always pay cash," Floyd would say.

Our office was on Main Avenue in an old building made from Lake Mary brick on what is now a parking lot just west of Keaveny Pharmacy. It had a small makeshift darkroom where I spent many hours developing film and making prints for the next paper.

Floyd's best friend, electrician John Parten, would often stop by for a visit and coffee. At one time, the three of us had a contest going of who could re-use his Styrofoam coffee cup the longest. I don't remember who won, but it went on for weeks.

"Pete" Peterson of the Howard Lake Herald would also stop by for a chat and to exchange commercial printing jobs that needed numbering, since only Floyd had the right equipment for that. Pete made it a point to leave soon enough so he "wouldn't be late for quitting time."

In those days, the area communities were more self-contained and most had independent newspaper owners.

"Barney" Barnaal of the Cokato Enterprise would conduct an invisible parade every year on St. Urho's Day. We looked forward to reading his description about the details of the Winsted Journal's float each time.

Floyd and JoAnn were also friends with Don and Carole Larson, then owners of the Delano Eagle. It seemed unusual to me then that they would know someone from so far away as Delano.

The Journal carried a line on the front page noting that it was "McLeod County's first offset newspaper" referring to a new method of printing that had come around in the '60s at a central plant in Hutchinson rather than each office running its own hand-fed press.

Floyd taught me a lot about the postal system. We didn't just send the paper off to press and that was it. After it was printed, it came back and we ran each copy through a stenciling machine to imprint each subscriber's mailing info on it. Next, the papers had to be grouped into bundles and bags fitting the post office's distribution scheme, and then we pushed a cart of papers half a block down the sidewalk to the post office.

Then we were done . . . no, then we had start on the next one.

That was in the heyday of community newspapers when there were many more local businesses to serve. Winsted even had a jewelry store at that time.

There was a period when we had five full pages of grocery advertisements each week. Both grocery stores in town ran two-page spreads, and the new Tom Thumb convenience store also got in the act with a full-page ad.

The Sneers were involved as the transition to multiple ownership of newspapers grew. In 1980, Bill McGarry bought the Lester Prairie News and moved it to Glencoe to compete with the Glencoe Enterprise, renaming it the McLeod County Chronicle. By doing so, he was able to maintain the status as a newspaper qualified to publish legal notices, which otherwise took a one-year waiting period.

At the same time, the Sneers started from scratch the Lester Prairie Journal. A few years later when Pete was ready to move on, they acquired the Howard Lake Herald. For those of you who don't know, those are the roots of the Herald Journal.

All of that is the background to get to Floyd.

The last time I saw him was several years ago when we got together to catch up over lunch at Blue Note.

Floyd wasn't just a newspaper publisher for Winsted. He was a person for Winsted.

If there was any type of effort to help the community, he was involved, and more than likely had a part in starting it.

He was very active in the Winsted Civic and Commerce Association, served on the public school board (when Winsted had an independent district), and frankly, too many other boards and committees to even try to list.

He also served as mayor of Winsted, and of course, was one of the world-famous Bratbusters.

Although I've stayed in the newspaper industry my entire working life, I think those first three-plus years with Floyd and JoAnn were the most enjoyable. Eventually I left for an editor's job up north; then received the welcome of a prodigal son upon returning.

When the winters got nasty, Floyd would often tell me "yeah, but it's a dry cold" referring to what he was told when he had worked on the Iron Range in northern Minnesota. Between us, that comment later morphed into "it's a dry heat" and even "it's a dry ___ (fill in the blank)" as a light-hearted explanation of anything.

Standing under an umbrella at the cemetery, I couldn't help but think he would tell me "Dale, it's a dry rain."

There's only one fitting way to conclude this, and it is the same way Floyd signed off on his "Thoughts on Things" newspaper column:

That's it. FS

One of the first people I came in contact with upon learning that I was the new reporter at the Winsted Journal asked: "What's there to write about here?" Turns out there was quite a bit.

Getting High

During my first winter, Winsted was in the process of building a new water tower. I was able to interview the colorful construction crew, and was escorted on a climb to the top for a photo op.

That's not me on the top of the water tower, but it was a nice view.

A picnic every day for water tower 'family'

Jan. 18, 1979 • Winsted Journal

By now, you've probably seen the men working on Winsted's new water tower and you should have reached a decision as to whether you'd like to do that yourself or not.

"There's no training. If you're nuts and crazy, it all goes together and you work on it," said Lee Anderson, foreman of the crew from Chicago Bridge and Iron Co., which is building the tower.

One day last week, the crew came out of the below-zero temperatures to meet with local press in their small warming shack during their half-hour lunch break. Amid a constant flow of good-natured ribbing between themselves, they talked about water tower-building at its best — and worst.

"It's a picnic every day!" laughed John Shewchuk, placing his homemade sandwich on a small heater. "You can look around and see that there aren't too many brains here."

"Yeah," joked Chuck Hagen pointing to his neck, "they hired me from here down."

"You know, this is the first time anybody's interviewed us," Anderson said. "Usually they just come and snap their pictures and go. The papers always say that the tower looks like a rocket and then a champagne glass as it's being built."

"It don't make any difference how cold it is," he continued. "If they want a tower built, you go build it. And we work all the way up to the Canadian line. Look around, everybody's noses are frozen."

"What happens," he explained, "is that the salesmen go up north during the summer and sell the towers and take in their fishing trips. Then, by the time everything's ready, we work on it during the fall and winter. We go south in the summer and north in the winter."

The steel is usually shipped to the site before the crew arrives. Other times it comes by railroad car and the crew unloads it, like they did for this tower when the shipment came to Howard Lake.

Each week an inspection is made. The welds are checked and sometimes x-rays are taken.

The workers have a set of instructions to follow but "we build so many of these that we don't look at the prints anymore," Anderson said. "They're all the same."

Protection from the cold amounts to just "putting on clothes 'til you just stand there."

"By the time you put enough clothes on and crawl up the ladder, you're steamed up and hot," Hagen said. "Then you start working and freeze."

The workers also voiced displeasure with the steel being cold and slick, and getting wet on the job.

"There aren't too many fatal accidents, maybe one a year," Anderson said. "When you get in a nasty place, you're supposed to have a safety line and belt on."

"You're on your own," Hagen added. "You watch your own personal position so you don't get someplace where you can't get back."

Finger and eye injuries are the most common, one man said, upon which two others promptly produced hands with abbreviated fingers.

"Everywhere you go, people ask 'What happened to the guy that fell off the top?'" Hagen said with a touch of sarcasm.

"Just tell 'em he sprained an ankle," laughed Shewchuk.

Like most occupations, water tower construction has its own terminology and nicknames. "Widow-makers" are ladders the men lay on while welding outside. "Canary swings" hold "chicken ladders" which are used when welding inside the ball.

"Everybody thinks we get $25 an hour," Anderson said. "I tell them we just get $12 and they think we are liars, that nobody would do it for that. There are different salaries for learning. If you work a month and they think you know something, you get more. We do this work for the money – certainly not prestige."

"Most of us come from economically deprived areas where the most you can make is three bucks an hour," Hagen added.

"I used to be working for a dollar and there were these guys around building a tower and getting $4.50 an hour. So I just jumped into it," Anderson recalled.

"We're the last of the traveling gypsies," Hagen laughed. "Some of us don't like to be inside or stay in the same place for three months."

The company covers 17 states so workers may not get home for a couple months at a time. For instance, Roger Wilburn of Clarksburg, Ohio, has been home three times since November. Occasionally, local guys are hired at a site, but they must be willing to travel with the crew.

After "eight hours a day and that's it," workers who live close enough drive home. Others make it home on weekends, or like Wilburn, less than that. During the week, some workers stay at a motel in Hutchinson or have trailers in Lester Prairie and Howard Lake.

The present crew ranges in age from 23 to 51 and sort of considers itself "one big family." The same group isn't always together, but they're all in the business of building water towers, flat bottom tanks, reactors, smoke stacks, etc.

"We're pretty much normal," Hagen said. "We all got homes and families. It's just a job you go to. Somebody's got to do it."

Quotable

Dick Genty was a prominent Winsted defense attorney whose career deserves a book of its own. The often-repeated local line of "If you're guilty, get Genty" was meant as a sincere testament to his ability.

Known for his witty remarks, Dick didn't anticipate while speaking at the 1979 secretaries luncheon hosted by the Winsted Civic and Commerce Association that a young reporter would take what he said and put it in the paper. It provided some chuckles over the next few years every time it came up, recalling that Dick told the group of secretaries being honored: "Secretaries are more important than wives. Wives are optional but you need secretaries."

Back to School

"Participatory journalism" is when a reporter joins in a certain activity and then writes about it from that perspective. I gave it my best shot in kindergarten.

My first day of school
Aug. 30, 1979 • Winsted Journal

As I look back at it, today was a turning point in my life. I started kindergarten at Winsted Public School.

I'm 5 ½ years old now – almost six – and I met the challenge of starting school confidently. Most of the other kids had their moms along, but I was a big boy and went on my own.

I took my notebook and two brand new number-two lead pencils just like you're supposed to have for the first day of school As we came in, we got some name tags, but I couldn't read mine anyway.

For awhile, we were just playing around on the slide and stuff when this lady started ringing an awful loud bell. I sure hope she puts that thing away from now on. I don't know if I can stand that all year.

First, we had to sit on the floor and this lady starts telling us about caterpillars. She said she's a teacher and there's one in every room. Then she showed us a picture of a teacher and asked what one was. Some girl said "It's like a person."

Anyway, she told us we're supposed to look for caterpillars at home and if we find any, to bring them to school 'cause then we'll make butterflies out of them.

Also, she said she'll teach us to read, but we got to learn a lot of other things first. Sometimes we'll be in small groups, we can bring pictures from vacations, and we should respect each other. She said so many things I don't know if I got them all straight.

If we get in trouble, we won't get spanked, but we have to take time out like in a ball game and sit in the corner and think about what we did. She said that with 21 boys and girls, we all have to behave, but I don't know if there are enough corners for all of us.

Finally we got our own desks. Yessireebob, my own desk at last! Even got my name on it.

Then she told us about the bathroom. We're supposed to keep it clean and wash our hands before we go. There's nothing worse than a bathroom that hasn't been flushed, you know. And we're supposed to be quiet so we don't have any accidents.

This lady, the teacher, then told us her name. It's Missus Stre-Tess-Key. We had to try to say it a few times. Then there's Missus May-Han whose title is One Helper.

Teacher said there's another Missus Stre-Tess-Key who teaches music. I wonder if they are all named that.

Next we had to do some exercises to keep our interest. Then we looked at a flag which is for the United States of America which is a long name but a neat place to live. Then we pledged our allegiance.

Then we did something real neat. We went in straight rows and made a circle. Everybody got a colored thing and a record told your color to stand up or sit down. Teacher said it was good for us to listen.

Then we had to make two lines by the door – one of girls and one of boys. We were going to see Mr. Pearce and Jim somebody. We went down this long hall for a couple miles and then into this big room. I wish I had one like it at home.

This guy, Mr. Pearce, made us stand on the black line and hold hands. We're gonna have to do that every day so we got to make sure it's on the black line and not the green or red one. We have to remember not to forget tennis shoes either.

He made us do some stretching and hopping just like in the classroom. Then he looked at our name tags and said he knew some of us. Then we got to do different walks and some running. I lost my name tag but found it on my back.

After that, we got back into lines again with boys in one and girls in the other. You know, that whole time we were in there, I didn't see anybody named Jim.

Then we went down another long hall and this time a lady gave us some milk out of a big white box just like the one at home. It's called a frigerator I think. But we couldn't have any milk until we got back and washed our hands and found our desks.

While we were drinking the milk, Teacher kept asking us things about our vacations. Then we had to rinse out the cartons and put them on a table.

After that, we got five whole minutes to do whatever we wanted to. Then we had to sit down and find out what August is. August is number 27 and it's almost over with.

Then we saw a movie about chickens and other animals, but we didn't get any popcorn. It was during the movie that I first realized I didn't bring a hanky today.

When it was over, Teacher said there were some grapes on the bulletin board for each of us. We had to draw ourselves on a paper plate and she stuck the pictures on the grapes and said something about it being "our bunch."

While we were waiting for some other kids to finish, we played some more. Then she rang that stupid bell again. Gee, I hate that.

Then we sat on the floor some more and she read us two books about fat animals and an elephant that had to sneeze. He could have used a hanky, too.

Next she taught us a rhyme about apples in a tree and how we shook them down and ate them. Then we had to cut them out of red paper and paste them on green paper to take home. That wasn't too hard, but the boy next to me kept using his wrong hand, the left one.

Then this other lady, Missus Toto-Sheck, must have thought we were all bulletin boards 'cause she pinned some papers on our shirts. Then we had to line up again and "stay behind the person in front of you."

Then we went into another room and there was another Missus Stre-Tess-Key. She made us get in a circle and then skip around and hop and do it to a record. There's a lot of repetition to this kindergarten stuff.

After that, we sat on the floor and sang with a record about liking each other. Then we made another circle and did funny things and then lined up again.

Then we walked back to our first room and they let us have our coats. But before we could go, we had to give back our name tags and push our chairs under the desk and line up and listen to one more song. Then we could go.

I guess it wasn't too bad for a first day of school so I suppose I'll go back tomorrow.

Night Shift

Journalists work all kinds of different hours. This wasn't participatory in the usual sense, but I spent a night at St. Mary's Hospital and Home to write about what it's like for workers on the overnight shift.

Afterward, St. Mary's management was unhappy because it wasn't promotional enough, but that wasn't the point. It was just "a day in the life," or rather, a night in the life.

Full moon makes residents 'buzz' for nursing home night crew
March 8, 1979 • Winsted Journal

"All the weird stuff happens on a full moon," nurses' aide Rose Johnson said about nights at St. Mary's Home. "The residents are different on a full moon. Everybody buzzes a lot. They get restless."

LPN Nancy Cole confirmed it: "You'd be surprised what that full moon can do. The day before and a day of a full moon they get real happy or real crotchety."

It's after midnight on a Saturday morning and some members of the nursing home staff are talking about what it's like to work the 11 p.m. to 7 a.m. shift. Besides Cole and Johnson, aides Barb Robison and Cheryl Otto are on duty.

"It's spooky working nights," Cole said.

"Yeah," agreed Robison. "You hear the darndest noises."

"One night we each went and got a pair of scissors and took a baseball bat out of the closet," Cole added. "Sometimes the residents will cry out. Last week, the pipes were thawing going bang-bang-bang-bang-bang-bang-bang and it got closer and closer. Maybe you hear somebody walking or somebody pops out of a room. Or you go into a room and they'll be standing up in there – and old people don't look that good in the middle of the night."

At St. Mary's, the first floor (downstairs) is for skilled care – residents who can't feed or dress themselves and need a lot of help. The second floor is intermediate care. Residents there can take care of most of their needs with little assistance.

For nights, there are usually four or five staff members on duty between the two floors.

"I'm the charge nurse so I set up pills, and unless there's a critical patient, that's about all. Other than that, we just work together taking turns answering buzzers, change beds and wash linen together, clean and rub people. It's pretty much the same on both floors," Cole said.

"There's an RN on call or if we need something right away, we go to the hospital," she continued. "Nights aren't my favorite shift. I don't think anybody really likes nights that much."

The late shift workers come on at 11 and hear a report about how each resident has been doing during the previous shift.

"We do rounds about 1 or 1:30, then wash soiled linen and sit for awhile," Robison said. "We check the bath schedule and get the linen ready, make up bedding, and see that everything's clean."

"There's not much that goes on," Cole said. "About 3 or 3:30, we do another bed check, do the linen again, fill the water pitchers with ice and fresh water, and get sleepy. The sleepy time is about 4 to 4:30. Then the day shift comes at six and starts getting people up."

"We're busy if there's a sick resident or someone new who is confused," Johnson said. "It depends on the state the residents are in."

"It's busy with sick and restless residents," said Cole.

"People that crawl over the siderails or decide to go for a walk outside – that's restless," Robison clarified.

"The worst night," said Cole, "was New Year's Eve. Two single females were sitting here working and one guy came out and kept us entertained. He'd sing and laugh and go for a walk up and down the halls and shake our hands."

"I've never had a busy night that the work didn't get done though," Robison said.

"I had only one really busy night and that was because we were a little short-staffed that night," Cole said. "Also, the cops will stop in and visit five or 10 minutes when they come to check on doors."

"Their nights are usually as boring as ours," Robison added.

They also mentioned that channel five stays on the air all night and a thank-you letter to the station might be in order.

"It's not that we sit and watch tv all night," Cole said. "We have to get the work done. We can't say 'I'm not going to answer that light; there's something good on.' The tv is just something to have there, and we keep it low enough so the residents can't hear it."

"I was hired mostly for the downstairs floor," Cole said, "so I get pulled up only for emergencies and nights. There are only about two or three people who always work on one floor. If you're needed, you can go about anywhere. You have to be a jack-of-all-trades – a hairdresser, manicurist, and babysitter."

One problem about working the late shift, they said, is becoming confused about what time it is.

"Your days get screwed up," Robison said. "I don't know if it's six in the morning or six at night. Do I go to work or do I have off? Is it morning or afternoon? That happens to me all the time."

"Like now, we go to work Friday and don't get home 'til Saturday. Then we work Saturday and don't get home 'til Sunday. That's how it goes," Cole said. "Me, I have no trouble sleeping. I'm sleeping when I check out."

Ride-Along

One more hands-on story: McLeod County Sheriff Duane Kopesky arranged for me to ride along with one of his deputies for another overnight shift. Not much happened as for policing activity, but deputy Don Heimerl was able to speak from the heart about the lives of law enforcement officers.

McLeod: wide open spaces for a sheriff's deputy
March 6, 1980 • Winsted Journal

It's a little after 10 p.m. on a Friday night and Sheriff's Deputy Don Heimerl has just come on duty.

He's one of three McLeod County officers working the 10 p.m. to 8 a.m. shift. Another officer started earlier and is on until 2 a.m. Heimerl's partner tonight is Dewey Horsman, the newest member of the sheriff's department.

"I do mostly nights," Heimerl explained. "I prefer nights. I love nights. Never could go back to an eight-to-five job."

A resident of Hutchinson, Heimerl joined the sheriff's department in May 1979 after working with the Jordan Police Department. His father, Robert, left the Winsted area in the 1930s, and the family is now in its second generation of the plumbing business in Madison.

"We don't try to congregate unless there's a reason to," he explained while heading for Glencoe, where the sheriff's office is located. "If there's a hot spot, we'll maybe be there together. If not, we spread distance between us. But if another guy gets a call, we start moving in that direction so that we can respond faster if he needs help."

The first order of business is a stop at the sheriff's office to pick up a radar unit, portable radio, and check reports of what has happened since he last went off duty. Horsman is also there getting ready for his first shift alone after a breaking-in period.

Dispatcher Dennis Jensen advises that it's "pretty quiet, nothing going on."

Conferring, they agree that Horsman will head toward Hutchinson while Heimerl will work his way east and north. They note that the only dance going on in the county is at Pla-Mor Ballroom in Glencoe, where the rock group Magic is playing.

First, Heimerl makes a few routine checks for unlocked doors or signs of damage at Glencoe Motors, Littfin Building Center, and some implement dealerships outside the city limits of Glencoe.

During that time, he gets a call on the citizens band radio from a trucker he knew in Jordan who comes through in late hours. "Those guys tell me anything that goes on," Heimerl said. "One year, I got 13 DWIs (driving while intoxicated arrests) off the CB. They call if there's a stalled car, DWI, or just to chit chat."

"That trucker comes as far as Glencoe. Calling breaks the monotony for them," he continued. "A lot of truckers are good; they have no big beef with the law. UPS and Murphy drivers very much hold to the law. One ticket and they're off three days. An owner-operator can get caught speeding. It's an occupational hazard."

County deputies have jurisdiction throughout the county, or as Heimerl said, "It all belongs to me." Patrolling per se isn't done on state highways, he explained, but some county residents live there so deputies do drive on state highways. The primary objective is on county roads, though, he said.

Each officer in the sheriff's department has his own squad car and is responsible for all things right and wrong with it. "It's assigned to me like my patch," Heimerl said. "It's nice having your own car. I came from a department where we had only two cars. They were run around the clock and that way the maintenance goes way up."

Before leaving town, a Glencoe officer stops Heimerl for a brief conversation. He said it's been busy in town and asks Heimerl to be around about 1 a.m. when the dance is over.

It's a mutual aid," Heimerl explained. "We're not working it, but helping out. We do the same with Winsted – go poke our nose around a bit. It's a deterrent to make the bulk of them realize there's a badge around. The traffic will clear and so will I."

Next it's on to Plato for checks of buildings there and a trip through town. Then Heimerl heads north toward Lester Prairie, covering several gravel roads.

"I know ahead of time where I want to go," he said. "Near Lester Prairie there has been a rash of mailbox vandalism."

With no pressing business at hand, Heimerl starts talking about the life of a county law officer. "It's very different to have a passenger," he said. "For years, there was nobody over there. I'm used to being by myself.

"The general public doesn't have any idea what goes on in a squad car – night, day, or really any shift. The only thing they see is the car drive by," he continued. "A guy in Jordan that joined the reserve rode with me and he said 'This is different. I used to be standing on the street corner looking at the squad. Now I'm looking at those on the corner.'

"You get some people who, even for a motorist assist, you pull up behind them and they get a little paranoid. A lot of people see the red lights and no matter if they're guilty or not, right away they tense up," he said.

"A traffic stop," he explained, "is the only time you can be at the right place at the right time from law enforcement's point of view, but from the driver's point of view, you're at the wrong place at the wrong time. They'll say 'Why don't you go out and arrest a burglar?' Great, tell me where there is one and I'll go get him.

"For speeding, I'll say 'Good evening' to break the ice and get them to relax. They're not a hunted-down criminal," Heimerl said. "Some are irate – 'What the **** do you want?'

"And many people I've stopped have thanked me. That's a part of law enforcement a person doesn't see," he said. "A person just thanked you for a ticket. You slide back behind the wheel and think 'He thanked me.' It gives a police officer a sense that there's a citizen who's responsible and an okay person. You get the feeling he knows what the hell I'm doing out here.

"But your guard can be let down, too. Many officers have been shot on traffic stops. They go up to a car sober and just interested in doing their job, just saving his tail end so he can put food on the table," he said.

"The first time I slid into a squad car, I looked down and saw the buttons and radar and wondered what this is all about. As time went on, I got used to it and it grows on you. It's like getting into your own car," he continued.

"Cops are human, no doubt about it. Just plain human. There are good cops and bad cops," Heimerl said. "But they have a heart, a soul, believe in God, have a family, children – just like a carpenter. But the occupation of a cop is probably getting shot.

"You have to be professional all the way, fine and simple," he said. "I personally don't believe in coming on like gangbusters. You know, Johnny Law steps out of the car and is gonna break everybody's head, that's not it. But he's not going to take any crap either.

"A police officer is not a punching bag, but we'll give a guy or a woman a fair shake," he continued. "Say, I'm called to a bar. I'll give the guy a chance, but if he's gonna take a swing at me, I'm not going to say 'You hit me. Don't do it again, please!' I'm not out here to get hurt. If a guy wants to punch, then he bought some trouble.

"I have good friends in Minneapolis, and we talk and exchange ideas. Down there they have very high respect for the outstate officer. In the metro area, back-up is very close. Here it's not as close," he said.

"A cop is a different breed out by himself. He doesn't expect anybody to feel sorry for him. If I didn't want to be here, there are plenty of other jobs. I'm out here because I want to be – and because Duane hired me. I didn't have to apply. My interest is in law enforcement. I believe in it and like it," Heimerl said. "You gotta like people, no matter if they're pointing a gun at you.

"To me, it's a treat to work here, working in the county. In a city, you come to the city limits and stop. After 10 hours, you get buggy," he said. "Here we got 550 square miles and there's no way you can grab every road in one shift, or even with three cars. Freedom, the wide open spaces.

"But there are times out here when it's boring," he said, "and different officers will get together to relieve a little pressure. Citizens don't really understand how much constant stress there is on a police officer.

"Take Horsman, he had his days off and now he puts on the uniform and gun and gets into his car. It's still normal. All of a sudden a call comes in, a domestic. Domestics have a high percentage of officers killed – and the man has a gun. He's thinking about it on the way there and his stress is up. He gets there and everything's okay. Then there's a burglary in progress. The guy is way up there in stress. By the end of the shift, he's at maximum stress and has to unwind,"

Heimerl explained.

"If you've ever been in a coffee shop and there are troopers or deputies, and you hear a loud laugh, they're just letting it out. You can't keep it inside," he said. "Police officers have the largest divorce rate in the nation, that's a fact. Any woman that stays with a copper for 20 years is one hell of a woman.

"Some cops don't realize how much stress they're under. To me it's fun, but it can be a pain in the butt sometimes," he said. "Personalities differ, the way we cop. I don't speak for all law enforcement, only myself.

"Sometimes people say 'All I see is that damn cop sitting in there drinking coffee.' But maybe he's conducting business, talking with another officer, or else there's an individual in there he wants to keep an eye on. People get the wrong impressions," he said. "Sure, they're in there drinking coffee, but they're either on break or conducting business, exchanging notes.

"Crimes are committed at certain times on certain nights in certain places – modus operandi. In rookie school, they told us an officer will come across a crime in progress once in every 14 years. I have yet to have mine. One other deputy already had his quota," Heimerl said.

By now, Heimerl has traveled county roads to near Silver Lake. He heads back for Glencoe as the dance will be over soon.

"Dances aren't the big thing, bars are too," he said. "You get a large group of people condensed in a small area with alcohol, people get screwy.

"That's something else – drunk drivers. I do not like people drunk behind the wheel. If they have the sense to get drunk, they should have enough sense to get someone sober to drive," he said.

He also noted that on DWI stops "with guys you put on the red lights and they pull over, but females take off. The three females I gave DWI tickets to, I had to chase at speeds over 100 miles an hour. Can you figure that out?" he asked.

Comparing McLeod County people to metropolitan residents, Heimerl acknowledged that there are differences. "Generally, they're down to earth here, and I might even say they respect the law more. But there are fruitcakes here, too," he said.

Before going to the ballroom, he also spoke about McLeod County's jail situation. The old jail was condemned last summer so prisoners are kept in surrounding county jails. Hutchinson has a holding facility, but prisoners cannot be kept more than 72 hours there.

"Having no jail is a pain," Heimerl said. "It ties up an officer on duty. Myself, I spend about two hours a week transporting prisoners, but there's not much at night. Day shift is different.

"We bring them from Sibley, Meeker, Carver to court and that deputy is tied up literally babysitting him, at lunch, everything, moving him around and wiping his nose. The county definitely needs a jail," he said. "It's tying up too much of a deputy's time when he could be other places. And if you figure we've had as many as four prisoners. One deputy watch four prisoners? No way.

"Whenever anybody's charged with a felony – a serious crime – we need security. We can't have Joe Blow come in to report mailbox vandalism and we got a felon sitting there," he said.

"They're working on getting a jail, and I'm glad of it. I don't know if the people will vote for it. But when they get a jail, we better have one that will do some good 25 years down the line or it's wasted money," he said.

At 1 a.m., Heimerl drives to the Pla-Mor parking lot where patrons are leaving after the dance. With two Glencoe squad cars already there, the arrival of a county squad naturally attracts attention.

Heimerl follows one car out of the parking lot, but doesn't have enough reason to stop it. He goes back to the Pla-Mor where Glencoe police have arrested a young man for disorderly conduct.

As things die down, Glencoe police take the man back to the sheriff's office and Heimerl goes there. After the arresting procedure is complete, Heimerl gets the task of transporting the prisoner to Hutchinson for an overnight stay.

On the way, the prisoner (who is from another county) asks why he is being taken to Hutchinson. He is informed that McLeod County has no jail.

Also along the way, Heimerl gets a call from another truck driver who talks awhile.

Near Hutchinson, Heimerl's radar unit starts beeping and shows that an oncoming car is traveling 66 miles an hour. But Heimerl just flashes the red lights and explains: "I don't make traffic stops with a prisoner. You don't know who you're stopping and you're endangering the prisoner. It could be armed burglars you're stopping."

After seeing that the prisoner is admitted to the Hutchinson holding facility, Heimerl goes to check out a prowler in rural Hutchinson. A man had called saying that a car had driven into his yard twice.

Heimerl makes a couple trips through the area, but nothing turns up. On another road, he notes some garbage dumped on the side of the road and in the ditch. Then he radios Horsman to meet him at a restaurant in Hutchinson.

"It's all downhill from here," he said, referring to the lack of activity. After coffee and a light breakfast, he drops off his guest at about 4:40 a.m.

"This night was slower than usual," he admitted. "You should be around in the summertime. That's when it really gets going."

Bargaining Table

A scene that stuck in my mind was the teachers contract negotiations one year when Winsted still had its own school district.

Representing the district were the superintendent and two board members, all who were tall, husky men. The teachers were represented by petite females who barely cleared 100 pounds each.

The physical dynamics of them negotiating was a stark contrast, compounded even more as the groups repeatedly referred to each other as "men" and "girls."

I took no sides, and still don't, but it was a scene that probably won't ever be repeated.

Larry Kettner

Larry Kettner was "the blind guy" in town who everyone respectfully knew to be aware of when he was walking the sidewalks. It was rewarding to be able to tell his story. This one has a special meaning for me as it was my first award-winning piece.

Larry Kettner on being blind: 'There isn't such a thing as a handicap if people give you a chance to prove your ability'
Oct. 2, 1980 • Winsted Journal

Larry Kettner can't read this story about himself.

Kettner, 40, moved to Winsted in February 1974 because of a work opportunity. Now unemployed, he spends much of his time weaving and doing other craft projects.

Larry Kettner is blind, and this is his story:

Born and raised on a 145-acre farm near Chaska, Kettner didn't even wear glasses until about seventh grade. At that time, a problem with the nerves in his eyes was diagnosed and he was told he would be blind within 10 years.

"There wasn't much I could say," Kettner recalled in a recent interview. "If it's gonna happen, it's gonna happen. Like when you find out you have cancer. Kind of a shock, you know."

The prediction wasn't exactly right, but Kettner did become legally blind (20/200 vision) in 1970. Now his vision has grown worse to 20/400. He sees only shadows and light, and only in a five-degree path.

"I can see people walk by me as shadows. When I hear them talk, I know who they are, just like on the telephone," he said. "I can still see my shadow in bright sun, but very slightly."

Kettner wears glasses, but it's more out of habit and for protection than for corrective purposes, he said. "I can see a window frame a little better with glasses, a little improvement but not much," he said.

The cause of his vision problem was not found in a family history, he said, but it may have had something to do with his parents' genes. "Some doctors say it was and some don't. I don't quite understand," Kettner said.

So at least for now, there is no chance of correcting or replacing his vision. Doctors have told him that if surgery was possible, they would do it, Kettner recalled. "Maybe someday there will be something," he added.

Kettner eventually became the owner and operator of his father's farm, until he had to sell it in 1971 because of his faltering vision. "People didn't want me on the road with machinery. I was too dangerous," he said. "I had to hire somebody, but expenses were too high."

Then he applied for assistance from state services and that led him into a series of events he would prefer not to remember.

After a long testing and physical examination process, he was sent to the Minneapolis Society for the Blind (MSB) to receive occupational training and instruction in reading Braille. He then planned to attend a vocational school in St. Paul, but a counselor told him to get a job instead.

Kettner found employment at Animal Fair in Chanhassen working with foam rubber for stuffed animals. However, a couple months later, the firm purchased a larger machine that eliminated his position and he was laid off.

He then went back to the Minneapolis Society for an occupational treatment and training program. The society has a workshop where blind persons work at factory-type jobs subcontracted from private industry such as light assembly, packaging, or wrapping.

Wages are according to ability, and that is a sore spot for Kettner. "I took home $80 in two weeks. How can anybody make a living on that?" he asked.

Kettner has a phonograph record of a speech read at the 1974 convention of the National Federation of the Blind (NFB) in Chicago, which tells about his

case at the Minneapolis Society.

Kettner underwent an evaluation period in January 1974 which was to determine his ability at factory-type jobs, and thus, his worth in wages.

The record alleges that the society "fixed" the evaluation so he would not score well, and would then receive lower wages than he deserved.

It goes on to say that during the 14-day evaluation period, Kettner was tested on the third, fourth, sixth, and eighth days. His duties were changed, the equipment was faulty, and he occasionally ran out of supplies and had to wait for more to do.

Still, his productivity rose from 42-52 percent in the first test to 79 percent on the eighth day. Then the test periods were halted with six days left in the evaluation period, the speech said; otherwise his rate would likely have been greater yet.

During the evaluation period, Kettner was paid at rates of 83 cents to $1.57 per hour. After the evaluation, he was paid 90 cents to $1.24 per hour, while working at the society's workshop until a job came along, it said.

Also, Kettner was forced into signing a wage waiver admitting that he was capable of only 75 percent of normal productivity, while his test rates were 79 percent and climbing, the speech said. He was threatened with loss of wages he had already earned, it said, but he needed the money and signed the waiver.

Kettner told of how he then heard of Sterner Lighting Systems, which had subcontracted some work at the society: "I told my counselor about it and she said to go there myself. So I made an appointment with Jerry Sterner. We talked about my condition, and he hired me. I made $1.90 per hour for days and more at night, $2.17. Then I got a raise to $2.25."

At that time, Kettner could still read and was able "to see Hirsch's (now

G&K) from the drug store," he recalled. He worked on the assembly line in Sterner Lighting's globe department for about two years until a major layoff took place, he said.

Since then, he has been unemployed and has sought work unsuccessfully. "Usually somebody looks up in the paper and tells me (about job openings). Last year I tried a lot of different places, but there was nothing available. This year I didn't call much 'cause of the layoffs," he said.

"I'd rather work than sit around," he continued. "Keep the mind occupied. I try to get jobs, but they always say they'll leave you know, or there's no opening. Then they never leave you know."

In 1978, Kettner spent about three months at a school for the blind in Sioux Falls, SD, taking classes about home management, mobility, crafts, Braille, aptitude and interest tests, workshop time, and a group session.

In the home management course, Kettner made pancakes ("I made too much and had to eat it all."), cakes, pork chops, chicken, macaroni and cheese, and pizza, among other dishes, some in a microwave oven. "I have a microwave, but that was different from mine," he added.

Also, he was instructed in vacuuming, washing and drying clothes, and similar tasks, although he already knew how to do them, he said.

The mobility class dealt with protecting oneself while walking. The participants would walk throughout the building, then outside and in an area where they would bump into things.

"You had to remember all the streets, and always know which direction you were going," he recalled. "I'd go almost twice as far as others 'cause I went so fast. Once I ran into a tree so I backed up and hit it again. It was right in the middle of the sidewalk, and the sidewalk went around it. I thought that must be a stupid town."

Kettner makes use of his mobility by taking frequent walks around Winsted, often to Green Giant or the hospital on different ends of town. His five-foot mobility cane is used to reach ahead of the opposite foot to make sure the path is clear for the next step. He recalled a woman at a Twin Cities bus stop once asking him if the unusually long cane was a fishing stick.

Living alone on the second floor in the library building, Kettner manages the steps by knowing how many there are and following the rail. He relies on sound when crossing streets, except at night when he can see car lights.

"I know the town. I wouldn't walk around in a strange town 'cause I wouldn't know where I am," he said. "I know my distance pretty well, but sometimes do a little bumping. I know where I'm at and know most of the places in town. Like inside your house at night, you know. But sometimes you bump your toe. That happens."

Also at Sioux Falls, he worked on punching rivets in the workshop. Doing one hour a day for a week, he was able to get up to 86 percent efficiency, he recalled.

One of the classes he seems to have gotten the most out of was crafts. He has more wood reed woven lampshades and baskets than he can use in his small apartment.

He also proudly displays a billfold, coin purse, and a pair of moccasins that he did the lacing on. Also, he has a nearly completed floor mat that is about three times larger than normal size, and a few hot plate holders made of small tile pieces.

"The hobby runs in streaks," he said. "It gets kind of boring sometimes. It takes a long time to make that, maybe five or six hours steady to make something. But it's fun. It keeps the mind occupied."

Kettner hopes to return to Sioux Falls for more instruction in Braille. He knows it somewhat, with a workbook and Braille deck of cards, but wants to learn it better.

"I have big fingers and sometimes I hit more than one letter at a time," he said. "And you lose it if you don't keep it up. Some letters – H and J, F and D – are opposites and you have to know them at different angles. Playing cards you get goofed up 'cause the 9 and 5 are opposite.

"Maybe this sounds stupid, but it's hard if you don't know which word you're on. You have to spell out the letters and think what it means. Sometimes it's the simplest word and the teacher is embarrassed to tell you the word," he continued. "If you knew the (Braille) figures, you could read it with naked eyes."

Noting that he is on the first book of Braille and there is a more difficult second book, Kettner recalled a man at a convention he attended who "could read Braille I bet faster than you can read words," he said.

Also at home, Kettner has a clock with the hands exposed so he can tell time by feeling it. Dialing a telephone is done in the same manner, by feeling and counting the holes for each number.

For other tasks, like keeping money, Kettner relies on memory. After someone tells him which bills are which, Kettner keeps them in order and remembers how much he has.

He spends a lot of time listening to the radio, which also helps him keep track of time, besides keeping him entertained with football and baseball games.

In addition to the radio, Kettner has a cassette player and phonograph for which recordings of books are available through the library system. The cassette player has four tracks rather than the conventional two, and the phonograph operates at 8 rpm to allow longer playing time.

Kettner has a couple records that are special to him. One is the recording of that speech at the National Federation of the Blind convention in Chicago telling his story with the Minneapolis Society for the Blind to the convention assembly.

Kettner has also attended national NFB conventions in California and Minneapolis, the latter was this summer at which about 2,000 blind people walked approximately two miles one way to picket MSB offices. The picket was in protest of alleged mishandling of proxy votes in an election of MSB board members. Blind persons are trying to gain authority in MSB, and that case is still in court.

His other record is of another NFB convention speech in which the speaker relates a letter he received from a woman who married a blind man and recounted the various attitudes blind people and their families are subjected to. "I listen to the records over and over," he said.

Kettner plans to stay in Winsted and continue seeking employment. "I get along with everybody and I don't think I have any enemies. That's why I like the town," he said. "Everybody knows me and my condition."

On the other hand, Kettner adds: "Some people think blind people can't do anything. But there isn't any such thing as a handicap if people give you a chance to prove your ability."

The Ol' Professor

In the '70s and '80s, Walt Brovald was a journalism professor at the University of Minnesota who took on the laborious task of receiving and reading virtually every newspaper in the state.

What Brovald did with them enhanced and motivated those in the newspaper industry. When he saw something that was done well, he would send a personal postcard acknowledging it.

Prof. Brovald also wrote a column for the newspaper association titled "The View from Murphy Hall" in which he would mention newspapers and their staff members for instances of high-quality journalism.

It was always a thrill to get an occasional card or mention. The positive reinforcement went a lot further than I realized at the moment.

Who's Got Gas?

Gas prices were going crazy, approaching $1 per gallon, and a shortage was forecast. I made the accompanying illustration for our story with comments from local gas station operators.

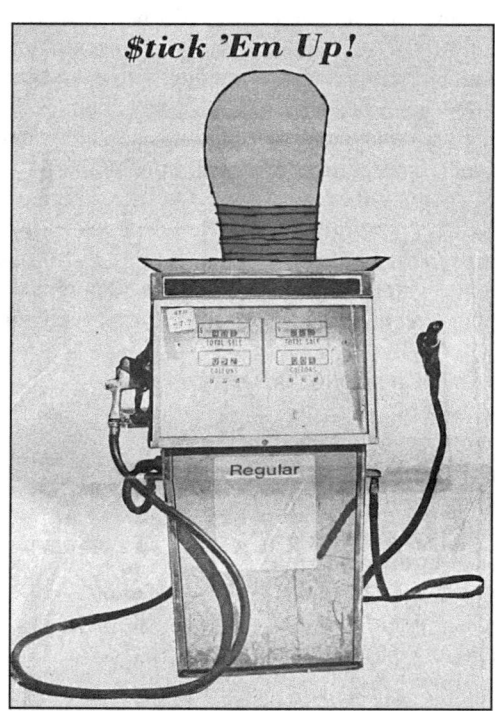

Gas shortage in Winsted? Yes and no
March 15, 1979 • Winsted Journal

Predictions of rising gas prices and complaints about a created shortage were the most common responses made in a survey of local gas stations by the Winsted Journal.

Of six Winsted gas station operators, three felt they would have an adequate supply, two were less optimistic, and the other has already felt a shortage.

The main points repeated by most of the dealers were:

1) Prices may continue to rise, possibly as high as $1 a gallon or nearly that, and

2) There is no real gas shortage, just a "created" one by large oil companies to raise the prices.

Locally, Sterner Garage has been the hardest hit, having experienced a 68% cutback in allocations. The garage ran out of regular gas for a while over the weekend and will be out for the rest of the month by Wednesday.

"We've gotten cut 68% on all gas right across the board – unleaded, regular, fuel oil. That pretty much kind of puts us out of business," said George Knott of Sterner Industries, which operates Sterner Garage. "They're cramming it down our throats. That's supposed to be all over. Everybody is supposed to get cut."

Mike Artmann of A.A. Auto Service has been cautiously awaiting notification of being cut 40%: "I don't know whether we're cut, but they follow in line," he said. "One guy heard on the radio that he had been cut 40% and he wasn't aware of it until then. Then he called and found out he was cut. That's how out-of-touch everybody is. I don't think anybody really knows."

"I read an article in 'Motor Age' magazine that said there's a 30% more supply of oil in the country this year than last," said Doug Kurtz of Kurtz Service Station. "All it is are the big oil companies

giving us the shaft. I think we're getting ripped, but I don't know if there's anything we can do about it."

Most dealers noted that prices have been consistently rising and probably will continue to do so.

"They push the prices up and as soon as they get the prices, there'll be no shortage," Kurtz said. "There isn't one now."

"Shortage? No, I think it's just driving up prices, personally," said Gene Fasching of Winsted Body Shop. "It's been going up a penny a week, but we can't really say 'just a penny' anymore,"

"They're talking a buck a gallon," Artmann said. "It'll probably go to that."

"I'm looking in excess of a dollar," echoed Knott. "By vacation time, it will hit the dollar sign – pretty darn close in July."

If it's any consolation, Paul Gatz of Pauly's 66 looked at it this way: "I figured what they'd do is get everybody worked up about $1. Then they'll get it up to 85, 90 cents and cut it off and everybody will be so glad it didn't make a buck."

Here are more comments by local gas dealers:

Artmann: "We're allocated for what we used last March, which doesn't create a big problem. But if it changes to a 40% cut, it's a big problem. Prices change every day. About every other week, we've been getting a raise. Today might come with another one. We backed off on hours during the big shortage four or five years ago when everybody ran out of gas. Since then we never went back to evenings or Sundays."

Erv Deidrick, Farmers Creamery: "We will have enough. We're not getting cut back so far. We only have six days of the week that the pumps are open. We have no plans for cutting back. Ours is mostly for agriculture. Agriculture is going to be all right, so they tell us. Prices – they'll be going up. I don't know how fast. We have no indication at all. Looks like it could go to $1, they predict."

Kurtz: "As far as I'm concerned, I have three suppliers and there isn't gonna be any problem. One guy wants to take over for us. Last time there was a shortage, we closed Sunday and some nights, but I don't see any reason for that now.

"Prices – you're looking at once a month for sure to go up one or two cents. One supplier is putting in an extra 20,000 gallons for diesel just because they're crying shortage. Gasohol isn't the answer either, by the way. It costs $1.45 a gallon to bring it in by tanker load.

"They say Iran is cutting us off, but only 5% is from Iran. Where is the rest from? At the rate it's going now, dealers are making less. The assumption is that if the prices on the pumps are up, then the dealer makes more, but that's not true."

Gatz: "It's a day-to-day thing. This could be our roughest month. Everything's been good up to now. We're working on last year's allocation. If we get through this month, we should be in good shape unless we get another setback.

"Our number one fuel oil has been out for two weeks. Otherwise, it looks good in prices. We just had a 1 ½-cent increase. The increases have been so common, and there could be another one coming. We will be cutting back one hour during the week and 1 ½ hours on the weekends."

Andy Anderson, Sterner Garage: "We got a load (regular) in Saturday, but now we'll be out about Wednesday and don't look for any more. The way it sounds, we're out for the rest of the month. Just said 65% from last year. That's a hell of a cut. I guess we pump 1,500 gallons a day, so 65% is quite a cut.

"Myself, I think it's a created short-age to get the prices up. It's gonna hurt everybody. I would say if they get it (price) up there, there'll be no shortage. Four or five years ago they got it up 50 cents and then we got gas.

"I don't think it will affect people's driving. They're still gonna drive. People have to work. Unless we get like Europe and go on bicycles. We'll see more motorcycles and people will go to smaller cars."

Knott: "You kind of hear in a roundabout way that refineries have it and are operating at only 75% capacity. It'll be less than that. It's bound to have an impact on industry. I hope to God it doesn't go to rationing. There'll be more darn stealing than you've ever seen. The only thing would be to buy enough to go wherever you're going."

Fasching: "According to the guy who supplies us, we can sell all he can get. He says 'Sell all you can,' believe it or not. But the last week of February, we ran out. We're usually not open evenings or Sundays anyway. We don't intend to close unless there isn't any gas to sell.

"We've been going up a penny a week. I don't know what's going to happen. I imagine if that's where they want it, that's where it will end up."

Jill of All Trades

There's an adage in journalism that every person is a potential feature story – there's something unique about everyone. In a small town where "everybody knows everybody," it's easy to get leads on interesting people like this.

Bought car for 60 bucks, raised turkeys to pay taxes
Sept. 6, 1979 • Winsted Journal

Anna (Mrs. Norbert) Fasching paid $60 in dimes for a Rambler about 20 years ago.

"I've been driving it since," she said in a recent interview. "And I never had any accident, to tell the fact. Never."

"It still goes anytime," she added. "The bottom is falling out – rusted – for the second time. But the motor is good. I don't know, other people have so much trouble, but I never had any – winter or summer."

She got the car from Ed Kraemer who ran a gas station and car lot in Winsted. Kraemer was collecting dimes and Mrs. Fasching happened to be saving them, so the deal was made.

"I drive all year 'round. Had some pretty tough streets in winter, but I always got through them," Mrs. Fasching said. "I haven't gone out of town the last couple years. The telephone is too handy for me nowadays."

Mrs. Fasching recalled her first experience of driving a car: "We had this old-time Ford car. Norbert went up north with a priest to visit for a week, so I was home by myself. We lived on a side hill and the Ford was parked there.

"I had wanted him to show me how to drive it 'cause in those days there was nobody to show you. Well, I thought, 'Gosh darn, I'm gonna learn how,' so I loosened the shift and it started to go down the hill easy and pretty soon it was running," she said.

"I didn't know how to stop it and I was afraid to go on the highway, so I turned among our apple trees. It wasn't going fast, but I'll be a son of a gun, we had a clothesline and it didn't stop and I heard a crash and the top got crushed off. The kids were standing there laughing at me," she said.

"That's how I learned to drive a car. Things like that I never forget," she laughed.

Mrs. Fasching, 87, was born on the farm where her brother, Alois Remer, now lives. She lived in rural Winsted until about five years ago when she and her husband moved to town.

"We had to walk to school and took shortcuts across farms," she recalled. "We had to be in town for church every morning at eight o'clock. We missed it very few times."

She only put in three years of school and then started working, at first doing a lot of babysitting for neighbors. Also, she recalled this from her younger days: "We had a ball team of girls with some neighbors and I was the pitcher. It was a regular team playing."

She became Mrs. Norbert Fasching at age 22, and they bought a farm near Winsted. Norbert farmed many years and then went into the business of moving buildings. He moved about 25 or 30 into Winsted, she said.

Meanwhile, Mrs. Fasching kept busy at home with various activities. One of her main projects was raising turkeys, geese, ducks, and chickens for sale.

"I hatched them in an incubator. I had as many as 75 to 80 turkeys at a time," she said. "I'm trying to remember the price; I know I got more than what they've been getting here lately.

"The turkeys would lay eggs. I'd put

them in the incubator, and it took four weeks to hatch. That was something terrible. I had to put kerosene in the lamp every morning and turn the eggs once a day. There were about 100 eggs in the incubator. And the temperature had to be just so," she said.

"Usually didn't have too many ducks," she continued. "The darn things always ran away from me. We had ponds of water and they knew how to get across them. The turkeys ran away in fall when we were getting ready to butcher. Sometimes they'd come back, sometimes they didn't.

"That was a lot of noise when the turkeys were gobbling around," she added. "In spring when they were laying eggs, the gobblers got so darn mean. They'd go after the kids and myself and just about chewed us up."

The birds were sold through stores and produces for roasting. "That was my business," Mrs. Fasching said. "I raised turkeys to pay taxes most of the time."

While the turkey business took up her mornings, Mrs. Fasching turned to sewing in the evenings. "At night I made rugs. I had a loom, crocheted, and did all my own sewing for all the kids. That was my work at night 'til about 12 o'clock," she said.

Among other things, Mrs. Fasching raised and sold poppies ("I did anything for money"), drove the kids to school with a horse and buggy, hitched up the horses and went plowing, played harmonica, and made several hundred gallons of molasses for her family and neighbors.

She was also quite handy at making toy jigglers from pre-cut patterns. And, in later years, every grandchild received a chair made by Mrs. Fasching. She has the first chair she ever made in her kitchen and "makes use of it every day" to look out a window that is too high for her.

She also recalled having a billy goat

at one time: "It followed the kids in and out of the house, and would ride up on the hay wagon. I thought anyone with kids should get and train one and keep it around town. I always had the notion to get one here and tie it up in back," she said.

"Everything changed so much," she said speaking about Winsted. "I used to go through town every direction and knew who lived where. Now the houses are all painted or have a porch built on."

On living in town, she said: "It's no difference. I never missed the country a bit. Since we moved to town, I've been more busy than on the farm. A lot of times I'm still looking for things when we moved out of the country. But I really do nothing, to tell you the fact. Just piddle around."

Variety

Part of the fun of writing is employing different formats and styles.

News reports need to be straightforward and written in an "inverted pyramid" with the most important information first and descending from there. Columns and opinion pieces go a different direction.

I once compared an editorial in the newspaper to a sermon in a church service, but Pastor Bill Metzger quickly set me straight on the difference between man's opinion and God's sacred word.

Sometimes there's room for creativity and fun, like leading our year in review story with a poem:

1980 – the year in review
Jan. 8, 1981 • Winsted Journal

Compiled here is a year of news
Plus a poem intended to amuse.
So now, good people, read and recall
Of things that happened, big and small:

This year we expanded our knowledge by far
And we also found out who shot J. R.
An elderly housing project was funded at last
To help us forget rejections in the past.

City council members were busy all year
As DAC completion grew near.
A city administrator was hired in spring,
And Win-dustrial Park is another new thing.

Firemen occasionally used their hoses,
And the Census Bureau counted our noses.
The Winsted community got a plug for its name
With Denie being inducted into the Hall of Fame.

Athletic success for some was the fate,
Sterner softball players were best in the state.
All the award winners took their bows
Including Francis Schommer and his cows.

County voters said "Yes! We want a new jail,"
And thanks to nine, the referendum didn't fail.
Politicians weren't the only people running,
The girls cross country team was stunning.

So what kind of impression does all this give?
Just that Winsted's a nice place to live.

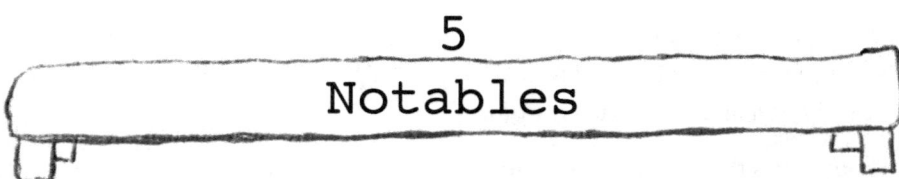

5

Notables

Road to Success

The timing couldn't have been better. Winsted's centennial in 1987 was a few months away, and one of the main events planned was a concert in the Holy Trinity gym featuring Winsted native Paulette Carlson and her band Highway 101.

With the success of Paulette's "The Bed You Made for Me" followed by "Whiskey, If You Were A Woman," Highway 101 was on the fast path to national popularity.

In preparation for the concert, Paulette came in to the Journal office for an interview. At the time, I didn't know much about country music. I'm sure she noticed the blank look on my face when she told of Highway 101 opening a show for Randy Travis.

Rising music star to return for hometown performance
April 28, 1987 • Winsted Journal

When Paulette Carlson was growing up in Winsted, she used to go to neighbors' houses and ask to come in and sing for them.

This summer, they'll be coming to see her when Paulette and her band perform a special concert during Winsted's centennial observance in July.

Paulette's band, Highway 101, is drawing national attention with its recent single, "The Bed You Made For Me," which reached number four on the country music charts. Now, Warner Bros. is pushing the band to complete its first al-

bum, which is planned to be released in early July.

Just a week and a half ago, Warner Bros. threw a party for Highway 101 in honor of making the top five on the charts.

Last week, Paulette was back in Minnesota to visit Winsted and attend the Minnesota Music Awards Thursday where she performed "The Bed You Made For Me" for the audience at Northrup Auditorium. Highlights of the program including Paulette's singing were televised late Thursday night on channel 4.

Saturday, she returned to Los Angeles for two days of rehearsal. By now, she's in Toronto where Highway 101 is playing a few dates with Randy Travis, another Warner Bros. artist.

That's a sample of the busy schedule Paulette is living as her lifelong dream turns into reality.

"I started out singing when I was a little kid. I always knew what I wanted to do," she said. "My mom sang a lot. She'd always sing for parties around town and Al Littfin would play the organ. I guess I took after her."

Herb and Madge Carlson operated Herb's Bakery in Winsted for a number of years. It was located where the telephone company's office is now. Paulette recalled Helen Mochinske, Loretta Janisch, and Lyd Laxen working at the bakery.

When Paulette was entering eighth grade, the family moved to Moose Lake to take over a bakery there, and Paulette graduated from Moose Lake High School. The Carlsons later returned to a farm near Winsted where Madge resides. Herb passed away four years ago.

Paulette began singing professionally right out of high school, working bars in the Fargo area while in college and later in Minneapolis. Then, about seven years ago, she packed up and went to Nashville, the home of country music.

"I felt I needed to be around a music center," she said, "so I quit my job and moved to Nashville. If you want to be in the music business, you have to be where the industry is. You can't just work a club in Timbuktu and expect some record company to come out and find you."

Following the move, Paulette worked with Gail Davies on the road for a year and a half. Later, she signed a production deal with Duane Allen of the Oak Ridge Boys, and a publishing deal with Silverline Music, the Oak Ridge Boys'

publishing company.

From there, she had three singles on RCA "that charted but didn't go real high."

She went on to hire a manager, Chuck Morris, who also manages the Nitty Gritty Dirt Band, Leo Kottke, and Lyle Lovett. Morris suggested that she work in a band situation, and from there, Highway 101 was formed.

Auditions were held in Colorado and Nashville. The group spent about a month in Denver putting the band together, and then signed with Warner Bros.

Their first single was "The Bed You Made For Me" which was written by Paulette right after she moved to Nashville, but it hadn't "hooked."

"All the producers and managers I played it for said 'Boy, that's a song that will break a new artist,'" Paulette said. RCA had the rights to it at the time but didn't put it out so it reverted to Paulette.

"It's such a simple straightforward song, but any time anybody wanted to work it up, they wanted to add too much to it," she recalled. With Highway 101, she said: "'Listen, let's do it very simple' and it worked great. The manager and producers said 'That works' and we went into the studio and cut it."

"The Bed You Made For Me" was released just before the holidays in 1986. Charts and record companies closed for two weeks during Christmas and New Year's, Paulette explained, and the company came back to work, finding the song taking off with much production yet to be done.

"They rushed us back into the studio – got to get the album out now," she said. "That was a treat for our first charted record to go to number four."

That's how her schedule started becoming so busy. Another example was a 10-hour photo session recently for publicity pictures.

In writing for Warner Bros., Paulette

has her own publishing company, Sportsman Music. The name comes from her father's love for hunting. "I figured I'd call it that so I could get all my dad's animal trophies. Poor Mother doesn't have a place to put them all," she said. "Dad was in the sportsmen's club here, and I thought it would be a good thing to do for him."

Paulette learned to write songs by doing it. "I'd write them and forget them, or forget the titles. After I realized everybody liked my songs down there, I thought I should put them down and remember them," she said.

Moving to Nashville, which she considers home base now, meant not knowing anyone there at first.

"You get to know people just from being there," Paulette said. "If you want to be in the music business, you have to be where you can meet people. The best thing about Nashville is it's small enough where you can meet whomever you want to – in restaurants, go to their office, whatever."

The success of late is also cause for some reflection: "I see a lot of work ahead. It's like all of a sudden – did I really ask for this? You've got to watch what you ask for. Evidently I'm going to get it," Paulette said.

"I'm busy all the time. I have to get up early all the time. I get to bed late. It's rewarding being able to get your music out there. This will be my first album. But all of a sudden my schedule became real busy. It takes a little adjusting to. I always have to wear makeup now because people recognize me, she said.

Among Paulette's other credits are having been named Minnesota's Female Country Vocalist of the Year just before she moved to Nashville. Recently, she has been writing songs with Don Schlitz, whose string of number one hits includes "The Gambler."

Other members of Highway 101 are guitarist Jack Daniels, Scott "Cactus" Moser on drums, and Curtis Stone on bass. Moser is from Montrose, Calif.; the others are from Los Angeles.

Moser and Stone appeared in the band scene of Rodney Dangerfield's movie "Back to School" with Stone singing "Twist and Shout." Stone's father managed Tennessee Ernie Ford for many years, as well as being a music publisher.

"They're a great bunch of guys to work with," Paulette said of the other band members, "and they love to party so I'm sure they'll have a great time in Winsted."

Looking forward to the centennial performance, Paulette said "it'll be very nice" and hopes to see a lot of old friends. "I wish my dad was here," she added.

The album should also be out by that time. Paulette wrote one song called "It's About Time" – "I felt it's about time I got an album," however, that song wasn't cut for the record.

With or without that song, it seems Paulette's time has come. "This is what I've been working for years," she said.

The concert had a packed house and was the highlight of the centennial weekend.

A couple years later as Highway 101 continued its success, the band was booked for a grandstand show at the Minnesota State Fair. Linda and I got tickets and enjoyed their high-energy performance.

The following act was a guy who just sat on a stool and sang. After about three songs, we looked at each other, then got up and left. We walked out on George Strait.

But after that, most likely spurred by Highway 101, I developed an interest in country music. Although I had worked my way out of the grind of the reporter role, I was substituting in covering the Winsted City Council when this topic came up:

Major country music festival planned for Winsted this summer

Dec. 27, 1993 • Winsted-Lester Prairie Journal

A major country music festival is being planned in Winsted this summer as a fundraiser for Holy Trinity Schools.

The event – to be called "Winstock" – would be patterned after similar festivals, on the order of WE Fest in Detroit Lakes though not on that large a scale.

Tuesday, organizers of the event sought approval to have the festival at the Winsted Airport. The city council was agreeable, pending details to be worked out regarding liability coverage, possible damage to the property, etc.

The city would be paid at least $4,000 in rent for use of the land for approximately two days. If Winstock meets its budget goal, up to $5,000 in rent would be paid, organizer Dick Langenfeld told the council.

Russ Paschke of the airport commission said his group is satisfied with the plans. The biggest concern is not to have the runway damaged because it would take too long to repair.

The festival is set for Friday and Saturday, June 24 and 25. "We're not looking at this as a one-time shot. Hopefully it will go on as a regular thing," Langenfeld said.

There will be a Friday night session, and then music from noon to midnight Saturday. Camping on the grounds would be allowed.

Possible entertainers include Paulette Carlson, Waylon Jennings, and Crystal Gayle, along with local bands, Langenfeld said.

Set-up work would begin on Thursday and everything should be gone by sometime Sunday afternoon, organizers told the council. The airport would only have to be closed for 1 ½ days during that time.

The airport location has electricity available, and is nearby but still in town so that traffic through Winsted wouldn't be a problem.

Winstock hopes to draw 4,000 to 6,000 people. "This close to the cities, we maybe could get 12,000 or 15,000, but we are thinking of limiting tickets to 7,000 or 7,500 at first until we learn how to handle that many people," Langenfeld said.

The group already has a commitment from a company to provide the stage, sound, and lighting equipment – the same company that handles the state fair concerts.

As you may well know, Winstock Country Music Festival is what puts Winsted on the map. The story is often told how Dick Langenfeld and Tom Ollig noticed the Cornstalk Festival in Regal, Minnesota, and wondered if they could pull off something similar in their town.

They did! Organized as a fundraiser for Holy Trinity School, the event involves hundreds of volunteers year after year to make it an annual destination for country music fans. Winsted is a little over 2,000 in population, but on Winstock weekend, it tops 20,000. Of course, it took a few years to solidly establish itself.

In the first year of 1994, held at the Winsted Airport across from the current festival site, it was only fitting that one of the headliners was Paulette Carlson.

The other big names for the first Winstock were Waylon Jennings and Crystal Gayle. As fate would have it, Myron Heuer was a columnist for us who had retired back to his hometown of Howard Lake after a career as a radio disc jockey. Myron was in Des Moines in the '60s and '70s as Waylon's career was taking off, and the two got to know each other then before going their separate ways over the years.

As part of the hype for the first Winstock, Myron got an interview with Waylon. Then the two were able to reunite in person when Jennings was in town for the concert.

The festival went on to thrive, and it would be remiss to write about Winstock and not mention . . .

An exhaust-ing week: 'Tail pipe girl' goes viral
June 15, 2018 • Herald Journal

By Ivan Raconteur

With Winstock, as with any large event, there are small dramas that play out against the backdrop of the main feature.

One such minor drama went viral on social media Saturday. The incident quickly escalated to show the incredible reach of the internet and social media.

It started when a young woman from Litchfield got her head stuck in a truck exhaust pipe at a campsite on the Winstock grounds. Emergency services were called, and a recording of that 911 call was shared on social media.

A short video showing an emergency responder preparing to cut the exhaust tip with a power saw in order to free the woman was also shared on social media. That video has reportedly been viewed millions of times.

After she was rescued, the woman, Kaitlyn Strom, posted a photo of herself holding the cut-off piece of the exhaust pipe on social media. In a caption on the photo, Strom declared, "I am the tail pipe girl."

This triggered a rash of comments. Some were hostile and abusive in nature. Others were more lighthearted responses noting many people made poor decisions when they were young, but there haven't always been cell phones and social media to publicize the consequences of those decisions. Finally, there were those who defended Strom.

Strom herself posted a comment. The story continued to draw attention through the week, and was picked up by news outlets across the country.

Locally, the owners of the Darwin Tavern posted a photo of the cut-off section of tail pipe on the tavern's Facebook site, noting "The owner of the tailpipe, Mr. Tom Wold, has graciously lent the tailpipe to us for all to see."

And a personal note to George Strait: if you ever come to Winstock, I promise to stay for the entire show.

Seeing Purple

Holy Trinity High School has had a number of outstanding athletes over the years. The most successful, in terms of a professional career, was Neal Guggemos, class of 1982.

After running through high school defenses, he continued wearing purple football jerseys at every level during a fine college career and two seasons with Minnesota Vikings. I went to the College of St. Thomas to catch up with Neal for this interview and covered one of his games.

All-American cornerback turns tables on opponents – now he's a receiver, too

Oct. 9, 1985 • Winsted Journal

A good athlete often excels at more than one sport.

Neal Guggemos went to the College of St. Thomas wanting to play basketball.

Since then, he's achieved All-American status in football and track, his name being mentioned as a pro football prospect, and as for basketball – well, it just got left behind.

Between the end of football season and the start of indoor track, there just isn't time left for basketball, but he "can't complain," said the Winsted native, son of Art and Donna Guggemos.

In high school at Holy Trinity, Guggemos was an all-sport performer, perhaps most noted for his open field running and kick returns in his senior football season. For example, in the homecoming game of his senior year, Neal scored touchdowns on a 55-yard kickoff return, a 19-yard run, a 36-yard interception return, and a 53-yard punt return. The latter three were all in the third quarter.

That kind of success didn't stop with high school graduation as it does for many athletes. After overcoming a knee injury in his freshman year at St. Thomas, Neal has been starting since late in that season.

Until now, he was attracting attention for his defensive prowess, particularly interceptions.

He led the Minnesota Intercollegiate Athletic Conference (MIAC) in interceptions the past two seasons. Coming into this year, he held five school records for interceptions – most career interceptions (18), most interception return yardage for a season (131) and career (230), most interceptions in a season (10), and tied for most interceptions in a game (4).

The single-game record came with all four interceptions in the second half against Hamline in 1983 to help the Tommies win the MIAC title. Earlier that year, he returned an interception for a touchdown against St. John's to win a crucial game. Last year, against Concordia he had three interceptions in one quarter and another that went through his hands.

For efforts like that, Neal was named to the Kodak All-American team last season.

Then this fall, injuries hit the St. Thomas receiving corps, so the coaching staff decided to use Neal's speed (he runs the 40 in 4.45) by making him a receiver in certain situations.

Going into Saturday's game with Carleton, Neal was leading the conference in receiving. Complete conference stats after last weekend weren't yet available when the Journal went to press.

In four conference games so far, Neal has 21 receptions for 424 yards and three touchdowns. Overall through five games, he has 22 receptions for 497 yards and four touchdowns. He leads the Tommies in receiving yardage, average yards per catch (22.6), and most touchdowns.

Defensively, he has four interceptions, three in conference games.

The addition of offensive playing time has been a fun one for Neal, giving him more chances to handle the ball.

"It's kind of nice to be playing both ways my senior year," Neal said. "It gives me a little more incentive to play. I look forward to games more each week. It involves more concentration being on offense."

At practice during the week, Neal now spends most of his time with the offensive unit. He already knows St. Thomas' defensive strategy well enough to play it in games, but spends practice time offensively.

"The thing that most impressed us about Neal was his ability to pick up things so quickly," said St. Thomas receivers coach Greg Capell. "The first time we used him as an outside receiver we came to him on a Monday and asked him. We worked on it that week, and he had two touchdowns that Saturday. Our offense is pretty complicated. It's tough enough to pick up in a year, let alone a week."

A player going both ways isn't too common at the college level, maybe only about one person in the conference does it each year, Neal guessed.

"Defensively, teams don't throw my way that much anymore, so the coaches take me out on a series now and then," Neal said.

Capell noted that in early games this year, both offensive and defensive coaches were afraid to use Neal too much. Because of that, along with a couple runaway games when reserves got into action, Neal was missing some playing time.

Each week follows a typical football player's schedule. Monday is a light day with a lot of film-watching. Conference rules prohibit scouting, but teams exchange two game films. St. Thomas has a new film room with a big screen, and films are now on VCR tapes rather than 16mm projector films, making it easier for players to watch at their convenience as well as at team sessions.

Tuesday through Thursday are the hard practice days with a lot of preparation for the next game. Friday is a lighter day with special teams work before Saturday's game.

Preparing defensively starts at the beginning of the week. As a senior, Neal said, "I know the other receivers – what they can and can't do. Depending on how fast they are and their size, I can play them different ways. And it depends on the rest of the team, what our team defensive plan is.

"We play a lot of man-to-man. I take my guy and adjust to the rest of the game plan. Some teams throw a lot, some don't. The last couple years, I always get the other team's best receiver. Coach just gives me his number."

Combining football, college classes, and a work-study job can get to be a hectic schedule, Neal said, noting that sometimes he leaves his house a half-mile off campus at 7 a.m. and doesn't get back until 10 p.m.

"Being it's my fourth year, I'm pretty well adjusted to it," he said. "I always seem to find a way to get my schoolwork done . . . well, maybe not always," he laughed.

A major in finance, Neal shares the house with a couple of his best friends who are also receivers on the football team.

Making the transition from high school to college football came fairly easily for him. "It's just a different level, a little tougher, but things always seem to be going my way," Neal said.

Though he played one year of nine-man football in high school, it wasn't difficult switching back to 11-man. "You don't have to punt as much with the shorter field in nine-man" is the main difference, he said.

He chose St. Thomas because of its campus and the Twin Cities location. Division III schools aren't allowed to give scholarships for athletic ability. Neal had offers from other schools but picked St. Thomas because of the area.

During Neal's tenure at CST, the Tommies won the MIAC in 1983, and placed second each of the other years. They were co-favorites this season with St. John's, but the Johnnies won the head-to-head meeting a couple weeks ago 16-15 on a last-second field goal.

Asked what Neal means to the team, Head Coach Mark Dienhart said that besides Neal's statistical excellence, "there's a more substantial contribution. He's an impact player who has the ability to change the nature of the game, to put points on the board, to change the way everybody else is playing."

In the conference opener against Gustavus, it was a close game until Neal scored twice on long passes, big plays that had a big psychological impact, Dienhart said.

"He's not a very vocal person. He leads more by example. He was elected captain, so he's popular obviously, and the best athlete on the team. He puts his abilities to use better than most folks do," Dienhart said.

With the prospects of a professional career ahead, both Neal and his coach try to keep the focus on this season.

"I wouldn't say there's pressure," Neal said, two days after the Minneapolis Star and Tribune headlined "Tommies' Guggemos called a possible pro candidate."

"I'm just taking it as an extra. I've got to play each game for the team this year.

It would be nice to get drafted or sign as a free agent. I have to play each game and have a good senior year to have any hopes. I don't think I play any differently because of it," Neal said.

Dienhart said: "My suggestion to him and other players is not to count on it. It's a long way between having a couple scouts come and look and actually being drafted. There are a lot of contingencies – injuries, lack of injuries, the type of year, the type of individual wanted, owners cutting down on the number of active players, the number of rounds in the draft, etc.

"Neal has the goal of having an opportunity and there's nothing wrong with that. It's important to concentrate on having the best year he can now," Dienhart said. "The best football player ever to come out of Winsted or St. Thomas may or may not ever get a chance. It's a matter of timing, and it has nothing to do with ability."

Neal has enjoyed the attention, though, saying he's gotten letters from friends in Winsted.

"It's nice to know someone from Winsted is interested," he said. "When I left for college, some of my friends in high school said 'Maybe someday we'll see your name in the paper' as a joke, and now it's really happening. I'm always trying to talk up Winsted, and when people ask, I make sure they know where I'm from."

More Purple

Another Holy Trinity alumnus made his name not in sports performance but in taking care of professional athletes. Larry "Stosh" Neumann was a trainer for the Vikings.

Stosh's brother, Dean, took me down to Mankato for a day at the Vikings training camp, getting close up to the likes of Tommy Kramer, Chuck Foreman, Ahmad Rashad, and Sammy White.

A few years later, Stosh also had the honor of singing the national anthem at a Vikings game.

Hard work but fun says Larry Neumann, Vikings trainer
Aug. 23, 1979 • Winsted Journal

Working for the Minnesota Vikings football team is something Larry Neumann never thought he'd be doing, but he's sure glad he is.

The 23-year-old Winsted native is now in his fourth year as an assistant trainer for the Vikings at their preseason training camp in Mankato.

He's been part of one Super Bowl, seen several other professional stadiums, and virtually lives a few weeks a year with the players that thousands of people throughout the state spend their autumn Sunday afternoons watching.

Neumann graduated from Mankato State University (where the camp is held) last spring and is seeking a teaching position. This may be his last year with the Vikes.

"I started in high school (at Holy Trinity) as a manager-trainer and liked it," he recalled. "Father Hillesheim suggested I go to Mankato for athletic training. I majored in physical education and minored in athletic training.

"After my second year, the head trainer asked if I was interested in working for the Vikings. I said yes and went for an interview in St. Paul and got the job," he said.

Getting the job means spending about six weeks with the Vikings around the clock during training camp at Mankato

State. Neumann has been working all pre-season games plus home games during the regular season. However, that may change this season if he gets a teaching job.

Neumann has acquired the nickname "Stosh" in the Viking camp. "It's Polish for friend, I guess. The equipment manager named me that the second day 'cause my mom is from Silver Lake," he said.

He described a typical day at the Vikings training camp this way: "I get up about six, shower, have breakfast, then come over and start taping to get ready for morning practice. Rookies start coming in about 7:30 to 8:30. The next hour, the vets come in so they all get taped for practice.

"From 9:30 to 11, we're on the practice field," he continued. "I carry a walkie-talkie hooked up to an ambulance service so we can call. We're there mostly if someone gets hurt, needs a Band-Aid . . . We never had any serious injury, but we're always ready.

"Then from 11 to 11:45 we give treatments like ice therapy, whirlpools, rehab exercises, stretching. Lunch is at noon. I go from about ten to 12 to five after. Then the rookies start coming back to get taped for the afternoon practice. About 1:30 the vets come so they're all taped and ready to go by three," he said.

"Practice is from three to five, treatments again from five to six. We eat at six. Then anything we want from 6:30 to 8:30 while the players have meetings. About 8:30 we have treatments again, and after 11, we're free," he said.

"That goes seven days a week, practice every day. The majority of my time is spent taping and giving treatments. On a busy day, I'll do maybe 80 ankles," he said.

Besides training, Neumann's other responsibilities include packing equipment for road trips, ordering supplies, and teaching new trainers the system. He and the other assistant trainers arrive at camp three days before everyone else to unpack all the equipment and supplies to get ready.

"In high school, we'd buy 32 rolls of tape at a time," he said. Here we orders 100 cases at a time. Since camp opened, we've already gone through 150 cases of 1.5-inch tape plus we have two-inch, three-inch, and elastic tape. I can tape an ankle in a minute and a half."

About 95% of the players get taped every day and most of them go to the same trainer each time. Some of Neumann's regulars are Steve Riley, Charles Goodrum, Dennis Swilley, Fred McNeill, and a lot of the offensive line.

"For practicing a few hours a day and meeting at night, they're usually pretty pleasant. It's a long day for them, too. Most sleep during the day," he said.

"You see all the rookies come in and get to know them fairly well. You like to see who will make the team, the long shots, and the dark horses," he said. Last year, a classmate of Neumann's, Mike Keating, was in camp but didn't make the final team. There are about 71 players in camp but that must be cut to 45 for the regular season.

In addition to the Vikings and Holy Trinity, Neumann has been a trainer for the Mankato State basketball team, and last year he worked Friday nights at Edina West football games. "They (Edina) just called the Vikings and asked for someone so I went," he explained.

The Vikings practice in Mankato until Sept. 1 and then go to Midway Stadium in the Twin Cities until the regular season begins. "I usually quit there and started school the next day," Neumann said.

What are professional football players like? "It's kind of hard to generalize," Neumann answered. "It's a lot different than I anticipated. I thought they wouldn't have time for me, but they're common, ordinary people in a professional career. They're interested in you as much as you are in them."

Neumann also mentioned that Vikings Bob Lee (who's no longer with the team) and Stu Voight have visited at his home in Winsted.

"The players like to tease Offensive Coordinator Jerry Burns," Neumann said. "He's afraid of snakes and bugs, so when they find one, they make sure to throw it in front of him."

There isn't a lot of separation between rookies and veterans, Neumann said. Vets are willing to help, although the rookies have to sing once in a while at the dining table. Trainers don't have to sing, just watch, he added.

Neumann doesn't have much contact with Head Coach Bud Grant. "I never talk to him, but he's fun to watch, the way he manages things. And he's not such a stone-face; I've seen him smile," Neumann said.

One example of Grant's methods is teaching new players and rookies the Vikings' procedure for the national anthem. They line up and Jim Marshall checks them for heels touching the sidelines, feet at a 45-degree angle, helmet under the right arm, left hand at the side, no gum chewing, and looking at the flag. During practice, they face the crowd and sing the anthem.

The Vikings' practices are very organized, Neumann said. "They never go full board scrimmage, just three-quarters speed. But they do practice goal-line situations with the quarterback not liable. They don't try to hurt anybody, just do their job. Everybody's got a spot to be and there's never a lull."

Another enjoyable aspect of Neumann's job is the food served at training camp (he gained 20 pounds one year). Some typical meals include steaks, lobster, shrimp, and crab legs. Near the end of camp, a large "last supper" is served with about 15 kinds of meat and all the fixin's.

"When we travel, everything's first class. That's kind of fun, too," Neumann said. "We stay at the Regency, Registry, Hilton – the nicest was the Crown Center in Kansas City; it was just gorgeous."

Neumann's first pro game was at the Orange Bowl in Miami. He's also been in Kansas City, Cleveland, Cincinnati, Baltimore, Seattle, Buffalo, Tucson, Los Angeles, Oakland, and San Diego. "It's fun traveling and seeing those huge stadiums, being down there," he said.

Neumann described the travel schedule for the Vikings' first pre-season game at Seattle this year: "We left Mankato at 4:30 Friday and got on the plane at 6:30. The next day we started taping about 2 to 5 p.m." All taping and similar preparations are done at the hotel, he said. Very little is at the stadium. The players arrive, dress, warm up, and play.

"Kick-off was at 7:30, but we had overtime so we weren't in the air until 11:30. We got back to Mankato about 7:30 the next morning. Then we had to wait for the equipment and unpack it, help the equipment workers. So we got to bed about 8:45 a.m. That's a long day, but the rest of it we had off. It's fun. I kind of enjoy a hectic basis for two days," he said.

On the sidelines, the assistant trainers mostly keep drinks and towels ready for the players, and attend to minor injuries.

When an injury occurs on the field, the head trainer and doctor will go out. "We watch and try to anticipate what they will need," Neumann said.

During the winter, trainers on the sidelines "have to freeze like everyone else," Neumann said, although he added that it isn't so bad when dressed for it.

"I don't know if I have a favorite player, but the guy that impresses me most is Marshall," Neumann said. "His personality is really interesting and he's a good storyteller about being stranded in the mountains with snowmobiles and all the things he's done."

Neumann hesitated to predict the Vikings' record this year, but said "I think they'll do good, better than people expect. Kramer adds a lot with his arm. A lot of older ones left and younger ones are making themselves known. The offensive line has new blood. Bud never has a losing team. I expect them in the playoffs."

As a highlight of being with the Vikings, Neumann chose the Super Bowl against Oakland. "We could see the mountains over the back of the Rose Bowl. All the players were lined up. 108,000 people were standing there and Vicky Carr sang 'God Bless America.' Who would have thought that a country boy from Winsted would be standing on the sideline? It was quite a feeling."

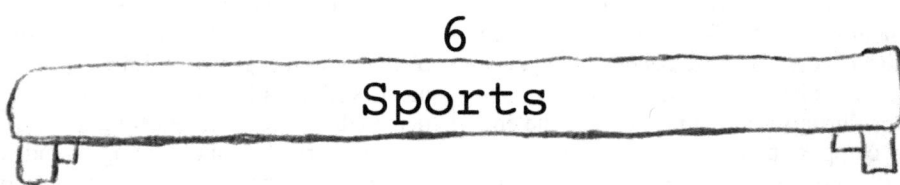

6
Sports

Special Kay

As girls basketball was becoming more popular in high schools, Kay Konerza of Lester Prairie was ahead of her time. A varsity starter since seventh grade, she could single-handedly dominate a game.

Early in the 1981-82 season, Kay became the fourth Minnesota girls basketball player to reach the 2,000-point mark, later climbing as high as second on the all-time scoring list.

When Kay led the Bulldogs to a sixth-place finish in the 1982 state tournament, I had already left mid-season for a job up north, but previously had the opportunity for this story.

Making basketball exciting is Kay's goal
Dec. 10, 1981 • Lester Prairie Journal

When you hear the name Kay Konerza, what do you think of? Basketball, of course.

When Kay reached the 2,000-point career mark in last week's season opener, she became the fourth-highest scorer in Minnesota high school girls basketball history, tops among active players.

Deservedly so, the event attracted a Twin Cities television station to cover it and report her accomplishment on three of its news programs. Similar attention came just 11 months earlier when she scored 54 points against Grove City to set a new single-game scoring record for Minnesota girls.

But that's the obvious side of Kay Konerza. Off the court, she gets letters every day and phone calls about four days a week from recruiters as she prepares to decide which college to attend.

More than 120 Division I schools – Big Ten, Southeast Conference, etc. – have sought her basketball services for the next four years. She has narrowed the list to about 10. March 1 is the earliest a letter of intent may be signed.

Following the lead of Janet Karvonen (New York Mills, 1980, 3,029 career points) and Kelly Skalicky (Albany, 1981, 2,704 points), Kay sent letters and resumes to about 100 colleges and universities last spring, including newspaper articles, stats, and personal information.

"In girls' sports, that's the proper thing to do," Kay explained. "In guys' sports, they'd laugh at it."

In her letter, Kay named the summer basketball camps she would be attending. The list included the B/C All-Star Invitational Camp, which is regarded as the number one camp in the nation, she said.

"There were over 60 recruiters there. You played for them and they watched you," Kay recalled. "If I wouldn't have sent that resume, I would have been just another face in the crowd. After that camp, I started hearing from a lot of schools."

The B/C camp, which holds separate sessions in Indiana and Georgia, rates all the participants by position as a college recruiting service. Kay was rated number 10 in the country at guard. The other nine had attended camp in Georgia; she went to Indiana.

While the B/C camp was basically one long performance for college scouts, Kay also attended some more traditional camps including a midwest-area invitational camp in Wisconsin and one conducted by University of Minnesota Coach Ellen Mosher. She also served as a junior counselor at a Penn State University camp, getting an inside look at that school in the process.

Under American Intercollegiate Athletics for Women (AIAW) rules, recruiters can communicate with Kay and her parents only by telephone and mail unless she is on their campus. For men's sports, "they can come knocking on your doorstep," Kay noted.

Earlier this fall, Kay visited Vanderbilt University in Nashville, Tenn. Under AIAW rules, she had to pay her own transportation to and from the school, but the school picked up costs during her stay on campus.

Men's rules of the NCAA (National Collegiate Athletic Association) allow schools to pay for transportation also, and there is a movement in women's sports to change to NCAA rules, she added.

During her visit to Vanderbilt, Kay practiced with the team's starters, talked at length with players and coaches, toured the campus, and had a welcome message to her displayed on the electric scoreboard during Vanderbilt's homecoming football game.

Vanderbilt, which is about comparable to the U of M, Kay said, is ranked fourth in the Southeast Conference, the strongest women's basketball league in the country.

Friday, Kay will leave on her last "big trip" which includes visits to Louisiana Tech, last year's national champion, and the University of Georgia, a team nationally ranked in the top 10. Later, she will make a formal visit to the University of Minnesota.

"This trip will tell a lot for me, what caliber of ball I can play, where I stand," she said. "I hope after this trip I'll know in my mind about where I want to go."

There has been some local pressure for her to "stay home" and become a Golden Gopher, she noted.

"At the beginning of the recruiting process, everybody had me signed, sealed, and delivered to the U of M. That's where Kay was going," she said. "Through (media) exposure, I've had more of a choice. It helped people to realize I can go to other places than the U of M.

"I'll take a good look at all the schools to make a fair choice for myself," she said. "The place that's meant for Kay Konerza is where Kay Konerza is going. My parents tell me as long as I'm happy, that's the place for me."

For now, thoughts of professional ball after college aren't a major concern for Kay, particularly because of the failing of the United States' pro women's league. She's leaning toward a career in business administration, possibly with a coaching degree.

Despite being the all-around leader on teams that won three conference and three district titles, it took until Kay set the 54-point scoring record before "the big time attention" came, she noted. "Ever since then, people have been aware of who I am and Lester Prairie for girls basketball."

This year, she is keeping a journal for the Minneapolis Tribune, which is running a series of stories on the recruiting process of Minnesota athletes.

"It's a compliment. I'm really appreciative of the exposure. It helps me as far as college. But I don't want people to think Lester Prairie is a one-girl team or anything," Kay said.

"It's five people that make a team. We're out there to make a team. I hope they (teammates) don't feel pressure from it. It's Lester Prairie. We're a team. I want to emphasize how important the team concept is. You can't get anywhere with just one person, that's for sure."

In the same modest manner, she shies away from comparisons to Karvonen and Skalicky – household words in Minnesota girls basketball.

"I don't look at it that way, comparing me to Janet and Kelly, being put in their molds. I don't look at the 54 points. I appreciate getting some exposure; it helped a lot of people know there are others who can play besides Janet and Kelly," she said. "I hate to try to compare. I want to be myself."

Acknowledging that some teams and coaches may be intimidated by the Konerza mystique, she noted the reverse is also true: teams with nothing to lose will go all out to beat Lester Prairie while Kay has the superstar reputation to live up to.

"With the television exposure and everything, people now at some schools, if I make a mistake, they say: 'Oh, Kay made a mistake.' Janet and Kelly, too. I talked to them. They were molded into superhumans, but they're only human, too. People try to build such a high picture that they don't see reality," she said.

"One year at regions, people were saying 'Gee, the girls could even beat the guys' team.' They've got to be realistic. We can do well, but we're not superhuman," she continued. "When I'm on the court, I try to put it in the back of my head. Pressure gets thrown in the lockerroom. Just so the team is doing well and we're winning."

If children are really born with basketballs in their hands, as the old saying goes, Kay must have been one of them.

"I enjoy all sports, the competitiveness, enjoyment, exercise. I was born with it, a first love," she said.

"I lived next door to the Dibb family and grew up in a neighborhood of boys. Kent and I were always good friends and we looked up to his brother playing sports in school. He set an example for us. We had an open lot next door, and we played anything: baseball, hockey, football, basketball. I guess that's where my start was," Kay said.

"Whenever people introduce me, it's 'our basketball player. This is our basketball player,'" she said. "But when I'm with my friends, I'm Kay Konerza the person, not Kay Konerza the basketball player, and I appreciate that. Now they give me a little rough time with 'Can I have your autograph?'"

But being Kay Konerza the basketball player is all right with her most of the time.

"There are times I like to be by myself, but the pressure isn't that great. Sometimes the recruiters are calling, and I want to do something else. But some coaches I could sit and talk with for hours. I enjoy 99 percent of the recruiting and one percent I want to be by myself. There are times I can put it aside," she said.

Other than some interest in art and drawing, Kay keeps busy with physical activities. "Most stuff I enjoy has to do with sports and exercise. I get bored if I sit around too much," she said.

"By accident, I learned to crochet. It's not a hobby, but more or less doing it to prove I could get it done. My sister's a housewife, domestic. I can't sit in the kitchen for more than a couple minutes to eat. I had to prove to her I can do something halfway like a housewife," she said.

When Kay isn't playing for LPHS, she's usually keeping statistics for whatever game is going on. "It helps the coaches out," she said, "and taking stats for football, that's the best seat in the house."

The old alma mater is important to her. "With the 2,000-point thing, I'm glad I got to do it in my home gym, wearing a Lester Prairie uniform," she said. "With the (teachers) strike, there was a little threat about when our season would start. There were rumors that Kay was going to Winsted, Kay was going to Mayer. I was proud to be in a Lester Prairie uniform. This is my home. The strike at Howard Lake and forfeit (the first game was to be at Howard Lake) must have been meant to be so I got to do it in the home gym. It means more with the home crowd."

Now, basketball is different for Kay than it was five years ago when she was a seventh-grader starting on varsity. "When I first started, Coach (Gary) Graham kidded me about getting 1,000 points. I thought 'Wow, a thousand points.' I never imagined 2,000 points. I couldn't imagine a concept that big."

Two thousand points and scores of victories later, Kay recalled: "Ever since seventh grade, I had the goal of trying to make girls basketball good for our school and town. I always enjoyed the boys' games, but the girls bored me. It wasn't as fast and exciting. 'Watching paint dry' is the comment we get a lot."

"I wanted to make it more exciting," she said.

The Fossil

Umpire Kenny "The Fossil" Norman claimed to have never missed a call. He wasn't that perfect, but the truth is he really was a good umpire. As many local baseball and softball players will attest, he called games very accurately, plus he was a fun guy to be around.

Umpire Ken Norman: he never blew a call!
June 19, 1980 • Winsted Journal

"You never blew a call, did you?" umpire Kenny Norman was asked.

"Never," he smiled.

Norman, who has quite a baseball history since he came to Winsted as a child, has been calling 'em as he sees 'em for the last 19 years in area ballparks.

Though slowing down to umpiring only about three softball and two baseball games a week, Kenny has had busy years of doing about 215 games from April through September. That includes high school and town team baseball and all types of softball. During other seasons, Kenny officiates volleyball and basketball games.

In a busy year, he puts on 3,500 miles going to ball games. Schedule-makers are trying to keep umpires closer to home in these days of energy conservation, but in past years, Kenny has gone to places like Hinckley, Northfield, Lonsdale, Red Wing, and even Wisconsin for baseball games.

Now he works in the Crow River Valley League (which the Winsted town team plays in), Ara Wilson, Wright Star, River Valley, Dakota-Rice-Scott, and Carver-Hennepin leagues.

He especially enjoys the Ara Wilson league (Arlington, Brownton, and southwest) because two umpires are used for a game. "That's nice. It makes it much easier," he said.

Softball games are closer to home for him, usually at places like Annandale, Maple Lake, Montrose, Hutchinson, Hollywood, Silver Lake, St. Bonifacius, Waconia, Cokato, or Waverly.

Kenny belongs to the Northwest Umpires Association for baseball and the Tri-County Umpires Association for softball. Scheduling is done through those organizations.

"When I started, I went in and a guy asked how much I played ball. There was no test or anything. They just screened you in a way," Kenny recalled. "They wouldn't know how good you are until you get out there and they heard about you later. You just pay your dues and assignment fee per game."

Officials for high school sports are required to take a test, register, and attend a rules meeting each year, however.

"I'd like to umpire every day with two guys. I could go 'til I'm 75 then," he said. "Two umps make a better ball game. You got somebody on top of all the plays. With one, you got to run for every play."

The hardest call in baseball for a single umpire at home plate is a sliding tag at second base, Kenny said. "Or a pickoff from the pitcher and they'll yell 'You blew it.' Well, I'm over 90 feet away."

Another hard call, he said, is at first base with a diving runner and high throw. Kenny contends a low throw seems to get to the base faster, although it shouldn't make any difference, he adds.

"Most of the complaining is from ballplayers that are mediocre players," Kenny said. "The good players won't give you trouble. It's the mediocre ones that are needed to fill out the team or the substitutes that give you static.

"The last five years have been a lot

worse," he continued. "You get some really hot-tempered guys. If it goes good and you call all strikes and all the right plays for them, jeez, you're great. But if you miss three or four out of 160 calls, you were really rotten today.

"You're not a good umpire if you try to even out calls. I believe some guys do that, but I don't know if I ran into it. Some might do it inadvertently," he said.

"Make one decision, make it tough, and make it strong," he stated his position. "Be loud so they'll understand you and don't have to ask again. If you hesitate, they'll doubt you. In this game, there's one guy out there. You're the boss. They're the ballplayers, and if not, they're soon out of the game. If they argue nice that's good, but some guys really get bad and you gotta throw 'em out.

"A lot of umps take too much, and that's why we're not getting as many umpires. They don't want to take the abuse. You got to enjoy the sport to take it Sunday after Sunday," he said.

Crowds get on umpires for certain plays, too, he said. "They'll yell 'You blind?' 'Where's your cane?' 'Can't you see?' A lot call you a lot of bad names, too."

He noted, though, that high school players are more disciplined. "High school ball is a lot different. It's the same strike zone, but a lot easier," he said. "We have two men umping. And the coach can tell the players what to do. In amateur ball, most guys tell you (the manager) to go to hell, or they'll quit. A lot of high school coaches are strict about it."

Through his year of umpiring, Kenny has seen about five or six triple plays and about four no-hitters, he said.

One of the strangest plays was about three years ago when a triple play occurred on a bunt. The batter laid down the bunt – not a popup – and a runner from third was out at the plate, he explained. Then the catcher threw the ball into the outfield and the next runner was thrown out trying for home; then the batter was put out going for third base.

The best type of ball game, Kenny said, is a 1-0 score. "The pitching has to be superb and the fielding excellent. There have to be a lot of good plays – outfielders run a mile and fall on their heads and catch the ball. 2-1 is good too, or 3-2. 1-0 is the most exciting.

"Now a lot of games are 18-3, 15-2, 22-6. One year, I had one that was 34-7 on a Sunday afternoon. There were four or five grand slams. Some guys had four homers apiece. And we got done at 10 minutes to five (games start at 2:00)."

Kenny played on baseball teams from about age 15 to 41 – mostly as a catcher, pitcher, third baseman, or shortstop – before taking on umpiring. Included in that career was Winsted's state championship in 1948 when Class A baseball was still popular in the area.

"A ball," as it is referred to, allowed for a certain number of players to be brought in by a team and paid, as much as $50 a game for a pitcher. However, in about 1950, Class A ball took a sharp drop in popularity and all town team baseball is now Class B with unpaid players.

Kenny contends that players aren't as good as those years ago. "There was so much better pitching and better ballplayers when I played," he said. "Then they wanted to play. Today, a lot like to play, but don't care if they miss. We had 14 to 17 guys and every one was always there.

"Town teams don't get the good high school players anymore," he analyzed. "Most go into slow-pitch or modified softball. Some teams have good pitching, but not hitting, or good hitting but not good pitching. A lot of teams have 24-, 25-year-olds playing so the younger guys don't get a chance to play and they quit. The younger ones are not coming out. You can't blame them in a way."

Getting back to umpiring and officiating, Kenny said basketball is the hardest sport to officiate. "In baseball, you just look for the ball and the plays. Basketball, there's a push here, grab there, traveling, the end line, on somebody's back – so many things to look for," he said.

And in today's world of shortages, Kenny notes there is a shortage of umpires developing as fewer people are going into it.

"It's been enjoyable. The most fun is meeting people, running into so many nice young teams and good people. I've even been invited out for supper, and you run into guys who played 12 years ago and are still playing," he said. "You got to like it, too. It was bred in me. Dad was a good player in his time. And you got to have a good wife. That's really important. You're away from home a lot."

Kenny plans to keep umpiring as long as he can, again noting that it's easier to do with two umpires for the same game. His career highlights are winning the state title and umpiring in state tournaments.

"I've had a lot of good years," he said. "We never miss any calls, but we do make mistakes. A guy I know asked me seriously if I ever miss a call. There's nobody that hasn't missed them – maybe seven or eight a year – but you can't tell them that. They know you do, ballplayers know you do – you're only human. But if someone asks, you never admit missing a call."

A few years later, we carried another story on the three-generation umpiring family of Kenny, his son Dick, and grandson Todd.

Getting It Wrong – Twice

My son, Kip, came across my column from when Lake City had defeated Howard Lake-Waverly in the 1979 boys basketball state championship game, and he took great joy in pointing out how far off I was in my comments about 7'1" Randy Breuer.

I had said Breuer would "never see action in a game as a Gopher" at the University of Minnesota, and if he did, he would be "eaten alive immediately." Well, as a freshman, Randy was a big part of helping the Gophers get to the finals of the National Invitational Tournament.

I apologized in a column the following year, but still didn't have it figured out, writing that Breuer "is still not a prime candidate for the pros." He proved me wrong again by playing 11 seasons in the NBA.

Some of the best moments in sports are impossible to anticipate. That spontaneity is what makes them special.

Long Night

In January 1979, we finished laying out that week's paper, and then I headed to the Holy Trinity gym to take in that night's basketball game. I was there longer than I expected.

Buffalo Lake tips Trojans in longest game ever
Feb. 1, 1979 • Winsted Journal

It was literally a game and a half when Buffalo Lake upset the Holy Trinity boys basketball team 98-97 in six overtimes Tuesday of last week.

Despite losing their second game of the year and possession of first place in the Circle Eight Conference, the Trojans earned a spot in history. As far as anyone knows, the Trojans' 98-97 loss was the longest game ever played in Minnesota high school basketball history.

The Minnesota State High School League does not keep records of regular season games, but Art Johlfs, a well-known Minnesota high school sports analyst, cannot remember a longer game. Johlfs has been involved in high school basketball since 1919.

If there was a chance that the Trinity players could forget the game, that possibility was dashed when the National Sports News Service awarded the Trojans a certificate for the trophy case to commemorate the game.

Trojan Mark Marshall also received an award as a member of the 40-point club for his 44-point performance.

From the beginning, it looked like Holy Trinity was taking a major step toward the conference title. The Trojans dominated the game early and led by as much as 14 points in the second quarter. Buffalo Lake had cut the margin to six by halftime.

Paced by 6'4" center Jay Bryan, the Lakers finally tied the game in the fourth period at 61-61 and took a four-point lead with 1:28 to play. Buffalo Lake could have put the game away in regulation time, but a Laker missed a free throw with 10 seconds left while leading by two. The ball was tossed to halfcourt where Marshall came up with it out of a group of players and raced down the court for a tying lay-up with two seconds to go.

In Overtime I, both teams squandered shots in the last half-minute. The Lakers had a chance to win in OT II, but, as in regulation time, a free throw attempt failed with eight seconds left and this time Jon Kohler pumped in a 20-footer to tie it for the Trojans.

With the teams tied in OT III, Kohler intercepted a late pass, but a long shot at the buzzer missed. If Trinity hadn't overcome enough hurdles, they ran into another obstacle when big Jim Fiecke drew his fifth foul just eight seconds into OT IV. The Trojans hung in though, and managed to extend the game again despite falling behind by four points at one time.

By now the score was in the 90s as Trinity took the lead in OT V, only to have Buffalo Lake's Bryan toss in a basket with four seconds left.

Bring on OT VI. The Lakers took a two-point lead followed by a single free throw by Kohler making it 96-95 Buffalo Lake. As time started running out, the Trojans had to commit a foul and they ended up tagging the wrong man: Bryan. With five seconds left, he sank both free shots icing the game. The Lakers gave Marshall an uncontested lay-up and let the clock mercifully run out.

Marshall was the star for Trinity shooting 58 percent from the field and making eight of nine free throws for 44 points, just one short of the school record set by Fiecke last winter. Fiecke had 24 points and Kohler added 13. Bryan netted 35 for Buffalo Lake.

Nice Shot

The next one wasn't a great moment in sports. In the 1981 football playoffs, Holy Trinity was handed a lopsided loss by Starbuck in western Minnesota. But I had the good fortune of capturing this action shot, which won an award in the state newspaper contest.

Nov. 12, 1981 • Winsted Journal
Trojan Al Sexton and a Starbuck player scrap for a loose ball in Saturday's tournament game won by Starbuck 56-14.

The A.D.

In order for us to enjoy sporting events, someone has to do the behind-the-scenes work. Fr. Jerry Hillesheim told of his love for athletics in the role of Holy Trinity's athletic director.

Athletics are fun for Trinity's Fr. Jerry

Sept. 18, 1980 • Winsted Journal

An athletic director does which of the following duties: a) sets up schedules; b) measures and marks the football field; c) sells tickets; d) keeps scores of games.

If you're talking about Holy Trinity High School Athletic Director Father Gerald Hillesheim, the answer would be e) all of the above.

For Fr. Jerry, now in his 13th year as AD at Trinity, being around athletics is fun. "It's something I enjoy," he said. "It's my form of a recreational outlet, in a sense – always being close to athletics."

Describing his job in a sentence, Fr. Jerry said he is responsible for the entire athletic program at Holy Trinity, and anything that pertains to athletics in any way.

That includes setting up schedules, preparing the field or court for games, and working at games, or finding people to help with those tasks. "My job is made a lot easier by all the dedicated coaches and volunteers helping out," he said.

Arranging schedules is one of the main duties of being an athletic director. That, of course, includes all 10 of the Trojan varsity sports, plus junior varsity and junior high as well.

Varsity scheduling is usually done a year or more in advance, Fr. Jerry said. Last week, he signed contracts for the first two football games of the 1981 and 1982 seasons with Howard Lake-Waverly and Mayer Lutheran.

That means next year's football schedule is taken care of, as well as the Circle Eight Conference volleyball schedule.

"The number one priority is the con-ference," he explained; non-conference games are then added to fill out the schedule up to the number of games allowed by the Minnesota State High School League (MSHSL).

The conference schedules do have a logical system that they are based on. Fr. Jerry explained that every two years the last two games are moved up to the beginning of the schedule so a team isn't playing the same opponent at the same time year after year. That is done in all sports.

Also, the schedules coincide with other sports in the same season. For example, Circle Eight volleyball games are played the Tuesday before the football game between the same schools, but at the opposite site.

This year, it is more complicated because Trinity is in the Tri-Valley Conference for football and Circle Eight for volleyball. Next year, however, during the week that Trinity plays football at Lester Prairie, the Trojan volleyball team will host Lester Prairie. Currently, the Tri-Valley has a junior varsity football schedule with schools meeting the following Monday at the opposite site of varsity games.

A similar coordinating pattern is involved in winter sports, too.

After Fr. Jerry gets notified of the conference schedules, he then hires officials (also a year ahead) and contracts for non-conference games. Travel and fan appeal are important considerations in choosing non-conference opponents, he said.

"Our athletic program is totally self-sufficient," he pointed out. "As opposed to public schools, there is no money for tuition or taxes for athletics. All the money is from what we can generate in the program itself. That's why we push season passes and have close-by games to draw fans."

For example, the girls basketball team this winter will play non-conference games against Mayer Lutheran, a traditional rival; neighbors Howard Lake-Waverly and Watertown; and Rockford, a smaller school in the Wright County Conference with which a tradition is being developed.

"Each year you're allowed so many games and you try to fill out as best you can with people close by," Fr. Jerry said. "Even though Howard Lake and Mayer are much larger than us, it's our best interest to play them (in football) for travel and fan appeal. The object is to maintain a balanced program and cut expenses."

In volleyball, it has become customary to have three matches for C, B, and A teams when schools meet to play each other. Transportation costs are reduced by sending all three teams on one bus.

Otherwise, junior varsity scheduling is usually finished during the previous school year, he said, while junior high games aren't set until right before each season when each school knows what kind of turnout it has.

So, now all the schedules are done and it comes time for a game to take place. There are still plenty of things Fr. Jerry has to make sure are ready.

For volleyball, the gym has to be set up, usually by coaches after school. People have to be found to run the scoreboard; keep the scorebook; for volleyball, judge out-of-bounds calls; and sell tickets.

The next step, he said, is to open up, usually 25 minutes ahead for volleyball and 40 minutes ahead for winter events. Fr. Jerry arrives in time for the opening and does a final check that everything is set up. "The rest runs pretty much by itself," he said. Afterward, he and a coach are the last ones to leave after shutting off the lights, locking doors, etc.

Fr. Jerry usually takes care of preparing the football field with a couple students, the day before a game when possible. That includes cutting and marking the field, seeing that all the lights work, restrooms are ready, and gates are working.

In winter, the boys and girls basketball teams take turns setting up the gym for each other's games, he said.

What's there to get ready for a basketball game? Well, the bleachers have to be pulled out, side baskets raised, floor swept, chairs set up for team benches, scorer's bench set up, and stage curtains pulled back.

"Ultimately, it's my responsibility, but the cooperation of all the other people makes it easier," Fr. Jerry said.

About the only thing Fr. Jerry doesn't get involved with is taking care of concessions, which is done totally by the school's student council.

Fr. Jerry attends all home events – there are 36 on the schedule so far this year. "I'm there to make certain things are working unless I delegate it to someone else. This is my 13th year and I can count on one hand the home events I've missed for some reason. I don't have time to go to away events except football and when our kids are in districts," he said.

For away games, duties are fewer: only arranging transportation and sending a roster ahead of time so the other school can make a program for an upcoming game.

Busing is arranged a month ahead of time, but isn't always the easiest thing to do – especially when several events are going on. By checking his overcrowded calendar, Fr. Jerry can tell that "Tomorrow we have a bus leaving for volleyball at 5:00 and the van going for cross country at 3:00." At times when both vehicles are tied up, he has to call parents to arrange for transportation.

And, of course, athletic directors aren't exempt from paperwork.

Fr. Jerry estimates he spends about 1 ½ hours each school day with tasks such as preparing game programs and sending reports to the MSHSL.

Each sports season – fall, winter, spring – he has to send eligibility lists, verification of physicals, parents' consent forms, insurance forms, participation numbers, and such to the state for all participants on all levels, including cheerleaders and the danceline.

Then there's the attendance of home events. For a volleyball match last week, he arrived at 5:15 and left the school about 9:15.

In addition, Fr. Jerry serves as announcer and scorekeeper for boys basketball, and keeps statistics for football. Speaking of the football stats, he said: "It's my way of keeping calm. I'd probably be the most enthusiastic fan around if I didn't have some way to tie myself down."

Except for attending an annual athletic directors conference, Fr. Jerry learned the duties by doing them. He came to Trinity in June 1968 and was Assistant AD under Fr. Edward Ardolf for the first year. He's had the position since.

"The only training I had was a deep interest in athletics all my life," Fr. Jerry said.

"There isn't really anything I don't like about it," he said of the job. "People might not think I care to go out and measure the football field, but I enjoy being in the fresh air and feeling I've done something worthwhile.

"One difficult thing is being on edge if an event will take place because of weather. Or if we have buses away, being on edge to see the bus return safely. Most of the anxiety is if something happens. My prayer before every event is for the safety of the individuals and fans."

Asked what he likes most about being involved with high school sports, Fr. Jerry said: "The opportunity to see and be with students enjoying themselves. I love young people. I love to see them having a good time, experiencing small and large successes. It's important that a player or student experiences the joy and happiness of doing something he might not have thought he could. It's not necessarily winning that is the most important thing. The most rewarding and satisfying is the amount of super-dedicated people, volunteers, and coaches."

Among his memories are games that drew large crowds; he mentioned a boys basketball game against Lester Prairie several years ago with both teams coming in undefeated. Also, he recalled the girls basketball team returning from winning the state invitational (private school) tournament several years ago.

And then there was his first year when the school didn't have a football field. One home game was played at Winsted's old baseball field in the south part of town and the rest at Howard Lake, some on Saturday nights. Except homecoming: "I remember going to Howard Lake for homecoming and there was a foot of water on the field," he said. "We had to postpone it, and it was played the next afternoon at Lester Prairie."

One other memory he mentioned, also from his first year, was when Roger Guennigsman made a basketball hook shot from past midcourt right before halftime during one game.

"That's typical of what I've enjoyed," Fr. Jerry said. "To see the expression of delight on a young man's face like that. Here's a kid out for athletics, willing to practice and participate, and to see him experience that satisfaction. Something he'll remember all his life."

Who You Know

For anyone with an interest in Minnesota sports, this next person needs no introduction:

Hartman: education important, so is hard work
June 2, 1987 • Winsted Journal

Besides talking about what he knows best – sports – Sid Hartman stressed hard work and desire, as well as education, to be keys for future success for today's young people, while speaking at the Holy Trinity athletic banquet Thursday.

Out of about 250 reporters at the Minneapolis Star and Tribune, Hartman is the only one without a college degree, he said. He started selling newspapers for the Minneapolis paper at age eight, and by meeting people in the newsroom got the break to begin his now legendary reporting career.

"Right now, if you don't go to college and want to get a job, you're going to have some problems," Hartman said, but adding that the person with a desire to work hard and do things can move up the ladder and exceed the top graduate of a class.

"If you work hard enough, you can accomplish something. I think I would be a lot better writer and newspaperman if I had gone to college. If you get a chance, get a college education," he said.

At the same time, Hartman pointed out "it's not what you know, but who you know," and playing sports helps you get to know people who can help you do well in the future."

The who-you-know principle was instrumental in Hartman agreeing to appear at the banquet, something he rarely does these days. HTHS alumnus Larry "Stosh" Neumann, currently assistant trainer with the Vikings, was able to convince Hartman to come to Winsted.

Noting that Neumann recently directed the school musical "Damn Yankees" at Holy Trinity, Hartman said "Stosh's biggest accomplishment of all time was getting Vikings Coach Jerry Burns to see that play."

Getting into his area of expertise, Hartman said: Those of you who read my column or listen to my shows know that my style is to be very positive. There are a lot of people in sports media today making a good living by being total negatives, just ripping people all the time, never talking to people. It's easy to be negative but it takes a lot of hard work to be positive.

"I think my relationship with athletes and sports in general allows me to lead a life that most people would envy. It's a lot of fun for me to go to work every day," Hartman said.

And it's long days he put in, starting with a 6:45 a.m. radio show on WCCO with Boone and Erickson. The station put equipment in Hartman's home so he can do the show every morning in his pajamas if he wants, he said.

Besides that, he does frequent "Lead-Off Man" and "Sports Hero" radio shows as well as his popular column in the Star and Tribune.

Hartman called the Twin Cities a tremendous area for sports with the professional and college teams playing here. "About the only thing that could make this area any better for sports is if one of these teams could ever win a major championship," he said.

Hartman also referred to another banquet guest, Winsted native Neal Guggemos, who spent most of last year as a Viking rookie on injured reserve.

"I think he's got a good shot," Hartman said of Guggemos." You have to be in the right place at the right time. The best thing that happened to Neal Guggemos last year was when he broke his wrist (in the Vikings' first pre-season game) . . . They put him on injured reserve and he got to hang out with the players and work out with the team, gained a lot of experience and I think he'll make it this year."

Telling of his relationship with athletes, Hartman said his closest friend is former Vikings coach Bud Grant.

Hartman began newspaper reporting about the same time Grant came from Superior, Wisc., to play football at the University of Minnesota, he recalled. "Grant practically lived at my house during the four years he went to college. When he wasn't home in Superior, we probably had every single meal together," Hartman said.

Recalling the scoop of Grant's first retirement, Hartman said: "One day Mike Lynn (Vikings general manager) called me into his office and said 'We're going to make a big, big deal and we want you to go out to California with us and report it.'"

Hartman thought a trade was in the works with the Los Angeles Raiders, so he got on the plane with Lynn and Grant where Grant said: "What's really happening is I'm going to quit, and I'm going to give you the story but we don't want you to print it until I get a chance to talk to Max Winter and tell him my decision."

They wanted Hartman to continue on to Hawaii with them. He refused, but honored their request to hold the story. Hartman flew back from Los Angeles, then got the phone call to go ahead, and "had probably one of the greatest stories ever.

"I learned you can be close friends with these coaches and athletes and still have a good relationship. My number one loyalty is still to the newspaper. If something happens that's news, I have to print it. One thing about Grant: he knew he had a job and I had a job. If I had to write a story that might be critical of one of the players, he didn't like it, but he went along with it. We still are close to this day," Hartman said.

As for others, "I get along with all the malcontents – Woody Hayes, George Steinbrenner, Billy Martin, Bo Schembechler, Bobby Knight. All these guys are very close friends . . . If you write a critical story and it's true, the facts are there, they're not going to get mad at you, but if you write something and just make it up, don't have the facts . . ."

Steinbrenner, for example, "gets nothing but criticism from the newspapers but has done more good things for more people," Hartman said. He told of how Steinbrenner read about a child with a serious disease and needed $28,000 for a year's treatment to keep him alive. The next day, Steinbrenner had the family come in and he gave them a check for $56,000. Another time, Steinbrenner was asked to donate $25,000 for lights at a college baseball field; instead he put up $125,000 for the entire cost.

Then there's Bobby Knight. "I saw Knight win the Final Four this year with less talent than any team in the Final Four. He knows how to discipline and handle people. He recruits the right kind of kid. In the 15 years he's been there (Indiana), three of his athletes have not graduated. He's kicked out some of the best players he's had because they wouldn't go to class. He does such a great job, and that's the way it should be," Hartman said.

"I just enjoy being with these people. It's fun knowing them. I don't think you can stab a guy in the back one day in your column, and write something accurate to pat him on the back the next day and go up and think he's a great friend of yours," he said.

Closing, Hartman gave a rundown on what he sees ahead for some of Minnesota's sports teams:

• Twins: "If they get some pitching, they might win the pennant. They've had trouble putting the hitting and pitching together."

• Gopher football: "They have a chance to be in the Rose Bowl this year. The first six games are all games they could win. John Gutekunst has done a heck of a job. They had a great recruiting year, and they're recruiting a different kind of kid right now – they're recruiting kids who can spell and write. They've got probably the best running back in the country in Darrell Thompson. If he stays healthy, they'll be tough."

• Vikings: "They've improved their team a great deal. They had a great draft this year. Greg Richardson from Alabama runs a 4.3 in the 40 which is very fast. They need some help in the secondary and that's where I think Neal has a shot to help them. Last year he showed them he can play. He's one of he fastest guys on the team. I think the Vikings are going to be the surprise of the National Football League if they don't get many people hurt. D. J. Dozier – you don't have a great team without a great running back and I think he'll make a difference."

• North Stars: "The greatest thing they did was hire Herb Brooks. I say Herb Brooks is the Bobby Knight of hockey. He coached the US Olympic team to the big Olympic championship with much inferior material to the Russians. The North Stars had a lot of problems last year that the coach didn't get along with the players, a lot of dissension. I think they'll do very well now."

• Gopher basketball: "It'll take a couple years for the team to come up. They have signed three or four outstanding players."

• Gopher hockey: "The team will do well, providing the Olympic team doesn't completely strip them of all their top players. Nine or 10 were named to the Olympic trial team; it's going to be tough."

"I could go on forever talking about sports," Hartman said. "I just want to impress on all you high school students: get your education, listen to everybody, don't go near drugs, don't drink, don't do things you shouldn't that you'll be sorry about. An athlete has a tremendous opportunity."

Real Sportsmanship

Silver Lake was in the midst of high school football dominance in the mid-'80s. In 1986, Holy Trinity came heartbreakingly close to pulling off a major upset, losing 14-12.

The next season, the Trojans came close again, falling 22-16. Then the teams met for a rematch in the section championship. Holy Trinity played tough one more time, trailing by only a touchdown at halftime, but the soon-to-be state champion Lakeites pulled away in the second half to win 37-12.

The point of this story is what I remember as one of the greatest moments of sportsmanship I've ever witnessed. During the awards presentation, the entire Trojan team spontaneously applauded as the Lakeites received the championship trophy.

This was before the scripted sportsmanship routines that teams are forced to go through now. It was a genuine show of respect after the two rivals had battled it out.

I added this sidebar to the game coverage in the next newspaper:

Class acts by class team
Nov. 9, 1987 • Winsted Journal

Besides the obvious accomplishments of an 8-3 record, the Trojan football team and staff should take a lot of pride in their character and sportsmanship this season.

Watching from the sidelines this season, I've noticed several instances that deserve mention:

• In an early season game, the referee lost track of downs and would have given the Trojans an extra play, but the coaches pointed out the error and punted instead.

• Many times when an opposing player went down injured, Winsted's coaches reached him first to provide medical attention.

• Saturday, after accepting their runner-up trophy, the Trojan players turned and clapped for their opponents who received the championship plaque.

Winning is nice, but it's just good to see a bunch of young guys who gave it their best shot and proved they are good sports as well as good athletes.

A Coaching Legend

There's more about Silver Lake's football success in this tribute to my high school football coach, Buz Rumrill, who passed away in 2023.

High school football memories: tribute to Coach Buz
March 24, 2023 • Herald Journal

Over 24 seasons in Silver Lake and five in Glencoe-Silver Lake under the guidance of Coach Buz Rumrill, hundreds of young men shared the joys and pains of playing high school football.

Buz yelled at us. He laughed with us. He taught us how to be good football players. First, he was our coach. As we grew up, he was a lifetime friend.

Every player has his own story about the experience of playing for Coach Buz. This is one of them.

Kicking it off

In 1970, a young South Dakota native named Burton Rumrill, who went by "Buz," arrived at Silver Lake High School to teach social studies and history – and coach football.

Victories didn't come right away, but when they did, they came in bunches.

Silver Lake had enjoyed a run of success in the '60s, especially the unbeaten 1967 team that only allowed one touchdown in its eight-game season.

But every athletic program goes through its up/down cycles, and so it was for the Lakeites. Yearbooks show that the team won only one game in each of Buz's first three seasons in Silver Lake.

After that, a winning tradition was established that lasted long beyond Buz's reign.

Cover the point

Buz preferred a style of we're-going-to-run-the-ball-and-you-can-try-to-stop-us.

He often said that three things can happen when a team passes, and two of them are bad – incomplete or interception. Still, his playbook had some options for when a pass was in order. Our go-to pass play was sending a tight end out about 10 yards and then cutting all the way across the field. High school defenses weren't too adept at covering crossing routes, so that play often came through when we needed it.

Playing under Buz, he instilled in me the most basic fundamental of football: "cover the point." Carrying the ball tucked between your arm and chest, keep your hand over the end of it as the most secure way to prevent fumbling when inevitable contact is made. When my boys stepped on the gridiron, that's what I harped on them most: "Cover the point!"

Buz taught us how to properly recover a fumble: you fall on the ground next to the ball and pull it in to you. The ball should not be underneath you, because a few hundred pounds of other players will be piling on top of you momentarily.

He insisted that we play at full speed rather than "pussyfooting." Buz liked to use the example, "If two cars collide head-on, one is going 90 mph and one is going 20 mph, which one do you want to be?"

That concept was reinforced in one of our pre-season drills in which the team would form into two single-file lines facing each other. Taking turns, one player from the first line would carry the ball between tackling dummies placed a few feet apart while a teammate from the other line would attempt a tackle.

After each turn, you went to the end of the opposite line, and it was luck of the draw who you would match up with for your next one-on-one encounter. Would you go 90 or 20?

Depending on the circumstances, both individually and for the whole team, Buz seemed to know whether a fiery tirade or a lighter reasoned approach was more likely to get his desired outcome. Sometimes he just made a simple observation, like that our offensive formation was "all wish and no bone."

Though he was a smashmouth football guy first, Buz also had some tricks up his sleeve to mess with an opponent strategically.

My all-time favorite Buz tactic was the year we committed to begin each play on the same snap count. It was "Down. Set. Hut." The ball was always snapped on hut, or "on one" as it was termed. This repetition trained the opposing defense into playing at that rhythm.

There would be two exceptions to that pattern. In the second half on third-and-four, we would go "on two" instead. Lining up, we were grinning inside our helmets, knowing that at least one duped defensive lineman would come crashing offside "on one" and give us a free first down.

The other situation was short yardage when a quarterback sneak would be adequate. In that case, we'd go on "down" before the other team had fully dug in.

As for school, even the girls seemed to enjoy that Buz's Friday social studies classes were primarily devoted to discussing that night's game. And Mondays were a good time to review what had happened. There were plenty of other days to learn about social studies.

Gaining momentum

As a sophomore in 1972, my first vivid memory of varsity football was seeing Lester Prairie's Dave Prehn coming straight at me, then darting to the side and into the end zone before I could react. The 90/20 analogy doesn't apply here. Dave was going 90 but I was parked.

That season was a time for taking our lumps and gaining experience as we finished with a 1-8 record. Cosmos must have been worse than us. We almost won a second game out in Milan in western Minnesota but let it get away at the end.

By the next year, we showed improvement and that there was hope for the future. It was also when we started playing home games in the evening under the newly installed lights at our field.

Our coming-of-age game was against Holy Trinity of Winsted. All week before, the hype was on having to face Mike Keating, who would later go on to try out for the Minnesota Vikings. Everyone was surprised when we not only upset the Trojans but did so convincingly 22-0.

Three weeks later in Lester Prairie, we gave the defending Cro-Hawk Conference champion Bulldogs all they could handle in a tense 6-0 thriller. The only score was a 59-yard screen pass play from Gordon Birkholz to Mike Foust in the second quarter. Joe Radtke made a late game-saving interception on our last-chance attempt. Maybe we shouldn't have tried to pass, huh?

We finished the season with three straight losses for a 4-5 record, but the pump was primed.

1974: first winning season

This was our time. We had eight seniors on the roster in a small school plus some talented underclassmen and a future hall of fame coach.

I was the other halfback alongside Alan "Butch" Pulkrabek. Butch was strong, fast, and tough – great attributes for a Rumrill team, or any team for that matter. There was no Mr. Football award in those days, but if there had been, Butch would have deserved to be in the conversation. In his senior year, Butch averaged 150 yards/game rushing and set a school scoring record of 102 points.

Our senior teammates were Doug Jurek, Scott "Cisco" Jurek, Greg Koktan (best man in our wedding), Bob Maresh, Roger Pokornowski, and Scott "Tedo" Stritesky.

This was the first year of the short-lived format of the 212 Conference split into two divisions. We were grouped with Lester Prairie, Brownton, Stewart, Buffalo Lake, and Cosmos. The west division was Hector, Bird Island, Danube, Renville, Sacred Heart, and Maynard. Scheduling was to play every team in your own division plus two of the others.

Before home games, while we walked the one block from the school to the football field, the entire team would shout in unison "GFN! GFN!" – a version of "Go Nuts!" with F representing the word it often does. I don't recall anyone ever asking what GFN meant. They either knew, or knew not to ask.

The coaches didn't acknowledge, encourage, nor restrict the chant. In the battle of strength and will that is a football game, having a group of teenage boys in a motivated emotional state is part of the package.

GFN became the unofficial, unauthorized theme of the season, with even the spectators joining in on occasion.

We opened in Winsted with a dominating 41-0 win. The Winsted Journal's report of that game brings up an interesting name: "Gary Fasching, 183-pound sophomore making his first start as middle linebacker, set a Trinity record with 30 tackles." Where is he now? Head coach at St. John's University.

The second week, we faced a larger school, St. John's Prep, in a game that was arranged to help us improve by playing stiff competition. The Johnnies were just that, and we lost 7-0. Another interesting name: their quarterback was John Gagliardi, son of the legendary college coach.

Next, it was revenge time against Lester Prairie with a 41-6 result. From there, we rolled through several games, with only Hector temporarily threatening to come close.

It came down to the Silver Lake

Lakeites vs. the Buffalo Lake Lakers in the next to the last week of the season for the 212 East title. Both teams entered that game unbeaten in conference play.

All season, we occasionally ran a flanker reverse which, unlike in today's game, was a somewhat unusual play call.

Buffalo Lake scouted us well, but Buz had other plans. When Cisco came from his receiver position through the backfield for a handoff and sprinted toward the other sideline, the entire Laker defensive unit swarmed after him in hot pursuit. Too bad, guys! This time it was a fake reverse.

Quarterback Tony Drahos kept the ball and was escorted 33 yards to the end zone by two unneeded blockers; none of the three was so much as touched by a defender. It was the defining moment of what became a decisive 27-0 Silver Lake victory, claiming the division championship . . . if we didn't screw it up in the last game at Brownton.

Teams coming off a big-game win are often vulnerable for a letdown. From memory, I would have told you that we struggled terribly in the first half against Brownton, that Buz lit us up at halftime, and to avoid further wrath, we got our act together and took care of business.

However, the newspaper accounts of that game portray it as an easy victory. There may be some truth in both versions. Either way, we won by 37 and got our trophy.

At that time, there were five classes of football. We were in Class C. The playoff system involved a computerized ranking based on teams' victories, victories by defeated opponents, and a bonus for beating schools from larger classes.

Only one team was allowed to advance from the whole 212 Conference and Bird Island slightly outranked us, so our season was over. Bird Island made it to the championship game, losing to Battle Lake in double overtime.

The following year, a post-season matchup of 212 division winners had been instituted with Bird Island, led by Dan Neubauer, defeating the Lakeites. However, even with a perfect 10-0 record and having outscored opponents 419-20, Bird Island still didn't place high enough in the computer rankings to qualify for what was then a four-team playoff field.

Carry on

Now on the right course, the Lakeite ship sailed on. In the 44 years from 1974 through 2017, the SL and GSL teams had 40 winning records and two seasons at .500.

As many schools faced declining enrollment numbers, 9-man football came to the area and a new Circle 8 Conference was formed. It originally consisted of the 212 East schools plus Winsted Holy Trinity and Grove City. Plotted on a map, they formed a vague circle.

With two fewer defenders on the field in the 9-man game, Buz's offenses thrived even more. In 1982, the Lakeites came within a game of making it to the first Prep Bowl played in the brand new Metrodome.

Immediately after that, the team did even better, advancing to the 9-man state championship game four of the next five years, winning twice. Talk was the 1985 team might have been best of all but key injuries at playoff time ended that season sooner than expected.

Scott Tschimperle, son of Buz's right-hand assistant coach Dan, was on Silver Lake's first two Prep Bowl teams. He later became head coach of Glencoe-Silver Lake from 2008-2022. Scott holds the distinction of having been part of state championship teams both as a player and a coach.

In that mid-'80s stretch, the Lakeites put together a 56-game regular season winning streak which was finally snapped in 1988 by Holy Trinity, coached by Jim Brown, with Luke Schoenfelder's five-touchdown performance.

Sometime in that era, another Buz creation, the famous Silver Lake Fake Punt, appeared.

The ball was snapped to the upback who would quickly tuck it between his legs, and then pretend to make a half-hearted block attempt toward anyone who came near. Meanwhile, the punter and some decoy blockers would make a mad dash for one of the sidelines. When the coast was clear, the player with the ball would head the other direction for an easy first down, often a touchdown.

To be effective, a play like that can't be overused, so Buz patiently kept it in his pocket for the moments when it would have the most impact. For fans, getting to see that play was like a hole-in-one – rare, impossible to anticipate, and exhilarating when it happened.

New teammates

When Glencoe and Silver Lake joined for football in 1994, Buz was named head coach and took his show to a bigger stage.

The first-ever game for the GSL Panthers was a 6-0 win over Mayer Lutheran and its longtime coach Dean Aurich, who recently joined Buz in the hall of fame.

My brother-in-law, Gary Kosek, was on the early paired teams so the whole family followed along closely.

1996 was Buz's best season at GSL. Josh Monahan was the quarterback with Gary, Nate Parpart, and Aaron Schultz (not the former HJ sports editor) in the backfield. Any of those four could break a long touchdown run at any time, and they often did.

A highlight was beating archrival Hutchinson twice – in the season-opener and again for the section title. Other than a two-point squeaker against St. Michael-Albertville, every other win was by two touchdowns or more.

Heartbreak happened in the first round of the state tournament though, with the Mahtomedi Miracle. After slugging it out all night, the Panthers went ahead with about a minute to go and it seemed a trip to the Dome for the semi-finals was in hand, only to have Mahtomedi steal it away in the closing seconds.

To come full circle, Gary Kosek, another Buz-coached alumnus, takes over this year as Glencoe-Silver Lake's head coach.

Buz stepped down from coaching after the 1998 season. He hadn't won another state title, but the seeds of success he planted flourished even more under Dave Dose and Scott Tschimperle. GSL became a dynasty making seven state championship game appearances from 2000 to 2009, winning five of those.

Honors

Buz was inducted into the Minnesota Football Coaches Association Hall of Fame in 1999 (along with Hutchinson's Grady Rostberg), and the Minnesota State High School Coaches Association Hall of Fame in 2012.

In 33 years, his career record was 233-108-3, according to MFCA.

Buz Rumrill passed away Feb. 18, 2023, at age 83. A celebration of life is being planned for June at Rumrill-Tschimperle Field in Silver Lake.

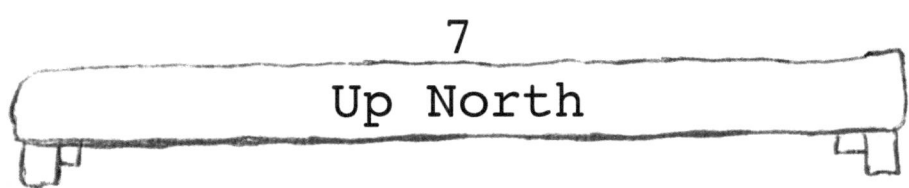

7
Up North

Linda and I spent a week in Duluth for our first anniversary.

One evening, after having grilled burgers on a small Hibachi, we stood on Park Point, admiring the Duluth skyline in the setting sun. Out of my mouth came the words: "How would you like to be from northern Minnesota?"

It was just a crazy thought at the time, but I followed up on the idea. Duluth was larger than my taste, but I identified Two Harbors on the north shore of Lake Superior as a place of interest. I subscribed to the Lake County News-Chronicle to get a better feel for the area.

Guess what? Just a couple months later, there was an ad for an editor opening at the News-Chronicle. "I'll just check it out," I told Linda.

In the interview with Publisher Ken Cronk, I saw him flinch when I mentioned I was a subscriber because I was interested in the area. It was like setting the hook on a nice walleye. The job offer came soon after.

Linda and I had a big decision to make. Would we leave jobs that we both really liked, our close-by families, and circle of friends to trek off into the north-woods so I could pursue a wild hair? It came down to a mild 55/45% but we decided to go ahead and move to northern Minnesota – in January.

Weekly journalism works best when staff members are connected to their communities. Over the years in hiring, we saw that often the choice was between someone who had the skills but knew nothing about the area, or a person with local knowledge but no experience. Neither is the right answer; it just depends.

In Two Harbors, I was the outsider who knew enough about newspapers but lacked in other areas. Life often teaches the best lessons through trials and tribulations rather than successes.

I had no formal party associations but I didn't fit in with the dominant political leanings – it was more than "leaning" – on the North Shore.

I got a first-hand look at union groupthink at a Two Harbors City Council meeting. A senior citizen had built a couple of nice park benches and donated them to the city to be placed in a convenient public spot. Someone actually lobbied the council to reject the donation because those benches "should have been built as a union job."

Also, Linda worked at one of the Duluth hospitals where the nurses weren't allowed to plug in any needed equipment. Instead, they were required to summon someone from the maintenance union who would have to find his way to the room on the correct floor to insert the plug into the wall socket.

At another time, she was criticized by a co-worker for even being there because in the time of a poor economy with scarce jobs, it wasn't right that both a husband and wife were working. One of the jobs should have been left for someone else more needy.

Now that I was an editor, I had the mindset that I could write prize-winning editorials and tell people what to think. I was the young hotshot trying to make a name for himself.

1982 was a mid-term election year so politics was a relevant topic. I wrote a "Don't Vote for Joan Growe" piece, bringing up my encounter with her in Redwood Falls four years earlier. Someone passed it on to Growe, and she called me to apologize, stating that she didn't recall what was said but she didn't mean to offend. We made peace. I still didn't vote for her.

Knowing I was greatly outnumbered, I took a different approach in another pre-election editorial. This time, I argued that everyone should be a qualified, knowledgeable voter who understands exactly what every candidate stands for, and if you aren't extremely well-informed, maybe you should sit this one out and not vote.

As I spent overnight in the Lake County auditor's office watching election results come in, it was anticipated but still shocking to see margins like 85/15% in some precincts.

In my year and a half up north, I collected the anonymous hate mail I received as a badge of honor, but it wasn't all bad either.

On the positive side, with Cronk's support, I advocated a "Think Tourism" month promotion with intent of helping revive the ailing local economy. The North Shore is a gorgeous place to attract visitors and their money.

Since then, tourism has vastly developed further but I deserve no credit; it would have happened anyway. From Duluth to Grand Marais and over to the Boundary Waters and Ely, it's simply the best place in Minnesota for fantastic scenery. But be warned: the winters are long!

When Two Harbors hosted an all-class reunion, we did special sections, first promoting and then covering the major event. We also created a Lake Superior Vacationer guidebook that doubled as both as a resource for tourists and a souvenir for those returning to the area for the reunion.

Jean Krysiak did typesetting and ad design on our staff, and was a skilled artist. I had ideas but could barely sketch a respectable stick-man, so we ended up collaborating on some editorial cartoons. I would describe the concept and she would draw it.

The best one was titled "Everybody's Playing Courthouse Politics" and resembled an elaborate board game that poked fun at issues leaders in Lake County were dealing with. Players were to roll the dice in order of their salary and would land on spots such as approving a budget, bickering with department heads, seeking a legal opinion, raising taxes, etc. The goal was to move around the board and be the first to file for reelection.

My favorite though was another local subject. John Cox was a reinstated Lake County employee who had been embroiled in a years-long legal battle over veterans' preference rights. The mention of his name was a sore spot for anyone associated with the case.

At the time, American Express was running a "Do You Know Me?" campaign featuring people whose names were well known but weren't easily recognized. The commercials would end with the familiar name appearing on an Amex card.

So my cartoon was titled "Do You Know Me?" and pictured a Lake County Express Card with the name John Cox. If you knew the background, it was laugh-out-loud funny.

Eventually, Two Harbors would be rid of me if people just waited it out. In my farewell column, I described it "Just like the ships that come and go in the Agate Bay harbor, so goes another editor from the Lake County News-Chronicle."

While explaining that turnover in the newspaper industry was common, I was wrong in stating "Editors may come and go, but the News-Chronicle will continue forever . . ."

Turns out the N-C ceased publication in May 2020 as COVID was ramping up. Fortunately, CherryRoad Media started the Lake County Press in January 2022 so Lake County again has a local newspaper.

I still had more aspirations, and had contacted the Sneers about returning to Winsted. We made an unwritten agreement that I would work for them for five years and then they would sell the newspaper to me. Those plans changed later, but that's another part of the story.

I re-arrived in Winsted Aug. 1, 1983, and haven't left.

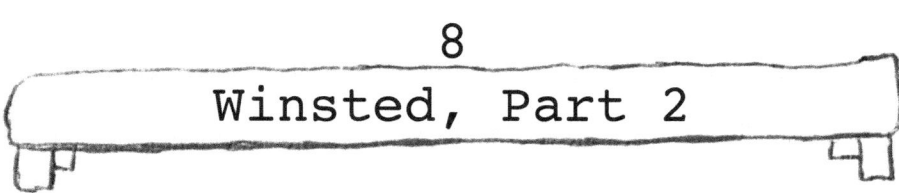

8
Winsted, Part 2

Life always changes. You don't go away for a couple years and return to where you left off.

After coming back to Winsted, over the next few years, I retreated from my ownership dream, realizing there were a lot of missing pieces in my puzzle. During one period, I interviewed for jobs in different fields for a potential career change, but nothing clicked.

The Sneers and I had agreed not to consummate our earlier deal, and when they were ready to retire in 1986, they found a buyer in Bill Ramige from neighboring Glencoe.

Bill needed employees. I had experience and local knowledge. It was a good match.

I became his general manager for Winsted Publishing, with a staff of about eight. I was in charge but also an in-the-trenches worker.

I had to submit and follow a budget, and as long as things were running smoothly, Bill gave me a lot of freedom to do what I saw was best. It was my training to operate a business, while still not being ultimately on the hook for it.

The Big Story

The biggest local news story we ever had was right before Christmas in 1989 when police officer Michael Hogan was shot and killed in the Hutchinson J. C. Penney store.

A few days later, the pursuit of suspect Phillip Cole resulted in a hostage situation at the Alan and Sandra Otto home along Highway 7, right in our area.

We rallied the staff to get all the details we could, and devoted the entire front page plus most of page two to that breaking story.

At the time, we were on an early holiday printing schedule Thursday night. Standard practice then was to hold the papers for distribution until Monday so readers wouldn't go to the grocery store for special prices that were advertised but not yet in effect.

With the significance of the news, we talked to our major advertiser, Jim Paradis of Jim's Red Owl, and he agreed that in this situation we could distribute the paper right away; he would deal with any premature bargain hunters.

Sheriff says hostage situation among most dangerous he's faced

Dec., 25, 1989 • Winsted Journal/Lester Prairie Journal

Duane Kopesky had planned to finish his Christmas shopping and do a few things around town last weekend.

With another week finished, he was enjoying a quiet Friday evening at home, reading a book. Then a phone call with the news that a Hutchinson police officer had been shot began a series of events that consumed all of the sheriff's time for days.

Before it was over, less than a week before Christmas, Kopesky found himself in a life-or-death chess match against an alleged killer who was holding a local family Kopesky knew as hostages.

"It was a stressful weekend," he said Wednesday, showing some signs of fatigue, in perhaps the understatement of the year.

It began Friday evening, Dec. 15. As McLeod County Sheriff, Kopesky's policy is to be personally called for major events such as that.

First, the dispatcher called and told him that officer Michael Hogan of the Hutchinson Police Department had been shot. Before Kopesky could get his uniform on, dispatch called again, informing him that his deputies were at the scene and a fatality was probable.

Kopesky rushed to Hutchinson to the command post set up by Hutchinson police and to view the scene. Though Hutchinson is within the county, this incident was in Hutchinson's jurisdiction and the sheriff's department acted in a supporting role, he explained.

Kopesky immediately assigned his four investigators to the case. By then, officers knew Hogan had died from the gunshot. Hutchinson police coordinated roadblocks, building searches, and gathering of evidence at the scene.

A couple hours later, he learned that officers had taken three persons into custody at a roadblock on Highway 7 east of Hutchinson.

Later, largely through interviews with those three, police determined it was Phillip Lewis Cole, 29, Minneapolis, whom they were after for the killing of a fellow officer.

Before Friday, Cole was an unknown in McLeod County. Kopesky said he never heard of him before, though Cole's lengthy criminal record was available in the files.

Knowing it would be an early start in the morning, Kopesky called it quits about midnight Friday. Other officers remained on the case during the night, and by morning "all these loose ends had been tied up except for the apprehension of Cole," he said.

Instead of shopping, Kopesky spent the weekend "living on the telephone."

He remained in constant contact with other law enforcement agencies as an intensive search for Cole continued.

"We were watching for Cole though we realized he wasn't here (in the county on the weekend)," Kopesky said. "But we felt confident that officers would get him. We thought it would be in the metro area since he kept popping up there. It was ironic that he came back."

Throughout the weekend, Cole had managed to elude two stakeouts of residences by Minneapolis police. A third was being set up Monday night.

Kopesky watched the tv news Monday and went to bed. He was awakened by a call from dispatch: Phillip Cole was in a farmhouse at County Rd. 9 and Highway 7 and had hostages with him.

"I knew immediately that the Alan Ottos live on that corner," he recalled. "There are other houses nearby but my thinking it was them."

Again he dressed quickly. Winsted Police Chief Mike Henrich had been called to assist. He picked Kopesky up at his home in Winsted and they rode together to the scene.

When they arrived, Kopesky was briefed by other officers already at the command post set up in the neighboring Ben Otto home, Alan's parents.

Cole had gotten into a high-speed chase in Minnetonka and ended up returning to the county of the original crime. He broke into the Ottos' home, bringing with him an adult female from Minneapolis whom he apparently abducted there.

A McLeod deputy aware the chase was in progress was already at the scene when Cole entered the Ottos' house. He set up the command post at the neighboring parents' home and made telephone contact with Cole. Other officers secured the perimeter to prevent another escape.

Negotiators were already on the phone when Kopesky arrived. "We had information that it might be Cole inside.

Police had identified him. We knew he was armed. We knew he had four people with him, and I knew three of them personally," Kopesky recalled.

As the chief law enforcement officer in the jurisdiction, Kopesky was in charge at the command post. With four or five key people at his side, providing information and their opinions, it was Kopesky calling the shots.

Yet after the fact, he praised the teamwork and assistance of many other officers necessary to resolve such a situation. All of his deputies where there, among dozens who helped. There were 18 law enforcement agencies that called and offered assistance, though all weren't used, he noted.

"It was helpful as incident commander to be able to bring in the expertise needed to handle it as safely and professionally as possible," Kopesky said. "We had negotiators and entry teams."

Other nearby residents were evacuated for their safety. One officer was assigned to make occasional reports to the news media present, which included tv crews from the cities.

Also in his favor was a good knowledge of the lay of the land, living only four miles away.

Working against him was the obvious. "We knew he was a fugitive, was armed, had allegedly killed before. We're dealing with a personality who was very calm and then very explosive. He was telling us he would take his own life, and he had nothing to live for. We were concerned about the hostages. We knew everything had to be done to perfection," Kopesky said.

Another factor was the below-zero weather. Not knowing how long the ordeal would last, officers securing the area had to be rotated for their own safety from the elements.

Several negotiators were used during the night. They were also rotated, Kopesky explained, "so that they didn't get too personally involved. Again, we didn't know how long we'd be there."

Negotiators would allow only what they felt was to their advantage, at one point providing cigarettes and later allowing Cole to speak to his family members.

"During the process, we were able to negotiate a successful release," Kopesky said. "He just didn't happen to walk out and put the gun down. There were several intense moments, but he was negotiated to the point of surrender. When he threw the gun down, our officers were there to apprehend him and verify the safety of the hostages within seconds.

"The victims reacted as well as they could for such a situation and should be commended for their bravery," he added.

On Wednesday, looking back, Kopesky said the incident was resolved relatively quickly. At the time, though, every minute and every second was long.

In his 20 years of police work, Kopesky learned to get dressed quickly in the middle of the night. He has been involved in negotiation and hostage situations before, as well as armed robberies.

"But nothing as complicated as this," he said. "None of the other situations were, in my opinion, as potentially dangerous to such a great number of people.

"The reason it was successful was not any one person," he said. "It took how bravely the hostages reacted, and a fine job by all law enforcement, dispatchers, and staff people. Everybody did their job."

Suspect's flee from police ends nearby

Dec. 25, 1989 • Winsted Journal/Lester Prairie Journal

By Rita Seymour and Rosalind Kohls

Everything was "please" and "thank you."

That's the way Sandra and Alan Otto of Lester Prairie described the behavior of Phillip Lewis Cole, the man who allegedly shot and killed Hutchinson police officer Michael Hogan, then took the Otto family and a Minneapolis woman hostage Monday night.

After gaining access to the Otto residence, Cole appeared to be two different people, said Sandra Otto. She said Cole was cordial and polite and that he played "peek-a-boo" with the couple's two-year-old daughter, Alaina.

Alan Otto said he was getting ready to go upstairs to bed at 11:30 p.m. when he heard sirens and saw numerous squad cars, flashing lights, and officers on Highway 7, about 200 feet from his home. Two people were walking down the road toward the house. Otto overheard an officer mention "Mr. Cole" and "get back."

Otto became frightened, locked the door, and took his wife and baby into the bathroom, where they locked themselves in. Soon, Otto heard pounding on the door and later, footsteps on their stairs. Otto also heard the woman with the suspect, crying.

Cole talked to the Ottos through the bathroom door, telling them he wouldn't hurt them and trying to coax them out. Meanwhile, Otto heard Cole rummaging through their dresser drawers, taking their loose change, and asking the Ottos if they kept a gun and ammunition in their home.

Later, after the Ottos came out of the bathroom, they gave him some money they kept downstairs to keep Cole from getting upset.

Throughout the night, the family and the woman Cole allegedly abducted sat in the bedroom and tried to calm Cole down. About 100 officers were gathered in the barn, an evergreen grove near the house, and at the Benedict Otto farm, where officers had set up a communications center. Benedict Otto is Alan Otto's father and lives a short distance away.

Benedict's wife, Irene, said officers asked her and her husband to leave the scene. They went to a daughter's home and simply waited until the ordeal was over. Police called Irene and her husband on two occasions to tell them their family was safe.

"We're just very thankful that he (Cole) let them go unharmed," she said. "We feel for Mr. Cole – he has some problems."

According to the Ottos, Cole wanted to say "goodbye" to his family, then kill himself. However, in the middle of a phone conversation with one of his family members, the telephone line was cut off. Cole became upset and sent Sandra Otto outside to tell officers to re-establish communications.

He got his wish, but when Sandra did not return, Cole became angry, Alan Otto said.

Sandra said she requested to go back into her home. But she was told it wouldn't be wise to do that, since Cole had already proven he would kill.

In an interview with Sandra Wednesday, she said her family is relieved and thankful the ordeal is over.

"Alan and I didn't get a chance to talk or be alone until last night," she said. "It took us awhile to fall asleep but we feel rested and good today."

She and her husband are also thankful to their friends and relatives in the Lester Prairie area.

Right Direction

For a different kind of writing, I prepared my own speech as incoming president of the Winsted Civic and Commerce Association:

Going in the right direction
Feb. 21, 1985 • Speech to Winsted Civic and Commerce Assn.

Tonight, our theme of the banquet is "Going in the Right Direction," and before we look at directions for us to go this year, I want to go back for a moment to a little over five years ago.

At that time, the Winsted Civic and Commerce Association under President Ben Weinbeck was lobbying hard with the city for the council to hire a full-time city administrator/coordinator. The purpose was to have someone working full-time on local projects, and being able to handle and coordinate much of the legwork in carrying out these projects to make Winsted a thriving community.

I share with you this quote from Mr. Weinbeck as he addressed the city council Dec. 4, 1979: "Without this experienced help, we find our community going backwards. No one here is properly educated or trained in city management, and should value the help an administrator can give in every phase of government."

Another excerpt: "Our community needs help, gentlemen, and you were elected to do that . . . If we'd done this three or four years ago, we'd be on a gravy train now."

So on Feb. 16, 1980, almost exactly five years ago today, a group of about 25 interested persons representing all facets of the community met for a day-long workshop with three consultants in the Holy Trinity social hall. They identified the major needs of our community on a point system vote, and it was ultimately decided that a city administrator would, indeed, be hired for Winsted.

It's significant, I think, that the people at the Feb. 1980 planning workshop collectively identified housing supply as the number one priority for Winsted at that time. A 1981 labor market survey carried out by the city confirmed that when it showed that almost exactly 50 percent of the people who work at our major industries live outside the city limits of Winsted, and a good number of them were willing to move here if there was adequate housing for them. So a grant was obtained, and as we were pleased to report in the Winsted Journal last month, 1984 saw nearly a half million dollars worth of housing construction in the Westgate project alone, and that was only the first half of the first of three phases for development there.

Now, no one person or organization can take all the credit for that accomplishment. It took a lot of hard, dedicated work by the elected and appointed city officials during the last few years, and the whole project itself was coordinated by the people who held the city administrator position.

The point I wish to emphasize is that it was the Winsted Civic and Commerce Association that gave the first push toward obtaining an administrator so that our community was better prepared to make events like that take place. I believe that was one of the right directions this organization chose to follow.

A couple years ago, I heard tourism consultant Jack Gray tell about an experience he had when he visited a large city in which there was a fantastic parade that drew three-quarters of a million people to watch. The event was a huge success. Gray looked over the throng of people watching the parade, turned to the parade director, and simply asked: "What are you doing tomorrow?"

And that's the question I bring to this organization tonight as we begin another year.

Many times in speaking about the C&C we talk about things we've done. Encouraging the city government to hire an administrator is one thing. There are a number of C&C-sponsored events that take place every year like clockwork along with a few other special projects.

So maybe we've been able to take a few short rides on that gravy train Ben Weinbeck talked about. But there's always another tomorrow and something to be done to ensure we keep going in the right direction.

I think it's important this year that the C&C not only carries out the annual events of the respective seasons, but is concerned with broader long-range issues for the Winsted community.

There are many outside factors that affect us as well:

• The difficult situations many farmers are facing.

• More and more government regulations and mandates without funds to carry them out.

• A change in American working society as a whole from industrial to informational and services.

Perhaps another planning workshop would be in order to again take a look at where Winsted is at, where it wants to go, and finding the right direction to get there.

One thing I hope the C&C will do this year is work toward being even better prepared to work with new industries or businesses that might be interested in coming to our fair city.

After all, Winsted is perfectly located just a quarter-mile outside the jurisdiction – and taxing authority – of the metropolitan area. We're in a nice peaceful, rural setting with a low crime rate, yet very convenient to metropolitan resources. There's a strong labor force here already. We have excellent public and private educational facilities, a beautiful lake, good airport and highway transportation, a full range of medical services, a growing housing supply, and a civic and commerce association and city government that are truly interested in the community's growth and well-being.

There just might be a few companies out there that would like to know this. And I hope our organization will continue to take an aggressive role in letting the world know what we have to offer.

Yet at the same time, it's perhaps even more important that we don't become so infatuated with the growth and development idea that we forget to take care of what we have here already.

There are plenty of issues that affect most of us as members of a business/civic organization, or important institutions in the community. And if the C&C's involvement consists of only taking a stance on a piece of legislation that affects our community, then we should be taking that stance and expressing it to the appropriate lawmakers.

Just in the past year, when the Alice Haney Home was threatened with closing, we joined with the Lester Prairie Civic and Commerce Association to discuss what that might mean for our communities. When the city council was looking at the possibilities of selling city hall, we hosted a public forum to increase understanding of the issue.

At our regular meeting coming up in March, we'll consider a proposal from the local Legion post to become more involved in the annual Legion Festival. We'll talk about things the C&C might be able to do to ensure that Winsted continues to have a growing summer festival rather than allowing it to die.

That's being issues-oriented, and it's something we should continue and increase. It not only creates the feeling among members that we do have a purpose, but it projects a good image to non-members that the C&C is involved in important concerns. And maybe just a few more good things will take place because the Civic and Commerce Association continues to give a damn about what happens to Winsted.

So, we're all here tonight presumably because we're interested in this organization. There are many other places in this state, this country, this world that we could be, but we have all chosen Winsted, Minnesota, as the place where we want to live and work. And it's important to us that we have a good thriving community with plenty of spirit and pride.

There's always something for us to do tomorrow. There's a long road to follow with no final destination. But with an interested active organization, we can always be traveling in the right direction.

Top Cop

I was just the warm-up act. At that same C&C banquet, we were privileged to hear from the colorful, candid Minneapolis Police Chief Tony Bouza, In hindsight, his comments about the deterioration of society ring alarmingly true.

Praise for the midwest, gloomy outlook for nation
Feb. 27, 1985 • Winsted Journal

By JoAnn Sneer

Tony Bouza, chief of police of Minneapolis for the past five years, lived up to his reputation as he spoke to an overflow crowd at the Winsted Civic and Commerce Association banquet last Thursday night.

Bouza, a native of Spain, grew up and was educated in New York City. Before coming to Minneapolis, he spent 24 years with the New York City Police Department, the last four as police commander of the Bronx.

He is known for his eruditeness, wit, intelligence, and bold and blunt manner in speaking his mind. All those qualities were at the forefront as he gave forth with his opinions of the now and his predictions for the future.

In introducing Bouza, master of ceremonies Dick Genty submitted him to a "roast" bringing in names of people Bouza has had run-ins and conflicts with since coming to Minneapolis. At one point, Genty played a recording supposedly of Ron Edwards, director of the Minneapolis Urban League, commenting on Bouza. It turned out to be a garbled tape.

Bouza, a man who seemingly does not give with the ready laugh, almost let loose a couple of times when his grins got wider and wider.

Genty is, himself, known for traits similar to those of Bouza, and it was an interesting match. He does not praise easily and gives it only when he thinks it is justified. Consequently, when Genty got down to the serious introduction, his words carried weight. He said Bouza had gone far in getting politics out of the Minneapolis police force. He summed it up by saying, "Bouza is a tough cop. He runs an aggressive police force. He's a good cop and a good man."

Then it was Bouza's turn to let loose with some barbs and quips, which he did in fine fashion. The laughs kept rolling along as he eased into his talk.

He related that he had recently spoken to 370 pastors from three Lutheran synods. He said they thought they were as different as Hindus, Muslims, Jews, and Catholics, and are struggling to come together.

Said Bouza, "They don't realize that to us New Yorkers, the Lutheran Brotherhood is just like a fighting street gang, and it's hard to tell them apart when they really all look alike. When we catch an occasional Lutheran in New York – we only have Jews and Catholics there – we used to put them under glass and put them in Times Square. People would actually come from miles and even bring their children – a genuine Lutheran in captivity!"

He added he was sure the Lutheran groups would be able to overcome their differences, and predicted that by 1989 they would elect a pope.

By this time, Bouza had the already willing-to-listen audience in the cup of his hand, and the laughter was rolling through the Blue Note.

He deftly turned the patter and jokes into the preface of his in-earnest talk about crime prevention, which he said has nothing to do with the police. "It fascinates me that the real experts know so little and the people who know so much and are so tough and smart are entrusted with so few decisions," was his lead-in comment. Portions of his talk, identified by quote marks, follow.

"George Clemenceau (premier of France in the early 1920s) once said that war is too important to be left to the generals. We don't know what that means and I kind of struggle with it. Except, in the Vietnam war we discovered we could not trust our generals to get us out of that mess . . . and in the final analysis, we could not even trust their word."

Citing the recent Westmoreland lawsuit against Time magazine, it was his opinion Westmoreland helped the magazine "win" the case by his statements, which he felt proved high-ranking officials not only lied to the American public, but also to the president.

"I think we see an analogy in the police chiefs in the United States who say to us, if you want to fight crime, the easiest solution is to hire more cops and increase the police budget."

It was his opinion this is not true, and is "subversive" because it undermines the search for the real cause of crime, which he thinks has more to do with the comments presented in the recent pastoral letter of Catholic bishops. The letter concerned social justice and the problems of poverty-stricken and those at the poverty level.

"The reality is that crime is a festering sore on the body politic, a symptom of underlying social problems that you don't see very plainly in Winsted, or even in Minneapolis, but you see them very clearly in the Bronx. The Bronx is today America's frontier.

"If America faces a tremendous outward danger in terms of the existence of another superpower in the name of the Soviet Union, and surely our foreign policy is much more complex than that . . . the internal threat is a threat that flies on the wings of violence and criminality which we call street crime.

"At this moment, it's declining because of a demographic glitch. My guess is your high school enrollment is declining and that it will continue to decline until 1992. That brings us a breather in street crime. That breather will not last very long since the most rapidly growing segment of our population is under age seven. With that new wave of under-seven population will come appalling levels of violence and criminality.

"We have doubled that prison population; we have not solved the crime problem. We haven't even touched the crime problem, and we may not even have defined it because I do not see the letter of the Catholic bishops being discussed too vigorously. And yet, it seems to me the fate of the nation is tied up with the meaningful discussion of its contents.

"If we continue to allow a large segment of our population, 35 million below the poverty level, millions more at its edges, to continue in a life of welfare, booze, television, exclusion, inadequate education, inadequate housing and unemployment, we are consigning ourselves to serious levels of criminality and violence . . . coming to this nation in the early 1990s. We can look forward to a very dangerous future.

"What to do? I think crime and crime prevention is too important to be left to chiefs of police. What we need is a national debate, a discussion, forums to take it to the street, the television, and the Blue Note Ballrooms for discussions to see where all this violence is coming from and what we might do to stem it.

"Crime prevention, speaking to such issues as the Bronx, means social glue. It means the things that hold a society together. I find it particularly frustrating to talk about crime and violence in Minnesota because there is so much social glue at work that it is hard to find models you can point to and say 'That's what I'm talking about.'

"The reality is we (Minnesota and the midwest) are a society very closely knit together with organizations, associations, societies, churches, and enormous stability.

"This is an island in the middle of the nation. It should not be taken as a model for what is happening in Los Angeles, Chicago, Detroit, Miami, New York, and Houston, where we are going to see a tremendous amount of society coming unstuck through such forces as the breakdown of family, neighborhood, community, influence of the church, morality – the breakdown of those virtues we seem to be rapidly moving away from family, God, country, community, neighborhood, friends. We're moving away from that system of values and moving towards a system that centers on the self.

"What crime prevention is all about is a society that holds together, takes care of its members, helps them up on their feet and insists they perform, provides education, housing, jobs, inclusion, a sense of community – yes, hold people to account.

"I believe we manufacture the monsters in our society we call criminals. If you want to manufacture sensible, law-abiding people, give them a town like Winsted, a closely knit community."

Bouza also made a declaration against the ownership of handguns, saying this country permits a proliferation of handguns that no other civilized society tolerates. "We have three times the murder rate of England, Germany, France, Denmark, and Japan in all weapons except guns. Where guns are involved, we have 50 times the murder rate, and the reason for that is those countries make the possession of a firearm a virtual impossibility.

"You'd be hard put today to identify who the winners and losers were in the second world war simply on the basis of who won or lost because defeat from without does not prove to be deadly to the organism known as a nation. It is defeat from within – a corrosion of the spirit – that creates a loss of national vigor as to produce death in the client.

"A prescription that appeals to me can be contained (in the words of) Minneapolis Mayor Donald Fraser. He talks about getting the dropouts into high school programs; jobs for youths and the unemployable; education; Head Start programs; day care centers for single mothers; get people off welfare and get them working, but give them a chance; decent house, to the degree the state is able to provide it; accountability to be served, not a free lunch; generosity of spirit and community sense.

"My own view of law enforcement is to take a tough approach. I'm a tough law and order advocate, and the fact is I am hired to attack crime . . . but I must confess we are simply attacking a symptom of an underlying social disease that is breeding criminality."

He commented that serving as police chief in both the Bronx and Minneapolis had been instructive for him. Stating that the job is not much different for him either place, the problems for the "cop on the street are totally different.

"There (in the Bronx) you are talking about shocking levels of violence and criminality, a society dissolving before your very eyes, every man for himself. Here (in the midwest) we have a 1935 America that still works, where the old values still remain, the values of farm, family, work, thrift, neighbors, God.

"It's really kind of amazing, and for me it has been a great voyage. So when I come to the heartland, it's almost like returning to 1935 America. This place still has a lot of energy, morality, altruism and decency, a sense of caring for the rest of the community. These qualities are rapidly disappearing on the horizon of the American perspective. That is very sad and very dangerous.

"It is what is going on in Winsted and Minneapolis and in the midwest and what is going on in the Bronx and Miami and Detroit that will settle the fate of this nation, not how many cops we hire.

"The fate of this nation, I think, really hangs in the balance. Although this midwest is not a good place to study it, it seems to me the future is a little bit bleak as the values shift into a darker future.

"We've got to be ready for that future. What we most desperately need is discussion, questioning, to see if our national leaders will not at some point come to grips with the serious internal danger.

"I get a kick out of examining the midwest. It looks kind of dusty in the sense that values are kind of old-fashioned, but to me it looks very real and very valuable and very useful. So, I think I'm going to opt for the populous midwest and the solid values I seek and hope that ultimately they will emerge strong and convince a nation to go back to them. I don't know if that will happen or not. The future, I think, is very much in doubt."

Immediate applause from a standing audience was the response to Bouza's talk. At that point, a personal gift from Genty was presented to him. It was a framed print of an Indian chief which Genty gave to him with the accompanying words "One chief deserves another." A surprised Bouza seemed touched by the presentation.

It should be noted Bouza does not charge a fee for his talks. However, he does accept contributions, which he in turn donates to a police fund.

Sudden Shock

I was getting ready to have supper before heading off to a city council meeting April 18, 1988, when the phone call came: my mother had passed away suddenly from a heart attack.

For nearly 13 years, she had been the family reporter for the Hutchinson Leader handling news items about births, weddings, etc., and writing feature stories about people. She also wrote a regular column titled "The Country Girl" and made that her identity.

In 1981, she took it to another level and self-published a book with that title, telling short stories of her youth in rural Silver Lake.

The Hutchinson Leader allowed me to write this guest column shortly after her passing:

What's forever?
April 1988 • Hutchinson Leader

Except in a few rare cases, death comes as a shock.

When my mother, Mildred Kovar, "The Country Girl," died last week, it was a shock to all of us who knew her and to many who knew of her. Aside from our shock, I was able to find comfort in what her death was not.

Indications were she went relatively quickly and peacefully. She did not have to suffer through months or even years on life-supporting machines. She would not have wanted to impose on anyone.

Had it been, say, a car accident or situation in which we could find fault in someone else's actions, it would have been much more difficult to accept. It was simply God's will that her time had come.

Mom was our babysitter the Thursday evening before she died. She brought Chelsea two new books and a toy. I won't forget how Chelsea beamed with excitement when Grandma walked in that night holding out a bright shiny new ball.

Chelsea happened to stay up way past her regular bedtime so they had a nice final evening together.

Last week, when we were going through Mom's things, I found another book, apparently purchased for Chelsea that hadn't been delivered yet. Titled "What's Forever?" it's a brief explanation of death in children's terms.

It reads, in part, "Most of us will live for a very long time. But someday we will die. That's part of God's plan . . . only one thing lasts forever – Heaven.

"When we die and join our friends and family in Heaven, we will be there forever. That's what people mean when they talk about eternal life – it goes on and on and on and on without ending. It's all part of God's plan for us."

I don't know if it was coincidence or premonition that Mom had bought such a book, or that it matters. Somehow it's just appropriate.

So was the poem with which she concluded her final Country Girl column last week. Yet no matter which of her columns would have been the last one, chances are there would have been something just as fitting in it. That's how she was and how she wrote.

Many of you who knew her personally must have marveled at times about
the contradiction of someone so shy putting her innermost thoughts and feelings
in print twice a week for all the world
to see.

That was the way she communicated
best, and she loved doing it. It was remarked to me last week that "she'll never know how many lives she touched."

I believe that is true, especially if the
correspondence she received is any indication. Mom was a saver. You can be
well-assured that if you sent her a card or
letter in the last 12-plus years, she kept
it. Even the smallest of notes meant a lot
to her.

My wish is that I could tell her all
about the last week – the outpouring of
sympathy through many acts of kind-
ness, written tributes, personal visits,
and a deep sharing in our loss.

But perhaps, from her place in Heav-
en, she already knows.

A Really Young Writer

Our second daughter, Alyssa, was born in 1989, and as we frequently remind her, she was two weeks overdue. That extra time prepared her well so I turned my column space over to Alyssa for her first published writing later that month.

Hello, world! Here I come!
July 1989 • Winsted Journal/Lester Prairie Journal

By Alyssa Kovar

Hi, my name is Alyssa.

Actually, my dad is helping me write this. I'm only a couple weeks and a couple days old so my typing and spelling still need a little improvement.

I guess you could say I've had a pretty good life so far. I've got food, clothing, shelter, and plenty of love. Mommy really takes good care of me.

Everybody says I was a couple weeks late being born, but I just wanted to be sure I was ready. Then I heard Mom and Dad telling everybody to come over and paint the house one Saturday morning, so I decided to come, too. You know what? Then they didn't even paint.

Instead, we spent the weekend at a hospital. My big sister, Chelsea, says a hospital is sort of like a hotel – a place where you pay a lot of money to stay overnight.

It was pretty nice except they only had one bed in the room so Dad and Chelsea had to go back home to sleep. Maybe next time we should reserve a room in advance. And besides that, they didn't even have a pool so Chelsea didn't get to go swimming.

I'm very lucky because I already had a big sister when I was born. Chelsea had to wait almost three years before she got a sister.

I like it when Chelsea holds me. Sometimes she hangs on real tight so I don't fall. Mom and Dad always tell her to be careful, but she knows what she's doing.

I've been sharing my toys with her since I don't have much use for them yet. This way, she knows all the good ones and when I'm ready for them in a few months, she can tell me which are the best ones.

My room is really nice. I guess the carpet is very soft, though I haven't had a chance to walk on it yet. There are lots of pictures. And Dad says Mom fixed my crib up really neat – "makes it look like a fun place to be instead of a jail cell behind bars."

Well, I guess I should be going now. I like to get up during the night for a snack, so I have to get some sleep now while I can.

I don't know if I'm going to write any more columns. Dad says there's plenty of time for me to decide what I want to be when I grow up. There are so many possibilities. I'll just wait and see what interests me most.

It's been fun talking to you. Catch you later,

Alyssa

In the late '80s, now with two children, I was able to switch jobs without switching jobs by replacing myself in the reporter/writing responsibilities and moving into a design/production role. Same pay, much better hours.

Name Games

At one time, we heard of a "hidden man" advertising promotion in which newspapers would include a very small drawing of a man's face in one of the ads each week and then ask readers to find him to win a small prize. The point was to drive increased readership of the ads.

Howard Lake

HAROLD

For our version, we found a goofy looking drawing of man's face and the name choice was obvious: we called him Howard Lake Harold. The tagline was "Find Harold in the Herald."

In another play on names, when Howard Lake started having a parade with its Good Neighbor Days celebration in 1990, we tracked down a gentleman from the Twin Cities whose name was Howard Lake and arranged for him to ride on our float in the Howard Lake parade.

Phone Poll

I made another effort at editorial cartoons, but lacking drawing ability and no staff artist, I went the route of text-based cartoons.

The political hype in 1990 was an accusation that governor candidate Jon Grunseth swam nude at a party years before. Witnesses claimed he did; others who were there swore he didn't.

At the same time, the trend on tv news was to do frequent phone polls with toll-free 900- numbers. I did this text-only cartoon and even got an award for it:

Phone poll: If you saw Jon Grunseth swimming nude in 1981, please call 1-900-485-2535. If you didn't see Jon Grunseth swimming nude in 1981, please call 1-900-543-2131. If you see Rudy Perpich swimming nude at any time, please call 911.

April Fool

When I was in Two Harbors, we happened to have a paper published on April Fools' Day one year, so we came up with the idea of doing a front page full of joke stories. It went over okay, and I filed the idea away for another time and place.

1991 was it, but I took a different approach. Having noticed this several months ahead, I had plenty of time to come up with a variety of phony news items. And I did it privately.

The way our newspaper production worked at that time was for our writers and typesetters to prepare the formatted items on computers. They were printed on paper which was then trimmed, an adhesive wax applied to the back, and the pieces placed on a layout sheet exactly as the paper would appear.

I was doing the layout every week in that period, so I went through the regular motions, and had a front page started on the paste-up board. It seemed routine enough that no one noticed.

They didn't know that I had an April Fools' front page already done and hidden away, only to send that off to press instead at the end. Only one other person from our staff, Mikkel Kelly, knew about it before the paper was on the streets.

Although I'd often get compliments on something that was in the paper, the April Fools' edition by far drew more comments than anything serious I had ever written.

The main item was a photo, manipulated in the darkroom, of Winsted's water tower on fire (see the back cover). There was also a story about the city developing the ability to reverse sewer flows to residences that were delinquent in paying their utility bills, and an announcement of my run for president as Kareem Abdul Co-Varr. And just for good measure, the nameplate at the top of the page was spelled "Winstead Journal" in homage to the common misspelling of Winsted.

City has big surprise for past due sewer accounts
April 1, 1991 • Winstead Journal April Fool's edition

By Otto Luck

If you owe the City of Winsted money for a past due sewer bill, you better look out.

The Journal has learned from a high-ranking source at city hall that a high-tech computer system in the new sewage treatment system allows the city a new unique method for collecting delinquent accounts.

Here is what the city is planning:

• when a sewer bill becomes 60 days past due, the computer enables the city to block the sewer line for any individual house or business place, thus cutting off service for those who don't pay.

• even more important, if the bill becomes six months past due, the city has the capability to not only block the line, but to actually reverse the flow to selected locations. In other words, if you don't pay your sewer bill, the city can literally back up the sewer right into your basement.

"Times are tough with state aid cuts and all," the city hall source said. "What it comes down to is if people aren't going to pay their bills, we're not going to take any crap anymore."

The collection method ushers in a new era of "reverse services," according to the League of Minnesota Cities spokesman William (Bill) Overdue.

Not every city has such a high-tech capability available, Overdue said, but many communities are looking into the reverse services concept for unpaid garbage bills. In that case, the hauler would be authorized to return garbage to households that don't pay their bills.

Fire!

Evelyn Fowler arrived at work the morning of Thursday, May 7, 1992, and found our Howard Lake office full of smoke.

Needless to say, that day didn't go as planned. Instead of sending our Laker Shopper off to press and then gearing up for the weekly cycle of newspaper production, we were scrambling for anything we could remember about what needed to be done.

While the Howard Lake Fire Department was subduing the flames, I summoned owner Bill Ramige. When the smoke was cleared and we were able to enter the building, there were a few charred papers we were able to retrieve to help jog our memories about what was to be in the paper that we were supposed to have completed the next day.

Fortunately with Bill also owning the paper in Glencoe, we had a place to go. Our whole staff went to the Chronicle office, and from scraps of paper and memory, we reconstructed what we could for the next edition, somehow miraculously still finishing by the end of Friday.

This is a good time to express appreciation for the men and women who serve as volunteer firefighters in our communities. They are forever on call, ready to leave their families, their work, their churches, their beds – wherever they are – so that on a moment's notice, they are facing serious danger in order to help someone else who is in need.

If you have had the occasion to summon a fire department to come to your home or business, you understand. If not, you are fortunate.

Fire destroys Herald office; those darn computers!

May 11, 1992 • Howard Lake Herald

By Tim Lammers and Dale Kovar

An early morning fire Thursday destroyed the contents of the Howard Lake Herald office including all equipment, furniture, and supplies.

Four computer terminals, all programs and files used for producing the Herald, the Winsted-Lester Prairie Journal, and the Laker Shopper were destroyed.

The fire was discovered by typesetter Evelyn Fowler who arrived for work shortly after 8 a.m. and immediately notified the Howard Lake Fire Department.

Fire Chief Dennis Bobrowske said that he and department members entered the building after crew preparation and were confronted with large flames.

"I took the first crews in (the building) about 20 minutes – they didn't even go through their first airpacks and they had the fire under control," he said. "After that, we put out some little fires and we tore open the floor."

All flames were out by approximately 9:15 a.m. Bobrowske and Wright County Detective Charlie Nelson both thought the fire had been burning for several hours, though it was virtually undetectable as the building's exterior was unscathed.

It appears there was tremendous heat inside the building as many items such as computer terminals, plastic shelving, and a microwave were melted like candles.

The building was fairly airtight and thus the fire was contained to the main office area. With more oxygen, it could have easily spread to the entire building.

A work station with two computers behind the front counter was pinpointed by the department and Deputy State Fire Marshal Tom Neudahl as the area where the blaze started. Investigators are still determining whether the origin of the fire was within a computer unit or the electrical connections leading to it.

Another employee, Sarah Niemela, had worked late the night before and no signs of the fire were apparent when she left.

A dollar amount of the damage has not yet been determined, though initially it appears insurance will cover virtually all damage.

Though all equipment was destroyed, employees were able to locate a surprising number of papers with news and advertising information for the coming issue. However, many original advertisements were burned and will need to be recreated in the coming weeks.

This issue of the Herald was reconstructed with pieces from previous weeks and put together at the McLeod County Chronicle office in Glencoe, which is under the same ownership. Much of it was rewritten from memory, and some photographs that had been submitted for publication were also destroyed.

The Laker Shopper, which was scheduled to go to press late Thursday morning, was cancelled. Instead, extra copies of the Herald and Journal are being sent to addresses that normally receive the Laker this week. The Laker will resume publication next week.

About a dozen bound volumes of the previous years' newspapers, which were located throughout the office for current use, received heavy damage. Most of the files were safe in a closet and received only a slight covering of soot.

All subscription and accounts receivable records are kept in the company's Winsted office and were unaffected by the fire.

Par for the Course

As golf became a mainstream recreational sport, courses began popping up all around our area, and we got one right in our backyard just outside of Lester Prairie.

Ed Mlynar of Lester Prairie was instrumental in arranging the establishment of ShadowBrooke Golf Course in 1993 by the father and son duo of Elmer and Tom Schmidt. I had covered Ed during his time as a councilman and mayor in Lester Prairie, but neither of us let the fact that we were distant relatives influence the situation.

My family got me a five-year charter membership to ShadowBrooke. I learned that instead of the sometimes painfully slow pace that golf proceeds at, I could play more and faster by being the first one out in the morning.

Arriving with headlights on, I could tee off on the first hole into a gray din and keep going, completing 18 holes in two and a half hours, and still making it to work before most of the other employees.

There's another connection to ShadowBrooke. Linda's third cousin Oral Oelke previously owned the house and farm, and we had rented it from him for a few years in the mid-'80s. I sometimes practiced in the pasture so I was able to claim I had lost golf balls on the property long before it became a golf course.

Going Online

I remember sitting in awe at a Minnesota Newspaper Convention session where a speaker was demonstrating on a projector screen how this new thing called the Internet worked.

If words appeared in blue and were underlined, you just click on it with your mouse, and it takes to you a file on another computer somewhere else in the world. The possibilities would be endless. And they were.

Dial-up Internet service came to our area through a company called Central Minnesota Gateway, formed by Dassel-Cokato newspaper publishers Dan and Carolyn Holje and their partners Paul and Marie Scivetti. We made a deal that we would help sell their service in Howard Lake in exchange for a free company account.

Bill Ramige wasn't as eager about it as we were, but as long as we kept the place operating well, he allowed us to explore the new frontier.

We figured it was more practical to create a single joint website for the newspapers in Howard Lake, Winsted, and Lester Prairie than separate ones. Although it had an awkward URL at first – www.cmgate.com/~hlhwlpj – it was the starting point for what would become herald-journal.com.

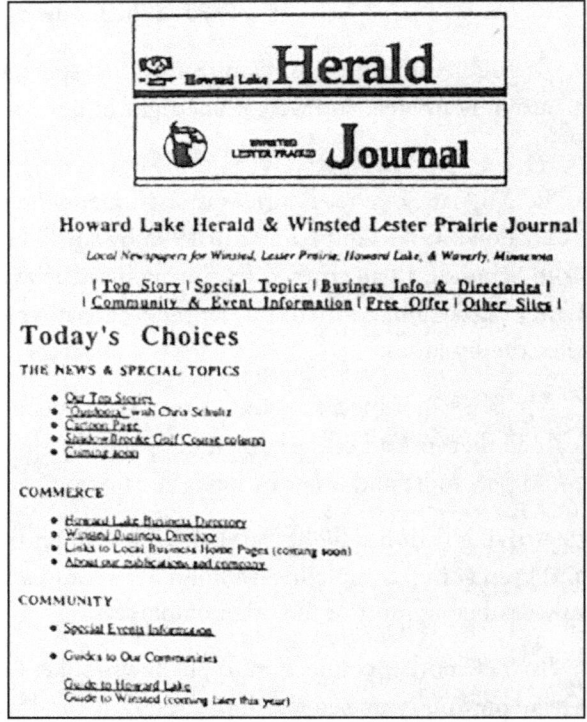

Our first website in July 1996, by today's standards, looks like a first grader did it. But we were literally beginners, and using beginner technology. We would have been the first newspaper in Wright County to have a website but the Monticello Times beat us by a week.

Elected

Journalists aren't supposed to hold elected office, at least not in their coverage area. We're the ones who are tasked to be scrutinizing those elected officials, reporting on their actions, and if necessary, exposing corruption.

Sometimes in the smallest of towns there needs to be an overlap. Chuck Warner was publisher of the Brownton Bulletin from 1953-86 and also served a number of years on the city council and as mayor of Brownton. Since he was re-elected multiple times, voters must have been satisfied. In all cases, citizens are to monitor their elected officials and remove them in the next election cycle if there is poor performance.

I ran for Silver Lake school board at age 21, under the opinion that I had been to enough meetings and could do a better job than most board members. Because I lived beyond my newspaper's coverage area, I avoided the ethical conflict. Voters knew better, though, and I placed fourth out of six candidates for two available positions.

Fast forward to age 42, and now with twice as much life experience, I ran again. We had lived in other places previously, but bought our first house in the Glencoe-Silver Lake school district.

There was a controversy heating up over where certain grades would be located, and from a group of unhappy parents, I became a candidate. We don't need to rehash that or other issues here, but there are a couple newspaper tie-ins I want to mention.

Andrea Vargo and Luis Puga were our editors in Howard Lake and Winsted. Andrea was hobbling temporarily from a foot injury she had incurred. In light of political correctness, the three of us joked together that I could have "a Mexican and a cripple" as my campaign managers.

As for the election, there were still three newspapers in the GSL district – McLeod County Chronicle, Silver Lake Leader, and Glencoe Enterprise – each doing its own version of coverage.

For the Enterprise, I knew its process wasn't computerized and that layout was still done by paste-up. I submitted my response to its candidate questionnaire in a column width exactly matching the Enterprise's format.

Sure enough, the elderly eccentric publisher, Annamarie Tudhope, clipped out my response and published it as it was without having to retype it. I had used 12-point type (intentionally) so my candidate profile ran in a larger font than the others that were typed into a traditional 10-point size. That is just a fun tidbit, and probably not why I placed first out of eight candidates.

Again, I was beyond the geography of my work responsibilities to avoid an ethical conflict. Although my boss owned one of the newspapers covering the board, I did not ask for special favors, and Chronicle editor Rich Glennie treated me fair and square, just like the others.

When I joined the school board, Glenn Gruenhagen, who is now a state senator, was the outcast board member who frequently fought for better accountability and transparency. Superintendent Mary Ann Straley wasn't too pleased to find that now there was someone else who would vote against her initiatives even more often than Glenn. However, I only served about half a term as I had to forfeit my seat when our family moved out of the district.

The big lesson I learned during my short stint as an elected official is that when you are in the minority, you are in the minority.

As it should be, "majority rules" from the smallest township board all the way up to Congress. That's why citizen involvement and election integrity are so vital in how our government performs. Unless enough courageous people step forward and attain a majority at many levels, we'll continue to have an ever-expanding government that taxes us more and serves us less.

Cliffhanger

The 2000 presidential election was a bitter battle that went down to the wire in which George W. Bush lost the popular vote but defeated Al Gore in the electoral college. The next morning, the Star Tribune ran an all-caps headline across the top of the front page "BUSH WINS CLIFFHANGER."

I decided to have some fun, and our paper that week used the same BUSH WINS CLIFFHANGER headline in all caps and a similar font – except that we were telling the story of Charlie Bush being re-elected mayor of Waverly, running unopposed.

It was enough of a gag that I was interviewed on Don Shelby's radio program. "Another 300 votes and it could have been a different story," I told him.

Nov. 13, 2000 • Howard Lake-Waverly Herald

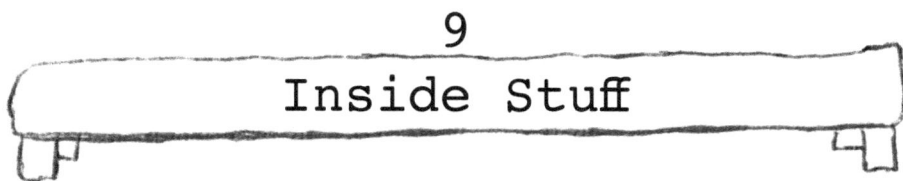

9
Inside Stuff

Classifieds

For decades, classifieds – aka "the want ads" – belonged to newspapers.

Besides a revenue source, they engaged readers with an active marketplace to buy and sell. Or for those who liked to be nosy, they could find out what their neighbor was selling.

In the late '80s, I attended the most valuable seminar of my career. It was about building and maintaining an effective classified ad section. I rushed back and changed almost everything about how we handled our classifieds, and we still follow that format today.

The key concept, the presenter explained, is about getting results for the customers.

Instead of charging customers by the word or line so that they try to keep an ad short or abbreviate to keep the cost down, the goal is to allow them enough space to write an effective ad that gets responses. Then price it to encourage repetition because multiple insertions work better than one.

We switched to allowing 40 words in the base rate, and an ad would run five times or until the item was sold. Each ad would begin with one or two words in bold caps – not "for sale" but the keyword describing the item: lawnmower, bicycle, etc.

We also strongly encouraged people to put their asking price in the ad because ultimately, that's one of the most important elements in making a sale or not.

Describe an item well, include the price, and run it multiple times was the formula for success.

Later, as the newspaper industry fumbled away its classified ad dominance to online platforms that were searchable and reached wider areas, we conceded that people weren't as willing to pay as much for newspaper classifieds, if at all, since there were free alternatives.

We began offering free classified line ads for subscribers for personal use. This was effective in keeping the readership of a healthy classified section while many newspapers saw theirs all but disappear.

We also ran classifieds in all our available editions to provide the largest circulation possible, plus the online version, and anyplace else we could get them more exposure.

We still charged for ads in certain categories, generally if there was an ongoing business aspect to them. For example, no one will run a help wanted ad because there is a discount. I've never heard "I didn't need to hire anybody, but the newspaper had a special going . . ."

Taking care of our classifieds has served us well and continues to do so.

Measure Twice, Cut Once

Unless you've worked in certain industries, you probably aren't familiar with picas and points. They are units of measure, sort of like a metric system of its own, that are used to define exact sizes without getting into thousandths of an inch.

There are six picas in an inch, and 12 points in a pica; thus 72 points in an inch. When you use a word processing program, that's where the size of fonts come from. A 36-point headline is one half-inch high. Most new employees needed to be trained on our measuring terminology.

"Column inches" is another term usually unfamiliar to those outside the industry that we had to teach to new employees. Simply, ads are referenced in the number of columns wide multiplied by inches high for the total column inches. A bit of a downfall in the industry is that newspapers have various page sizes and/or various column sizes on those pages, so if you work for an ad agency dealing with numerous papers, good luck!

Odd Layout

How is it that a newspaper always fits exactly into an even number of pages?

Once in awhile it's luck. More often it takes a lot of thinking.

I've always enjoyed the aspect of doing layout, partly because it is the final step of what all our other work becomes. There's also the challenge of organizing it well while trying to make it visually appealing. Readers should be able to find certain items of interest in predictable places.

A lot of decision-making goes into the layout. What are the lead stories that are most important or will be most interesting to most people? What else has to get in? How are ads placed in appropriate spots? Maybe we have to edit some items on the fly to fit a certain spot. And fix those errors that got past proofreading but are now visible. Then how do we fill whatever space is left? And does everybody have their work done on time or will someone show up at the last minute with something too important to leave out?

Computers made it much easier to make late changes in resizing, adding, or removing. My slogan was "miracles while you wait" when confronted with an after-deadline request.

I noticed when browsing old papers from a hundred years ago that publishers occasionally left a page blank when caught in the trap of not enough content. By my time, papers had gotten better at having various extra items on hand to fill both sides of every sheet of paper.

As digital publishing becomes more common, that's one of the most attractive details: there is no reason a digital-only publication has to have an even number of pages. Use what you have and then stop. If it's an odd number of pages, so be it.

Official Notice

They're called "legals" in newspaper office lingo. More formally, they're known as "public notices."

They are the items government units are required to publish so their citizens have the opportunity to be informed about the actions that affect them.

Traditionally, newspapers were the only practical choice because most people cared enough about their community to subscribe to the local newspaper. The aspect of it being printed made it possible to refer back as many times as one wished, unlike the spoken word which is gone as soon as it's said.

Like with many other things, the Internet became a nuisance to newspapers regarding public notices.

Government entities would claim they could put notices on their own websites cheaper. At first glance that might sound reasonable, but when you consider staff and technology costs, it is debatable.

A significant problem with government self-publishing – as anyone who has worked with website development well knows – it's pretty easy to place an item online so that it can meet a requirement of being posted, yet remain terribly difficult for a citizen to find. Along the same line, it's easy to change an official document after the fact when you have control of the publishing tools.

I concede that newspaper audiences aren't what they once were, but I've always argued that "third party" publishing protects the government unit from accusations of playing tricks with the notices. Just like a city or school district employs an outside firm to perform a financial audit each year to assure things are in order, an independent publisher adds trust to the process of government telling its citizens about itself.

Back in 2006, I took that position in an article that ran in the newspaper trade industry publication Publishers' Auxiliary.

Public notices must stay in newspapers
May 2006 • Publishers' Auxiliary

Regarding the "revamping public notice" topic (Pub Aux, April 2006), the best argument I've found for preserving public notice in newspapers is this:

Just as cities, school districts, and counties are required to have a third party accounting firm audit their books each year, their publishing should also be handled by a third party (newspaper) to provide a level of credibility.

Given the ability to self-publish, either on the web or in print, there is too much leeway for abuse, just like if a government entity audits its own financial records.

Council and board members with integrity should welcome the protection of third party publishing, as it removes the likelihood of being accused of hiding or omitting important information when a controversial issue arises.

Too often, newspapers' position on saving public notices comes off with a self-serving tone that sounds like we're really just interested in preserving the revenue.

Hammering the point of credibility by using a third party seems to me as the best approach.

Sell, Sell, Sell

I've done just about every type of job in weekly newspapering, and my weakest area by far is advertising sales. I know enough about it and can easily handle a transaction with a willing buyer, but I don't have the personality to be a good salesperson. I can ask "Do you wanna buy an ad?" but struggle going beyond that in explaining the benefits and marketing strategy to convince an otherwise uninterested prospect.

I can do effective copywriting and ad design though. In 1984, a goose wandered through downtown Winsted, which was unique enough that it was worthy of a photo in the newspaper.

Since some of the photos were with the goose apparently walking toward Citizens State Bank, my creative side took over and I pitched a few ads to the bank. With some darkroom trickery, I was able to place the goose inside the bank lobby and then wrote the copy for this award-winning ad:

The Story of the Goose, the Golden Egg, and the IRA
April 11, 1984 • ad in Winsted Journal

Once upon a time, a man had the great good fortune to own a marvelous goose – every day it laid a golden egg.

The man was starting to grow rich, but the more he got, the more he wanted. He started planning to kill the goose, cut her open, and hopefully find a horde of golden eggs inside her.

Now, every day the goose was sent over to the Citizens State Bank of Winsted to make deposits for the man so that he could get the highest interest rate and returns on his wealth. One day when the goose returned, she told him about the Individual Retirement Accounts (IRAs) the bank is offering.

Because it was nearly April, the man learned that he still had just a few days left to reduce his 1983 income tax before the April 16 deadline, and at the same time, he could increase his retirement income, all through an IRA.

The goose reminded him that an IRA means he could have a tax deduction of up to $2,000, even if he already had an-other pension plan or was a government employee. And together with his working wife, they could put $4,000 a year into an IRA.

"You can't go wrong," the goose told

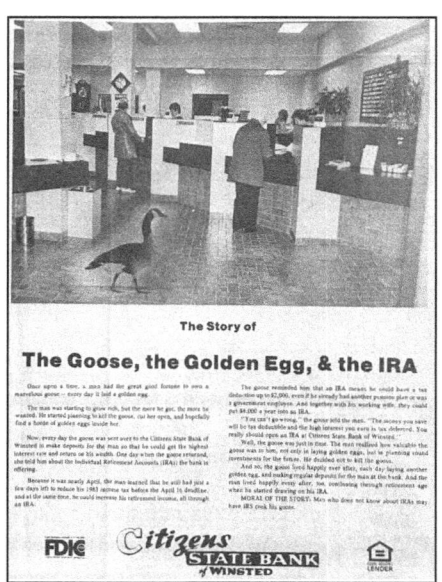

The Story of

The Goose, the Golden Egg, & the IRA

the man. "The money you save will be tax-deductible and the high interest you earn is tax-deferred. You really should open an IRA at Citizens State Bank of Winsted."

Well, the goose was just in time. The man realized how valuable the goose was to him, not only for laying golden eggs, but in planning sound investments for the future. He decided not to kill the goose.

And so, the goose lived happily ever after, each day laying another golden egg, and making regular deposits for the man at the bank. And the man lived happily ever after, too, continuing through retirement age when he started drawing on his IRA.

Moral of the story: Man who does not know about IRAs may have the IRS cook his goose.

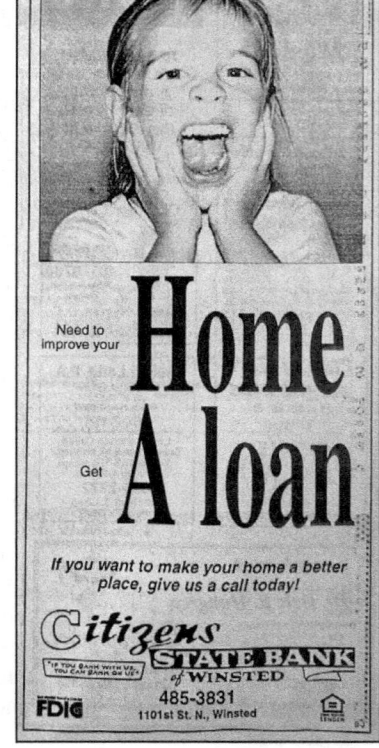

May 3, 1993 • ad in Winsted Journal
For a follow-up bank ad,
I enlisted my daughter Alyssa to
recreate the "Home Alone" movie
pose with the message "Need to
improve your home, get a loan."

Oops!

As newspaper employees, we make our mistakes in public.

Those can be a minor transposition of letters, crucial errors such as getting the date of an upcoming event wrong, or downright embarrassing (like pubic instead of public). Mistakes come in all sizes and shapes.

A lesson: if you are aware of a mistake and can inform the affected people before they find it themselves, it softens the reaction. Even better, present a resolution how you can mitigate the harm.

One error I'll always remember wasn't my fault but involved my photograph. In the newspaper production process at the time, photos were placed into the layout individually during the preparation for printing. We had to identify each one and note any size changes; then the production crew would handle the steps of shooting a negative and stripping it in before burning a plate for printing.

I had a photo of Redwood Falls gymnast Lorri Randgaard performing a handstand during her balance beam routine. But in the production process, the photo was inserted upside down so that when printed in the newspaper she was hanging from above. From what the paper showed, she really deserved a high score!

Due to a production error, this photo ran upside down in the Redwood Gazette in Feb. 1978. Sorry, Lorri – still didn't get it right.

Corrections

"Standing heads" are the labels newspapers put over items that appear frequently but with updated information – lunch menus, bowling scores, and such.

I've always refused to run corrections in the format of a standing head for one simple reason. By its existence, a standing head indicates that this is something that appears regularly. Although we all screw up sometimes and a correction is necessary, it should be the rare exception.

We should always get it right (thanks, Brent). It should be "news" that a newspaper made a mistake, not a regular occurrence that gets a standing head.

Past, Present, and Future

I was fortunate to have missed out on the hot lead era, although there were some Linotype relics still around the offices in my early newspaper days.

When I started, writing was done on a typewriter, edited on paper, and then another person would re-type the material into a Compugraphic typesetting machine which would arrange the words in a specific font and column size on a photographic-type paper which then was developed and then placed onto pages in a layout. Any corrections had to be set in the same format, and then stripped in line by line.

As computers became common, the ease of word processing with spell-check, grammar-check, etc. took over.

Negative scanning was the first step toward digital photography, and we went through some periods of let's just say, awful quality, as we knew little about resolution, brightness/contrast, file format, and such. Eventually we made it to digital photos, and along the way, learned how to handle them for better reproduction.

The layout process evolved into pagination, in which the entire newspaper is produced with computer software. This was a major advancement in the ability to make sizing adjustments instantly instead of having to re-do an item completely to make it fit differently.

The Internet also allowed us to send our finalized pages to the printing plant via modem instead of personally driving over pasted-up layouts.

As websites matured and technology continued to develop, it became apparent that society was shifting to digital formats for many purposes, including news.

I had thought we would have another generation before that transition would be complete, but the move to newspapers that aren't on paper is accelerating faster than I anticipated. In fact, we started publishing a few digital-only editions in 2024 simply as a cost-saving measure. A segment of readers didn't like it, of course, but it was a necessity in the current state of the industry.

Back to the Basics

Hey, you didn't think you'd get through this whole book without a rant about correct usage of apostrophes and grammar, did you? This should take care of it.

Here are some awesome language lessons
May 1, 2019 • Senior Connections

In the newspaper business, part of our job is to use language correctly.

I haven't been able to change the world the way I want, but maybe I can get through to you at least.

Let's start with the simple things.

Apostrophes: when correctly used, they are for abbreviations or to indicate possession, and in the case of possession, we need to be clear if it's singular or plural.

Frequent errors are on house signs, as in: **Welcome to the Smith's**.

Such usage would indicate the property belongs to just one Smith, so we are left to wonder which Smith. Or if there is only one Smith, why include "the" when **Welcome to Smith's** would suffice?

If the intention is plural possession, it would be **Welcome to the Smiths'**.

Next we get the card with **Merry Christmas from the Smith's**.

Of course, this is intended as a plural, not possessive, so it should be **Merry Christmas from the Smiths**.

So please . . . don't put apostrophes as decorations in every word that ends in s.

Another common error on apostrophes is with years. If you are talking about the **1990s**, there is no need for an apostrophe; it's simply plural.

If you want to abbreviate it correctly, it's **'90s** – the apostrophe is in place of what you are leaving out. If you make it **1990's**, then you are actually indicating possession of something that belongs to the year 1990.

Moving on to a higher level: bring/take.

Similar to come/go or here/there, the usage of bring or take is relative to a location and the speaker or writer.

You can **take** something **there** or **bring** it **here**, but you can't bring it somewhere else.

That leads us into word usage in general. Over time, it seems some words become more fashionable to use. Years ago, we didn't talk about a sports venue, or vetting someone who is seeking an important job.

Other words have become popular to the point of being terribly overused and misused – especially **awesome**.

The dictionary definition is: extremely impressive or daunting; inspiring great admiration, apprehension, or fear.

That's much different from the common usage where anything favorable or positive is "awesome."

For example: "I found a nickel on the sidewalk. That's awesome!"

Nice, yes. Maybe I just don't get extremely impressed that easily.

Next up: **random**.

Does anybody remember the chapter on probability in high school math?

If you draw one card out of a deck, there is a **random** chance that it will be any particular number or suit.

The dictionary definition has several parts:

1a: lacking a definite plan, purpose, or pattern

b: made, done, or chosen at random

2a : relating to, having, or being elements or events with definite probability of occurrence

b: being or relating to a set or to an element of a set, each of whose elements has equal probability of occurrence

In the last decade, the word random has become quite popular but very misused.

Example: someone comes up to me and says "I have a random question for you."

I'm (usually) too polite to correct him or her, but I'm already thinking "No, it's not a random question; you know exactly what you are going to ask."

Many times I can't even figure out why someone is using the word random. It appears to be an attempt at referring to some unknown aspect, but it still comes off sort of like a swear word that is included in a sentence but doesn't add any meaning to what is being said.

Maybe it's for emphasis. More likely, it's just a fun word to say, no matter what it means.

I'm afraid the next word to be popularly overused is **epic**.

I guess it's an alternative to **awesome** – but again it's frequently used to exaggerate something okay as if it were extraordinary.

Just one more note: I was going to use reaching into a bag of M&Ms as an example of **random** probability, but that leads to a discussion on whether there should be an apostrophe in M&M's.

Two inquiries to the manufacturer Mars, Inc., have gone unanswered (they must think I'm a crackpot), so I am left to reason it out myself.

The brand name is clearly spelled with an apostrophe – M&M's – which refers to founders Mars & Murrie, and in that instance is correctly punctuated as possessive.

On the wrapper – besides the logo which includes an apostrophe – the product is referred to M&M's Brand Chocolate Candies. In television ads, the candy is referred to by the brand name.

Now the dilemma: if a single piece of candy is an M&M, then several pieces of candy would have to be M&Ms – plural, but not possessive or an abbreviation, so no apostrophe. Right?

10
Failing Media

The one thing the media needs most is credibility.

People understand the media is operated by humans, and humans are fallible, but there needs to be enough trust developed that reporting is consistently fair and accurate.

Corruption has been around since the beginning of time, but in the last several years, blatant unfairness has become the new normal, particularly in larger media. Here are a couple pieces discussing that topic:

What has gone wrong with the media?
Dec. 11, 2020 • Herald Journal/Senior Connections

More than 40 years ago when I was going through journalism training, the most important elements were accuracy and objectivity.

If there was any type of "error of fact" in something we wrote, the entire piece received a failing grade, regardless of how well done the rest of it was. There was no alternative to being correct.

Next was objectivity. A reporter was never to interject his/her own views or thoughts into a story – simply report what someone said, accurately, and attribute it to the source.

These days, the fear of being wrong still drives me. Even in casual conversation, I notice myself qualifying statements in a way that can be defended so that I'm technically "not wrong."

Media objectivity is a different matter.

Journalism students start their careers thinking they know what they need to. Of course, we are objective, right?

I don't believe so anymore. Even with the best of intentions, every one of us comes with our own biases and frames of reference. Some have never seen a live cow; others don't know how to use public transit.

Whether it's political leanings, religious beliefs, or just plain life experience, reporters are influenced by what they know or what they want.

There is a huge amount of judgment involved – what is important? – and that's followed by how to clearly express it. At the individual level, good reporters can do a credible job, but true objectivity doesn't exist, any more than perfect, sinless behavior.

The media also faces its systemic

pressures. Being human, people in leadership have their own biases. Big-spending advertisers have clout. So do personal relationships – positive or negative. And those are mild influences before taking into consideration greed and corruption.

The media also faces a battle of having to fight for attention. Things should be interesting or important, but that quickly turns into being as shocking as one can get away with.

"If it bleeds, it leads" is the TV slogan for ratings.

Both the news and entertainment sides of mass communication push the boundaries of what's acceptable, usually in small increments, to compete for that attention. What was not allowed to be said or shown in TV's early days is vastly different from now. We see women in their underwear in a toothpaste commercial because . . . it gets attention.

But where I'm going is the disturbing trend I've noticed in the national news media, particularly this year.

In the midst of a pandemic and a highly charged election year, media biases have become blatant.

Many times I've been shocked to hear the way things are reported.

Instead of professionally reporting what the president said, they add words like "the president's FALSE claims."

It is not the reporter's role to color it as false or not. If it's in doubt, the proper way would be to follow with an opposing quote attributed to another presumably credible source, not for the reporter to attach words like "baseless" or "wrong" to a statement.

It's become outright discrediting as part of the reporting – not at all what journalism is meant to be.

Love or hate Trump, one must admit that Obama would not have been treated that way by the national media. He wouldn't have been accused of having no evidence for what he stated.

This happens at the Twin Cities media level, as well. It's often just one word inserted into a sentence that takes a legitimate news report and colors it with someone's opinion.

Example: in November, WCCO reported that "our neighboring states have FINALLY instituted mask mandates."

The actual news is that our neighboring states have instituted mask mandates. The word "finally" brings an overriding value judgment into it. Just tell us they now require masks; we'll decide if that's good or bad, or especially if it's finally overdue.

So much for objectivity.

Humans write and report the news, and humans aren't objective. There are too many opportunities to tweak things to one's own preference.

That said, credible balanced reporting is still possible. It's just hard to find these days.

Worst of all, I'm afraid many people aren't even realizing this shift.

The mass media are in crisis. The tools of smartphones and social media have given everyone a voice, and as we know, there is free speech, not responsible speech.

The one thing the news media used to have was credibility. Now even that is being thrown away.

WCCO needs to apologize for political censorship

Sept. 9, 2022 • Herald Journal newspapers

On Sunday morning, Sept. 4, governor candidate Dr. Scott Jensen was being interviewed on WCCO-TV by Esme Murphy, live from the Minnesota State Fair.

The tone of the interview had already been unusually confrontational, especially when compared to the cordial flavor the Sunday before when current governor Tim Walz had his turn.

Near the end, a gross breach of media ethics occurred when Jensen was cut off in mid-sentence, just as he was making the point that the media has been assisting Walz in avoiding debates during this campaign season.

Suddenly, the screen went black and the audio was gone. After a brief segue in studio, a Walz commercial was aired.

A bit later, the feed was restored. Murphy uttered an awkward apology and distanced herself from the situation. Jensen was allowed to finish his answer, and then the interview was declared over without the usual pleasantries.

We all know that technical difficulties occur during live television, but given the circumstances here, it is impossible to look at this as anything other than political censorship.

WCCO has already repeatedly shown itself in more subtle ways to favor liberal positions. Considering who was speaking, what was being said, and the format, there can be no other conclusion. This was too coincidental to be a random power surge or someone accidentally kicking a cord backstage.

No, someone on the WCCO staff with the means to do so must have hit the button to cut off the feed.

It is plausible that the Walz commercial that followed was already cued up, since his half-truth ads air at times such as this. Also, it's normal when tv stations have trouble to "go to commercial."

We can accept that the cut-off wasn't pre-planned. More likely, it was a heat-of-the-moment reaction, laced with poor judgment.

Some time ago, there existed a Minnesota News Council which offered a method to deal with infractions such as this.

For those who felt aggrieved by a media action, it was a hearing format in which the issue would be evaluated, and then a panel would rule on the validity of the complaint. The participating media entity agreed to publicize the result, whether it was found to be unsubstantiated or the media was determined to be negligent.

Unfortunately, the News Council was discontinued several years ago, so citizens are now left on their own to judge which media outlets are credible or not.

I write this not so much in defense of Dr. Jensen, but on behalf of all other news media whose reputations are harmed by bad behavior such as this.

Media has no regulating authority to answer to. Trust is its only asset. The news industry as a whole is already on shaky, sinking ground. When one entity goes way out of bounds, we are all tarnished.

At minimum, WCCO needs to step up as a station to issue a formal, public apology – both to Jensen and especially to the public – and provide some assurance that corrective action has been taken.

Better yet, the person or persons who were involved in the feed cut-off should personally come forward to confess, apologize, and resign.

C'mon WCCO, it's now up to you. Show us if you have any credibility and professionalism left.

11
Letters to the Editor

Free Speech

I believe free speech is one of the most important rights of citizens.

With only the most rare restrictions, we can say what we want, how we want, and when we want. When government makes any attempt to restrict or curtail our speech, we are in danger.

One could do many books on this topic and its related issues, including who censors whom when.

In August 2022, we received a letter to the editor from Jackie Young for our Delano Herald Journal. It was the best summary of free speech concerns from someone outside the industry I had ever seen. So much so that I had it enlarged and framed to be displayed on the wall in our office for staff and visitors to see and comprehend. Here it is:

Freedom of speech
Aug. 26, 2022 • Delano Herald Journal

Letter to the editor from Jackie Young, Delano

For a number of years now, we have witnessed attempts by some on the left to silence, demonetize, and de-platform conservative voices and right-leaning politicians, so-called "conspiracy theorists," Christians, and doctors and scientists who dare question the government's COVID-19 narrative.

Last week's letter to the editor calling for the DHJ to not publish an individual's letters to the editor because they do not deal with "local" issues is just another example of censorship.

It should be apparent that "national" issues do impact people at all levels of society and that people have a right to comment on them at the local level.

The First Amendment does not limit free speech based on someone's ability to articulate certain views or facts to someone else's satisfaction, nor does it limit it based on a person's level of education, income stream, occupation, or opposition to various political views.

Rather, freedom of speech is dependent on a free press and the ability of the people to gather in public and private forums without fear so they may express their opinions on the matters of the day. Isopolity is one of the fundamentals of any democracy.

A free and just society also depends upon a literate, knowledgeable citizenry whose access to information enables it to participate as fully as possible in everyday life and criticize unwise or oppressive government officials or policies. A citizenry must be free to express themselves – openly, publicly, and repeatedly in speech and in writing.

While it may be difficult at times, we should trust that members of the general public have enough intellectual capacity to give the appropriate weight or credence to something they read or hear and be able to form their own opinions based on their life experiences and research.

Who Wrote It?

During my Two Harbors days, I started putting the names of letter to the editor writers at the beginning rather than the end.

I reasoned: what's the first thing you do when reading a letter to the editor? Glance at the end to see who wrote it. Besides, we put our bylines on stories we write at the beginning. Why not letters?

It's at least convenient, if not imperative, to know the source when considering a point of view. We've been doing it ever since.

Determined Writer

Helen Bunge is a wonderful person who fills the unofficial job description of "the church lady" at our Zion Lutheran congregation in Mayer. She knows everyone's names, keeps up with what the children are doing, and seems to somehow be involved in just about everything. She is appreciated for the numerous personal notes she writes with a message of support or congratulations for almost every occasion.

Helen is also a frequent letter to the editor writer for our paper, usually near the Roe vs. Wade anniversary and National Day of Prayer. One year, Helen realized she was down to the deadline and hadn't submitted her pro-life Sunday letter yet.

So at 9 o'clock on a below-zero January night, there was a knock at my door. It was Helen with her letter. There wasn't time to mail it anymore, so this 80-year-old woman drove 20 miles round trip in the middle of winter late at night to deliver it personally to me. I made sure it got in.

The Phony Letter

Over a long career, one inevitably faces some difficult situations. The one that gave me the most anguish was getting burned by a phony letter to the editor.

The most significant lesson I learned in all the years of newspapering is to listen to your instinct. If you wonder about something, check it out; don't just let it go.

It was the summer of 1988 and the Lester Prairie Journal had received a letter to the editor from a former resident who had come back to town and expressed his disappointment about the lack of businesses, and the prices charged by the ones that remained.

It didn't seem quite right. I hesitated a bit, then put in the next paper. And paid dearly for it.

Not only was the reaction to the negative comments severe, but it turned out the letter was phony.

I made a visit to the hardware store that was mentioned to make an apology in person. Owner Wayne Bodenhamer was civil but visibly hurt and upset. We ran a front-page retraction in the next issue. We gave the original letter to the local police to check for fingerprints or anything to find the culprit, but no further resolution was reached.

Former resident shocked at town's digression

July 11, 1988 • Lester Prairie Journal

Letter to the editor from "J. A. Nelson," St. Paul

This past week I visited friends in the area and caught up on the news. I was amazed to see the number of old dilapidated houses for sale and empty. The town is dead in the evening.

My friend sent me to Prairie Hardware for some hardware for a project. They only had half enough, so I went to Winsted for more. I was astonished when Winsted's price on that item was only half of Prairie Hardware's. So, I decided to check prices on several other items in Winsted's store, then returned to Prairie Hardware for a price check. Yup, double on all items. Yowee!

As I related this news to a farmer friend, he informed me that the price of feed is half again as much in the local elevator as in neighboring feed stores.

I wouldn't be surprised if your town becomes another Plato, with all stores gone, school consolidated with Glencoe, and you don't even have a dance hall. Then they told me of the wild idea to build a bigger school.

You people better look around and see how the crops in the country have dried up. I think God is giving you a signal to tighten your belts and cooperate. Remember years ago there was a Red Owl, a Red and White, a Federated, and a Texaco store. Not much left in that department. I also seem to remember several other stores along main street that disappeared.

You don't need a bigger school. New Germany has a fairly new one sitting empty; go borrow that. Be sensible. I want to come back and visit again someday. I don't want to find a ghost town.

An apology for letting phony letter get in the paper
July 18, 1988 • Lester Prairie Journal

I got suckered and I apologize.

I was responsible for ultimately allowing the letter to the editor by "J. A. Nelson of St. Paul" to see print in last week's newspaper. There were some negative statements in the letter which reflected poorly on the community and local businesses.

My first mistake was not paying closer attention to the letter when it arrived. There were a number of ways it could have been handled. In retrospect, I made a poor decision.

The letter met our first test for publication of carrying a name and address. I cringed at the content, recognizing it as outwardly unpopular. But following the practice of allowing all opinions in an open forum, even negative ones, I let it go through for typesetting and publication.

After the fact, it became evident the letter might have been a hoax by someone trying to discredit our newspaper and/or holding a grudge against the other businesses referred to.

Is there a J. A. Nelson in St. Paul? Of course. The phone book lists three J. A. Nelsons, 10 more J. Nelsons, and when you add the Jacks, Jameses, Jerrys, etc., the possibilities are well over a hundred.

Later last week, I received further evidence that the whole thing was a scam.

Our policy on accepting letters to the editor requires the writer to give his/her name and address, and we handle it from there according to each situation. This was not a case of bad policy, but a mistake that got by me. My greatest error was not being entirely certain the letter was legitimate before allowing it to be published.

I apologize to everyone who was offended by the letter's appearance, and assure you that this is not our typical way of running a newspaper.

Our management concludes that if the writer's name was indeed a phony, then statements in the letter were equally fictitious.

In the future, we will still accept letters to the editor. Free expression of opinions is the backbone of the American Constitution, and our paper is one way in which people can communicate their opinions to others if they wish.

However, our staff and I will be much more alert in watching for bogus letters, and will verify them with the author if there is any doubt whatsoever.

So, if there really is a J. A. Nelson who wrote us a letter, please contact me.

More likely, though, I have to say this to the prankster: you got me – this time. I hope you had a good laugh at the expense of others.

Our attorney advises us there is a state law that makes it a misdemeanor to submit false letters to a newspaper. If anyone can supply us with information as to the true identity of the letter-writer in question, we would appreciate it.

12
Cast of Characters

We've had many baseball players on our staff. One year we had four employees who played in the state amateur baseball tournament. We often joked that the problem with baseball players is that they think if they do something right one out of three times they belong in the hall of fame. For better or worse, I can't mention everyone I have worked with. This is certainly not comprehensive, but here are a few notable stories:

Tim and the Cannon

Waverly native Tim Lammers was our editor of the Howard Lake Herald in the early '90s. During this time, he wrote some movie reviews in the Herald, and even had an interview with Clint Eastwood.

When he left, he pursued his passion and became a widely known movie critic, regularly appearing on a number of Twin Cities media outlets, and having conducted thousands of interviews with some of the biggest names in film and television.

More recently, he has been published by national entities such as Esquire.com, and is now a contributor to Forbes.com writing about movies, TV, and doing interviews. In 2013, he published an e-book about director Tim Burton's animated films, and an expanded print version is now in the works.

There's a story about Tim that surfaces in the office every once in a while, usually shortly before or after a new reporter is assigned to cover Waverly's Memorial Day program.

That event includes the firing of a large cannon as a special salute. When he was covering it, Tim anticipated the moment, drew up close, and crouched down to get the perfect shot. When the cannon was fired, the force of its blast sent Tim tumbling over backwards like a cartoon character.

Working Mom

Small weekly newspaper reporter/editor jobs are often best for young single people. The demands of evening and weekend work don't fit well with family life. It's part of the territory that many events and activities that deserve coverage happen when other people aren't working, meaning that our people are.

Lynda Jensen, who was editor of the Herald Journal (and its preceding titles) since we took over ownership, was one of the exceptions who was able to be both a mother and an editor, and do a fine job of both.

She was eight months pregnant with their third child in 2004 when her husband, Brian, was deployed to Iraq for 18 months with his National Guard unit. At least, the family was able to videoconference at times.

Lynda not only kept working and mothering during the deployment; we added to her load by buying the Dassel-Cokato paper a few months later. It was more than anyone thought was humanly possible. Yet she did it – happily.

Tragedy struck in 2010 when an accidental fall at home caused a brain bleed, and Lynda passed away just days later at age 42. Our staff members dealt with their grief by publishing tributes in the next issue. Here's mine:

Peace
June 21, 2010 • Herald Journal

This woman loved her job and was dedicated to a fault.

Even Monday morning when we learned she had gone to the hospital by ambulance, we thought there'd be a chance she'd be back at work the next morning. We even talked about whether we should allow her back unless she had a doctor's note, knowing she would want to be here.

Lynda would often go beyond expectation to make sure things were well done, or something extra was accomplished.

Just recently, one of her co-workers made up a framed special recognition certificate honoring her for "creating extra work for herself . . . through tireless dedication to ignoring the easy way of doing things."

In its playful way, it acknowledged how we could count on her to follow through and take care of everything that needed taking care of, big and small.

Putting together the above story, I more deeply realized how much Lynda was a part of Herald Journal's growth and success in the last few years.

Though Chris and I would make the final decisions, she was one of the key people who carried out the missions and got others to pull in the same direction.

We've gotten many compliments in the last few years on the amount of HJ's news coverage, but it was Lynda and her department that deserve the credit.

As with any management situation, we occasionally had some "spirited discussions" about what should be done in certain circumstances.

I always greatly appreciated that Lynda and I could have a pretty serious disagreement about something, and then just a few minutes later on another topic, we'd be right back working together with no hurt feelings or grudges to mess it up.

Once in a while, if she later felt the discussion was more spirited than it needed to be, a little bag of jerky would appear in my in-basket the next day.

Most of all, I admired Lynda's willingness and ability to publicly express her faith in Jesus Christ.

Sometimes Santa Claus and the Easter Bunny get all the press, but with Lynda's leadership, we were able to cover religious topics in more meaningful ways and use our media privilege to spread the "good news" of salvation.

My last words to Lynda in the office were something about classifieds or website updates.

My last words to her at the hospital were "God will give you peace."

Which she now has.

Another Loss

Another sad time was when we lost our longtime sign department manager, Troy Feltmann, when he succumbed to cancer in 2023. We again did the collection of staff tributes.

Dedicated sign dept. manager and community champion
May 5, 2023 • Herald Journal

Troy was our employee with the longest seniority, having just reached 20 years on April 14.

Not too long after joining our staff, he became our sign department manager as the company expanded its product offerings. In fact, he was our ONLY sign department manager through several moves, a new building, the branding of sister company Greater Minnesota Communications, and the constant changes any business goes through.

Troy was a dedicated, reliable employee. We never worried if he would show up. If anything, we sometimes wondered when he would go home. His habit to stay late and even work on the weekends was a topic of good-natured joking among employees, but also a point of admiration.

He would occasionally stop by my office to rehash a high school sports result, or see if I had caught the latest tidbit about the Twins. His proudest moments were when he would tell me he was a grandpa-to-be.

Beyond work, he was an unofficial "Mr. Lester Prairie." Whether it was the Lions, business association, school, park board – if there was a Lester Prairie project on the go, Troy almost certainly was involved in some manner. He did so constantly, but didn't seek to take credit for it.

That helping attitude was especially evident when a coworker became homebound, and Troy stepped in as a personal attendant, making frequent visits for companionship and running errands as needed.

When a family, a company, a community, loses someone like Troy, there isn't a replacement waiting to take over. We can only appreciate the gift of time we had with Troy.

So teach us to number our days that we may get a heart of wisdom. – Psalm 90:12

The Curmudgeon

A fellow by the name of David Cox started writing some stories for us as a stringer, a common way to fill in the gaps when we didn't have enough people to get everywhere people expected a newspaper reporter to be. After a while, it was agreed that he liked the job enough and we liked his work enough that he became a full-time staffer.

A few years later, he legally changed his name to Ivan Raconteur. The dictionary defines raconteur as "a person who tells anecdotes in a skillful and amusing way." That was an apt description.

He also dubbed himself "The Curmudgeon," but one could make the case that wasn't necessarily true.

Readers appreciated the weekly pub quizzes he would create. That grew out of his previous experiences conducting actual pub quizzes, an activity that became a tradition at our staff Christmas parties.

When Lynda was taken from us unexpectedly, Ivan was the logical choice to fill the hole.

Ivan also solidified himself as our most knowledgeable government reporter. He could sort out the actions of a city council or school board to boil it down to something meaningful and understandable for readers.

He and I would occasionally commiserate over something a local government entity did, especially the excessive compensation contracts some consultants were awarded. We grumbled that either of us could do the same thing for a fraction of the cost. Then we would go back to work, and the city would pay the consultant.

Ivan ran into his own serious health issues that caused him to cut to part-time and eventually pass the baton. He was able to continue raconteuring his weekly columns for a bit, and when that was no longer possible, we fielded many calls from disappointed readers.

There's a line from one of Ivan's columns I like to bring up regularly: "If a man says he'll do something, he will. There's no need to nag him about it every six months."

The Tweeter

In the spring of 2016, we needed to hire a sportswriter. Chris Schultz knew where to look.

My son, Kip, was writing sports for the Sleepy Eye Herald Dispatch, having graduated from Winona State the year before. He had developed a following with live tweets from games being covered. He was especially adept at mixing updates, comments, and details in an interesting manner – not just "the score is now 5-2."

Our staff was big enough that I didn't have to be both his boss and his dad, so we agreed to give it a go.

Kip's other big advantage was that we didn't have to tell him where anything was. He had most likely competed at all the local gyms and fields during his youth. He also knew much about local sports history that is always very helpful at putting some results in context.

When his now-wife Rachel Schuth was working at an internship in Pittsburgh, Kip made a visit and they attended a Pirates game at PNC Park. He told of the experience in his sports column.

Kip's Twitter audience grew exponentially, as he was able to cover both buzzer-beaters and tragic situations in the ups and downs of the sports world. He became an amateur baseball authority and made several radio appearances to discuss the state of baseball affairs.

With all the local teams we had to cover and numerous opportunities, Kip became an expert at state tournament coverage, even freelancing at times including reuniting with Sleepy Eye when its girls basketball team made it to the state championship game.

It was sometimes a frantic schedule, having to dash from a state tournament game in St. Paul to a section championship in Mankato to see if the next team would also make it. He was like a good-luck charm as his alma mater Mayer Lutheran won a state football title and several state volleyball championships.

Kip initiated the Herald Journal All-Area Sports Teams selections that are now published after each season, honoring the top athletes from the coverage area of five newspapers.

What's Going On in Delano?

As a high school student, Ryan Gueningsman started hanging around our newspaper office. We figured that he liked it better than being in class.

He helped us out, and we put him on the payroll. Eventually, he turned it into a full-time gig.

It took quite a while for Ryan to live down his famous radio interview. At one time, we had an arrangement with a local radio station to do a weekly wrap-up of news in the area, and it was Ryan's assignment.

As one of the radio interviews discussed upcoming events, Ryan casually mentioned that Delano's Fourth of July celebration was just ahead. The announcer asked a follow-up question: "What's going on in Delano?"

With no information in hand and not having anticipated needing details, Ryan was on the spot. On live radio, he froze.

For quite a while afterward, other staff members enjoyed taking any available opportunity to ask: "Hey, Ryan, what's going on in Delano?"

But Ryan was a good sport. When we started the Delano Herald Journal from scratch in 2006, Ryan was named our editor there, and recounted the radio story in the first issue.

Along the same lines as his newspaper career advancement, Ryan took his interest and passion for country music to another level. The Winstock festival was in its early years, and Ryan was able to secure interviews with many of the visiting singers. He wrote some professional interview stories that were as good as any you'll see in national publications.

He kept growing as the festival did, and became chairman of the Winstock committee in 2024.

Oh, and one more thing: Ryan and I go way back. I took his picture when he was the new year's baby at St. Mary's Hospital.

Best Wedding Advice Ever

At the rehearsal on the evening before our printing department manager Jami Berg's wedding, the scripture reader was reviewing his part, and asked: "Jami, are you sure this is the verse you want?"

There was an error in the program. The verse numbers and book from the Bible were mixed up, so what was indicated was a passage from the Old Testament about not having sex with animals.

When I attended the wedding the next day, they used a different verse.

The Dead Editors Society

The basement in our Howard Lake building was a dingy, dirty cavern filled with dust and cobwebs. No one went down there unless absolutely necessary.

I think this started with some staff conversations about an alleged ghost in the building. Eventually, the fable developed that when an editor left employment, he or she would somehow come back to haunt us.

To make it more formal, we created the Dead Editors Society, appropriately based in that filthy basement.

When someone resigned, on his or her last day of work, we would have the entire staff file down the creaky steps, turn on the single light bulb, and acknowledge the moment.

Each former editor's name and employment dates were memorialized tombstone-style, written with a Sharpie marker on an 8.5x11 sheet of typing paper, and then taped in place on the wall to preserve their memory for all time.

13

Herald Journal

I hired Chris Schultz as a part-time reporter in November 1992.

I knew his older brothers from the local softball league, and remembered his twin sister, Jenni, was an outstanding high school runner. Since Chris was from Lester Prairie, the interview included a screening question to make sure he didn't have any alliances to the competing Prairie Ad-News. When he assured me he wasn't a spy, off we went.

Later, I recalled a softball game in which Kendall and Chuck Schultz sent a short, young kid with a tiny strike zone in to pinch-hit late in a game I was pitching. I didn't realize it at the time, but it must have been Chris.

At the paper, Chris came with the local knowledge of a native, an education in public administration, a dairy farm work ethic, and much more. An outdoors enthusiast, he developed some hunting and fishing coverage that was nonexistent before.

I often teased him about his typing skills, but when proofed and edited, his writing was right on point. He did a feature story for our Farm Horizons publication by riding along with a milk truck driver. The lead for that story was one of the best I've ever seen:

> *"The rooster in the hen house is crowing; the dairy farmer has been hard at work; his bulk tank is full of milk. And down the road a bit, just over the horizon, the early morning sun glistens off the huge, shiny, silver tank of a milk truck rolling down the highway. Another day – like all 365 of them in the dairy industry – has begun."*

Just a few months into his employment, on the way back home from the state newspaper convention, Chris broached the subject of considering him for the opening we had as the company's salesperson. I wasn't too enthused with having to look for another reporter, but agreed to give him a shot. He sold me, and has been selling since.

With Chris putting his marketing expertise to work, our sales took off like never before. He didn't sell just newspaper ads. If a customer needed a sign or banner, he found a vendor to order from and fulfill that need.

At a newspaper convention a few years later, a colleague asked about our success. All I could answer was "I've got Michael Jordan."

In the late '90s, Chris was looking to raise the stakes and we started talking with owner Bill Ramige about Chris and me buying the company. I was hesitant, having been frightened by the advice that "you don't own a business, it owns you."

So due to my foot-dragging, it took longer than it should have, but when I realized we were near the point where Chris would move on to something else, I got on board. We agreed he would be the majority partner. The deal closed Nov. 30, 2001.

We were a good pair. He was the face of the company with an aggressive approach of becoming a full-service marketing company, not just a newspaper. I was pleased with a behind-the-scenes role doing a lot of the administrative tasks and inflicting my compulsion to never be late on the staff.

Many times I shook my head and concluded that the man must never sleep. Chris went to every community event possible, served a nine-year cycle on the Minnesota Newspaper Association board culminating in being president, and had several outside endeavors besides running a business.

Whenever I tried to do too many things at once, the most important ones suffered the most. Some people can pull it off.

With Chris's drive and vision, we had explosive growth in the mid-2000s as he further developed the sign, printing, and online services divisions. One day, a staff member introduced himself to who he thought was yet another new employee, only to find out it was the copier repairman.

We built a new office building in 2003 at the prime corner in town, and added a second building for the sign department in 2006.

To keep things in shape, we'd occasionally schedule clean-up days for the entire staff. I started the ritual of playing Barney the dinosaur's "Clean Up" song over the intercom. It was fun to see the reactions from new employees. The other ones were used to me.

When the real estate market crashed in 2008, we still rolled on. As the legal newspaper for Wright County, we sometimes carried multiple pages of foreclosure notices. Though a crisis for the individuals, those notices were revenue for the newspaper.

As the Internet matured, Google, Facebook, and others continued to hack away at the newspaper industry. There were fewer local businesses left to advertise, and technology gave people more media choices than they could keep up with.

Initially, the newspaper brand helped us sell the other marketing services and products. However, we started to notice more customers who were reducing their advertising because their "newspaper bill" had gotten too big.

To answer that, we began a separate company, Greater Minnesota Communications, which would primarily handle the printing, sign, and online work under a separate billing function. It was no secret that both companies were associated, but it helped change the perception of having to write a large check to one entity.

We started having some lean years in the late twenty-teens. Sales were harder to come by, and debt kept growing. Then we ran into COVID-19.

It was something no one had seen before. As good citizens and stewards, we complied with instructions from the government, not knowing any better in the moment.

We were especially fearful about the cancellation of virtually every event in 2020 as a good chunk of our business activity was tied to those events. A community festival not only needs promotion but signage, printing, etc.

But difficult situations can have good outcomes. The necessity of the circumstances forced us to make some staff reductions that should have been done anyway, and I'll admit that the government assistance programs for businesses helped us survive. We were able to get back to a sturdy footing.

Then about 20 years after starting, we looked at how the calendar kept flipping from year to year, and made a quiet agreement that Chris would take over my ownership stake and I would stay around a few more years in the same role. We didn't tell anybody except when there was a legal requirement.

In fall of 2023, the proposition of Herald Journal acquiring the southern neighboring Glencoe and Arlington newspapers surfaced, and it made too much sense to pass by. Such an endeavor requires consolidating all possible operations and expenses. We underestimated what resources it would take to pull this off, but overall, it was still a good idea.

Just a few months after that, the local media scene was turned upside down when the hedge fund, Alden Capital, suddenly announced it was closing the western neighboring newspapers in Hutchinson and Litchfield, as well as some in Carver County. They didn't sell those publications to someone else. They just shut them down and walked away. And with that, the printing plant in Hutchinson that printed our five newspapers was also abruptly closed.

With less than a month to react, we scrambled and found a new printing vendor in Cambridge, this one 80 miles away instead of 20. This clearly resulted in additional distribution costs.

There were a lot of community requests for us to start papers in Hutchinson and Litchfield, but we were still recovering from Glencoe and Arlington investments, and we wouldn't have had the available staff or resources to pull it off.

Fortunately, CherryRoad Media, which had started papers in the so-called "news deserts" before, stepped in to fill the gap. Our opinion was that if anyone could succeed in the industry, it would be a good thing, not a competitor. The dust is still settling for local newspapers in our area.

And as this book is published, Andrew Meuleners has taken over as general manager at Herald Journal Publishing, and I am remaining on staff during a transition period.

On the Job

During those ownership years, I did very little writing for the newspapers. I was occupied with being the HR guy, maintaining some website and online tasks, keeping my fingers in newspaper layout, filling in on delivery routes when a driver was absent, and whatever else a general manager generally does.

Just before COVID, after a rash of turnover in bookkeepers, I took a couple seminars about QuickBooks and moved into the bookkeeping department as one of my main duties. I found it to be a great fit as I've always enjoyed working with numbers. Knowing the customer names and internal company processes made it a simple transition.

Here are a few noteworthy items from the HJ years:

Discrimination Claim

In late 2007 and early 2008, we went through an interesting situation when a former resident wanted to announce a "commitment ceremony" for himself and his gay partner.

Same-sex marriage had not yet been legalized in Minnesota, so we balked on the grounds that it didn't involve a valid marriage. The exchange continued and the man stated he wanted to invite people from his hometown to the ceremony. We agreed to let him do so in a paid ad, but when we noticed that the "invitation" didn't include a date or location, we questioned the motive and pulled it.

From there, we ended up being investigated by the Minnesota Department of Human Rights, and had to travel to St. Paul for a conciliation meeting. As part of a discrimination claim, the man was asking that, in addition to other things, we publish the announcement and pay damages of $22,500 plus attorney fees.

We countered that the amount was excessive, as one could print and mail a postcard to everyone in town for $700 at current rates. Also, we asked why the newspaper from the partner's hometown wasn't involved, nor the newspaper of their current residence. Wouldn't the couple want to invite those people as well?

We sweated it out while attorneys for both sides wrote letters back and forth, and eventually the claim was quietly dropped with no further action.

Our front page from 2021. Amidst the many activities of the season, the real reason for celebrating Christmas is the birth of Jesus Christ.

The Real Reason

While our business was growing, so was my faith.

After the movie "The Passion of the Christ" came out, which was an unprecedented graphic depiction of the crucifixion of Jesus, Lynda Jensen wrote a feature story about the movie.

That was the turning point when we increased our emphasis of the real reason why Christmas and Easter exist. We still included photos of the fat guy in the red suit and the rabbit from community events, but Jesus is more important.

I compiled passages from the gospels into a chronological summary of the Christmas story which ran that year. We followed it up by doing the same for Easter.

Depending on how the holiday fell relative to publishing day, sometimes we devoted the entire front page to The Christmas Story; other times it started on the front page and continued inside. The Easter Story would run in the edition on Good Friday.

Each time we published the Christmas or Easter stories, we got a couple notes of appreciation from readers. Complaints were very rare but once every few years, someone objected.

If you doubt the importance of faith, please see the "Where do we go from here?" column in a later chapter.

Breaking News, Literally

There's a railroad overpass in Howard Lake for which the posted clearance underneath is 11 feet, 7 inches. From years of observation, I can say that measurement is a firm limit. It seemed at least once a year a too-tall vehicle would collide with that bridge.

One definition of news is "something that happens out of the ordinary." So when an 11' 9" truck or camper attempted to pass under, the result was "news" only to the driver, not the community.

Close to Home

My brother-in-law Mark Blazinski was in poor health and in need of a second liver transplant.

A loving, living donor stepped forward: my wife Linda. Besides being involved firsthand, I was able to share their story with our readers:

On the road to recovery
April 14, 2008 • Herald Journal/Dassel-Cokato Enterprise Dispatch

When asked what's ahead for him now, two-time liver transplant recipient Mark Blazinski quickly responded: "Everything."

After nearly a year and a half of medical complications, Blazinski, of Silver Lake, appears well on the road to recovery.

On March 19, Mark underwent his second liver transplant in less than a year. This time, a living donor process was used with his sister-in-law, Linda Kovar of rural Mayer, donating a portion of her liver.

"My prognosis is very good," Mark said. "I will heal to the way I was before, if not better."

There's still a long road of recovery ahead, but Mark and his family are the most optimistic in months.

"I was living on borrowed time. My liver was doing nothing but taking up space," he said. "It was like a plugged oil filter, and then you get high blood pressure, contaminated blood, no immune system."

Things started around Thanksgiving 2006 when Mark had his gall bladder removed. Though doctors couldn't say for certain why, it was right after that surgery that Mark's already compromised liver started failing, leaving him hospitalized for several periods of time, including a 37-day stretch from late July to Labor Day.

About a year ago, he was placed on the transplant list, a somewhat competitive process in which those with a need are given a ranking based on medical factors, to receive the relatively few organs that become available.

Last May 24, Mark got the call and received a liver transplant, from an unknown cadaver, at the University of Minnesota Medical Center - Fairview in Minneapolis.

Though it saved his life at the time, that liver proved not to be a long-term answer.

The family was told it involved a "preservation injury," meaning it was kept on ice for a lengthy time while being transported from where it came.

Recipients are told very few details about where donated organs are from. In this case, the Blazinskis only know it was from beyond the Minnesota-North Dakota-South Dakota area, and that some time also passed while the donor's family was making the decision whether to donate or not.

Over the next several months, Mark underwent at least seven ERCP procedures to place stents into his transplanted liver to help drain the bile.

After the summer, Mark's health suddenly improved in September and he was able to attend the large fundraiser event friends and family members put on in Silver Lake.

But within the next couple months, his condition again deteriorated, to the point that doctors determined another transplant would be necessary.

This time, use of a living donor was a possibility because Mark was still healthy enough to be able to use a partial liver.

Immediately, four relatives stepped forward, including Mark's wife, Deb, and son, Giles.

The first steps to be a living donor are basic lab tests to determine blood type and filling out a comprehensive health history. Only about half of the people who apply pass that step, for a variety of reasons.

From there, one person at a time goes through an extensive process of medical tests and interviews.

Initially, Mark didn't want to have any family members involved as a living donor.

"That day, when they brought it up, family was not an option," Mark said. "If something bad would happen to one (in the surgery), it would happen to two."

Mark recalled the reality of the clinic visit when a second transplant was proposed by doctors: "It wasn't said until then. But now instead of being assumed, it was said."

At the end of that appointment, Deb and her sister Betty walked ahead through a hospital tunnel, while Mark and Linda held back and had a heart-to-heart conversation.

"They were way ahead, and we put our cards on the table. I had to tell you some things on my mind," Linda told Mark, recalling that moment.

"It made it easier to accept that you were donating," he answered. "I wanted no family, and to be in control."

Linda had been deeply involved with Mark and Deb from the beginning.

"From going through it the first time around, I saw everything and how it played out," she said. "There was no way I could let that happen again.

"No way I could let Deb be without her husband, or Giles, Sarah, and Amy – my godchild – be without their dad. I felt deep down if I passed the testing, it was meant to be and would be okay," Linda said.

Being the donor for the transplant "was easier than to live with myself if I had not tried," she said.

The greatest advantage of using a living donor is that the person with the unhealthy liver doesn't have to wait for someone to die. Only about one-third of the people on the waiting list get a liver each year, according to the university, and about 20 percent of the patients on the list die while waiting.

The living donor method greatly reduces the time element of transporting the liver, improving the chances it will work correctly.

Also, every living donor transplant takes someone off the list, allowing others to move up faster.

Linda was so positive about the procedure from the start, Deb said. "I was very thankful for what she was doing."

That was early December, but it took over three months to get to the actual transplant.

Linda had immediately applied and was scheduled for the medical testing. But at one point, she realized that Mark and Deb's son, Giles, who had also applied, needed the opportunity to try to help his father.

Instead, Giles went through the testing first, but was not accepted. Unless an unrelated medical issue that needs attention is found, applicants aren't given reasons – just a yes or no.

After that, Linda went into the testing process. As she was finishing, there was some concern because Mark's calcium level was too high, so additional tests were ordered for him.

"They were digging around, looking for cancer," but didn't find anything more, Deb said.

Eventually, the transplant was set for March 19.

The day before, both couples went to the University's Transplant Center for a final round of testing to make sure nothing had changed, as well as final preparations. "Enema day," Mark called it.

The transplant day started with a 5:30 a.m. arrival at the hospital. Linda went into surgery about 7:30, Mark closer to 8:30, and a number of family members dug in for a long day of waiting.

Linda's surgery was estimated to be eight to 10 hours.

For Mark's, "they said we could go to 4 or 6, or midnight. They said, don't worry, even if it takes a long time," Deb recalled.

Linda had two surgeons, Drs. Abhinav Humar and Anthony Rezcalleh. Mark had three at his side – Drs. Hill, William Payne, and Raja Kandaswamy – with Dr. Humar also coming over after completing Linda's.

Because of Mark's previous transplant, removing his old liver was a more delicate procedure that took additional time.

Shortly after 3 p.m., family members were notified that Linda's surgery was in a waiting mode until Mark was ready. "She's circling the airport waiting to land," a nurse described.

At around 5:30, about 60 percent of Linda's liver was taken to the adjacent operating room for Mark.

Several times before and after the procedure, Linda jokingly referred to the old Pannekoeken commercials where waitresses in Dutch aprons would run – "fresh from the oven to the table."

Linda was out of recovery about 9:45 and family members got to see her, a few at a time.

Less than an hour later, barely out of surgery herself, she called her husband Dale's cell phone to check on Mark's status.

Doctors came out about 11 p.m. when Mark's surgery was complete, telling family members they also had to replace a portal vein connected to his new liver. The old one simply wasn't usable, so they retrieved one from the hospital's tissue bank.

Family members headed for home that night, but Deb had only gotten to I-494 when she was called back because Mark's heart rate had dropped quite low. By the time she arrived back at the hospital, two injections of Atropine had stabilized him.

"I don't remember what the nurse said, but it wasn't positive," Deb recalled. "I thought we were going to lose him, that he wasn't strong enough to survive the surgery. But then when I was talking with Mark's mom, I said 'I'm really scared, but I know he's going to be okay.'"

Deb described the three-day period around the transplant as "just stressful." She slept only about five hours in three days.

But after the first night, recoveries for both Mark and Linda went remarkably well.

The transplant was on a Wednesday. By Sunday, which was Easter, doctors already mentioned Linda going home, though she knew she wasn't ready for that yet.

Linda did make it home that Tuesday, and Mark right behind her on Thursday.

Mark's improvement was very noticeable to those around him, especially his eyes becoming white again instead of a yellow color, and the constant itching that plagued him before the transplant subsided.

Hospital staff commented on how quickly he improved. He was in intensive care only from Wednesday to Sunday, and when he transferred floors, he walked to his new room himself.

Now, Mark looks forward to getting on his motorcycle, hunting and fishing, and taking a family vacation.

"Last summer was just a blink of an eye. I hardly remember anything," he said.

Mark missed Giles' high school graduation, and daughter Sarah's participation as Pola-Czesky queen candidate in Silver Lake.

"I need money and a job and everything that goes with that, but the other things are what I have to have," he said. "Things have become more precious and dear – how can they not?

"We've got family. Without that, I wouldn't be sitting here," he said. "Money can't buy a family. They're the most important people in your life. I had people stepping up, and all they'd say is 'You'd do the same for me.'"

Mark won't ever be pill-free, but looks forward to reducing his medications from the current nine prescriptions to one, as well as regaining weight. He lost over 40 pounds since the ordeal began.

On being a donor, Linda said she felt she helped two people – Mark directly, as well as someone else who would get a cadaver liver instead of Mark.

"There's a lot of personal reward in donating. I have my secret little smile inside – how can you not think about it?" she said. "But there are some awkward moments when people over-acknowledge it. They said 'You're so wonderful, a saint, an angel.' I have a hard time with that. People say 'I don't even give my brother-in-law a birthday card, let alone a liver.'"

She also expressed thanks for cards and phone calls, some from people she hadn't been in touch with for years. "It's nice to know people sincerely care," she said.

Linda is off for 12 weeks from her job as a registered nurse at Elim Home in Watertown. She is slowly increasing activity, and has not had any complications.

The Blazinskis credited Ann Kalis, Mark's transplant coordinator, for seeing them through.

"She was always so positive, always there for us," Deb said. "We'd call and she'd call right back. She even told us things we didn't want to hear, but should. She's a wonderful lady."

The surgeons also get a lot of credit.

"I told them 'Do you know the miracles that you do?'" Deb said. "And they just said 'We're glad to be a part of it.' They're really humble."

In an adult-to-adult transplant, about 60 percent of the donor's liver is given to the recipient. The liver has two lobes, each with its own blood supply.

The recipient gets the larger portion. Both pieces regenerate to fill the original space within a few weeks.

The University of Minnesota does about 25 living donor transplants a year, the first one being in 1996. The Blazinskis were told this was the first re-transplant at the university that involved a living donor.

Nationally, about 500 living donor liver transplants are done each year.

As of last week, there is a national waiting list for livers of 16,385, according to the Organ Procurement and Transplantation Network website. In Minnesota, about 548 people are currently on the liver transplant list.

Mark passed away in November 2011 after contracting esophageal cancer, but the transplant gave him three and a half more years with his family.

14
Columns Intro

The Art of Column Writing

Looking back, I went through more names for my personal columns than I remembered.

It started with "Off the Bench" which was intended to mean off the bench and into the action.

Next, it became "On the Bench" referring to being an observer.

In Redwood Falls, I called it "Upper Dek," a play on my initials, then switching to "Foul Lines."

In Winsted, I went with "Between the Lines." Later on, it simply became "My Column."

And finally, there was no column name at all – just identified as my writing.

Writing a weekly newspaper column can be both a joy and a pain, and coming up with something meaningful on a regular basis is a demanding task. Once I confessed to coming up blank:

A slow week
May 21, 1981 • Winsted Journal

Column writing for me goes in streaks.

Sometimes I'll go for several weeks in a row with reasonably good ideas for columns. Then for a few weeks, I won't be able to think of anything.

This is one of those weeks I can't think of anything.

For quite a few years, my column writing was sporadic at best, but when our company started the Senior Connections publication in 2018, it was rekindled. The monthly (later every other month) schedule was more conducive to generating material I would be satisfied with, while keeping up with other more important duties.

That schedule gave me the time to develop a process: get the basic piece drafted, then let it age a few days before coming back to it fresh to make revisions, followed by a few more sessions to tweak the wording.

We'll finish with a series of my favorite columns, arranged in groups by topic.

15
Columns for Seniors

There was a Sunday morning in 2016 when I wasn't in church because I was running around in Minneapolis with a woman half my age. Wait, let me explain that differently.

The following column about how I took up running at age 53 mentions meeting a group of professional runners. As with any sport one gets involved with, it's natural to follow those who are the best at it.

In this case, it was Team USA Minnesota (now called Minnesota Distance Elite), a group of runners who train together in furthering their careers.

That year, the team hosted a series of group runs in which anyone who wished could join in for an informal workout. During my marathon training, I went once to participate.

In all, there were maybe 15 people that day. After brief introductions, everyone took off running around Lake Harriet and Lake Calhoun (that was still the name then). It broke into two groups with faster runners going on ahead and those of us comfortable with a nine-minute-per-mile pace trailing. As part of hosting the event, Heather Kampf stayed with my slower group.

Heather is known for "The Fall" in which she tripped to the ground during a 600-meter race at the University of Minnesota, but then recovered to breeze past the other runners in the last lap and win. She was then Heather Dorniden. Look up the video on YouTube; it's worth it.

Professionally, Heather was nicknamed "Queen of the Mile" for her numerous victories at that distance. Earlier that summer, she had just missed qualifying for the Rio de Janeiro Olympics when hampered by an injury at a most inopportune time.

Our group run had dwindled down to four, and about halfway through, two other runners decided to split off in a different direction for their training. That left Heather and me one-on-one for the last three miles. Unlike celebrity meet-and-greets where you are herded through a line for a quick handshake and photo, Heather was stuck with me for half an hour to get back to the finish. We got to talk about running and goals, and I found her running ability to be exceeded by her graciousness.

Running after 50 (5k to marathon)
Aug. 1, 2018 • Senior Connections

Returning from a vacation a few years ago at age 53, I stepped on the scale and it read 199 pounds.

And I felt awful, often not bothering to tie my shoes because, well, it was just easier not to.

Faced with "turning 200," I decided to try again at some exercise and dieting. I'd occasionally run before, but not consistently enough to do much good.

I adopted ex-Gophers coach Glen Mason's mantra: "I hate to run, but I love to eat" and set off jogging a 1.5-mile loop near our house.

This time, I was able to keep at it – as well as restrict meals to moderate amounts with no snacking – to make a difference. Within a few months, I had lost 30 pounds, the equivalent of carrying two bowling balls around, and felt tremendously better.

So I stuck with it. The next year, my daughter Chelsea talked me into running one of the local 5k (3.1 miles) races. It was free, so I agreed.

Then things got out of control from there.

I've always liked sports. I gave up softball after trying to field ground balls with bifocals. Even golf became pretty difficult with carpal tunnel.

I found running to be an easy, cheap, and convenient alternative.

For one thing, you can literally step out your front door and go running at any moment that suits you, not having to wait for a scheduled time or be dependent on any other factor.

You can also make it as competitive or keep it as casual as you wish, from striving to win your age group in large races to never looking at a stopwatch.

Warning: competing is fun, but no matter how good you think you are, there are many, many others of all ages who will be faster than you. Keep your expectations in check, and it will be more fun than frustrating.

And although there are numerous opportunities and gadgets to spend money on, you really don't need much more than a decent pair of shoes and comfortable clothes.

I say it's easy because you can go at your own pace. No one plays defense against you. It only takes the willingness to keep putting one foot in front of the other.

So when I mastered the mile and a half loop, I increased it to two laps, as well as entering some more 5ks.

Then I heard about the Twin Cities 10-mile, from the Metrodome (at that time) to the state capitol. Still inexperienced at the finer points, I proclaimed: "I run three miles, I can do 10!"

Turns out that each additional mile is just as long as the previous one. There's no volume discount or anything like that.

Eventually, Chelsea and I reached the goal of running a 10-mile race.

You see where this is going – next was a half marathon (13.1 miles). Repeat after me: each additional mile is just as long as the previous one.

Then I read about the Loony Challenge, which is a 10k and 5k back-to-back on Saturday and 10-mile on Sunday, for a total of 19.3 miles. The best part is that it guarantees an entry into the Twin Cities 10-mile rather than having to go through the lottery process, because, yes, there are that many people who want to run 10 miles.

Actually, the really best part is that you get to do three races in less than 26 hours, including the gorgeous finish stretch from the St. Paul Cathedral looking down to the capitol. The atmosphere of the whole weekend is sort of like getting to go to a state tournament at the end of a season.

Of course, this wouldn't be complete without one more progression.

There was talk of a group from our church doing a marathon. That didn't materialize, but truth be told, I was a year away from changing age groups (meaning I would compete against older runners), so I signed up myself.

Twin Cities Marathon was a natural fit because I was already familiar with the start and finish areas, plus it's close enough to drive in and out rather than dealing with hotel logistics.

So I trained and read everything I could and learned how to ingest gels while moving and which flavor of Powerade to drink and went to physical therapy for an injury and almost passed out from dehydration and met some professional runners at a group run and studied the course and got there and plodded through the first half and then had several miles that were a joy and then crossed the river and my back hurt and feet hurt and ended up walking most of the last four miles while my family was wondering what happened to me after the last tracking checkpoint, but I made it to the finish and then said I wouldn't do it again . . .

And I haven't – yet. But I would like another shot at it because I think I can do better.

In the meantime, I'm getting older every day, preventing the scale from starting with a crooked number, and running more days than not because, as I've stated many times, "It feels better than not doing it."

Things a non-runner doesn't understand

• Fun run: If you don't run, it's easy and common to scoff about running being "fun." My favorite part is, after a race, dripping with sweat, chowing down on the post-race food and feeling like I have done something.

• Injuries: You're not being tackled by a 275-pound linebacker or beaned by a 100-mph fastball, so how can you get hurt running? There are a variety of pains that come from repetitive use or overuse.

• Pace and times: So how long does a 20-mile run take – an hour? (Even the Kenyans don't come close to that.) It takes some experience to be in tune with what's considered a "good" time. For the elite runners, even reaching a personal best by a second can be a significant accomplishment.

Reviewing life's lessons

July 1, 2019 • Senior Connections

A social media poll recently posed the question: would you rather have a youthful body or the wisdom that comes from age and experience?

For me, this one isn't too hard to answer.

Although I'd love to be able to hit and pitch a baseball well again, and do away with the seemingly daily aches and pains (and prescriptions), there is a lot of value from the experience of life.

It can be regarding anything, like driving in the cities – knowing where certain places are, where major roads go, and just understanding traffic in general.

Or it can be the comfort of knowing what's really important in life, and equally so, what's not worth getting upset about.

There are the standard things everyone learns, like "Don't touch a hot stove."

Some lessons, like getting your private parts caught in a zipper, only take once. Others need to be repeated multiple times to sink in.

We draw on our experience to avoid pain, find our way around, or simply do things in easier or more enjoyable ways. We even learn to temper our reactions to many things.

If I was able to make a list of everything I've learned in six decades plus, hopefully it would be longer than we have space for here. But instead of trying to be comprehensive, here are just a few of the miscellaneous things that I've learned:

• One of my uncles taught me about cross-reference filing in both personal and business use. Simply, you leave notes in specific places where you might look for something with directions to where it actually is.

• I save myself time and aggravation by buying several pairs of white socks that are exactly the same and several pairs of black socks that are exactly the same. Then there's no need to try to match specific pairs, and if the washer or dryer eats one of them, it doesn't matter.

• In the heat of the moment after a youth baseball game that my son's team lost in an intense extra-inning battle, another parent remarked: "It's important now, but it's not important." Turns out he was right. More than a dozen years later, I don't remember the score or even the opponent, but I do recall that the heartbreak of a lost game passed with time while the memory of having been involved is still pleasurable.

• A basic understanding of financial aspects like insurance and deductibles, taxes, and financing and interest helps one make hopefully good decisions.

• Gather everything you need for the next day the night before. It's so much less stressful than running into a problem when you're trying to leave in the morning.

• Some of my wife's best advice for me has been "Don't believe everything you think."

Driving for a discount

Dec. 1, 2018 • Senior Connections

When you turn 16, it's exciting because you are finally eligible to get a driver's license.

When you turn 55, it's – (fill in emotion of your choice) – because you're now eligible to enroll in a driving safety course.

There are a number of names for it: defensive driving course, mature driver improvement course, smart driver course, etc. I just call it "old people's driving class."

There is a standing offer on the table of a 10 percent discount on auto insurance, which elevates it from a good idea to an action item.

Although it's hard to argue against safety, the insurance discount is the clincher that makes it worth pursuing.

The first time around, it's a full eight-hour course. After that, you only need a four-hour refresher every three years.

There are a number of approved providers of these courses including AARP and AAA, as well as some more local organizations.

In this day of many choices, you can do it either in a classroom setting or, of course, online.

I did my first round over two evenings in Waconia; then opted for renewals online in my pajamas.

If you haven't taken this class yet, it guides you through virtually every aspect of driving from traffic laws to vehicle maintenance to physical health issues to dealing with weather to driving etiquette to accident statistics, etc.

Both the classroom and online versions do a good job of mixing up the presentation format to keep your attention. It might be a stretch to call it entertaining, but at least it isn't drudgery.

There are quizzes along the way, but it's low-stress. You don't have to actually pass the course, just complete the course – which means if you put in the time, you'll absorb enough of the information anyway to be valuable.

Which is why the government and insurance companies want you to do it.

I'll admit I was there strictly for the discount, but then found myself reciting tidbits later in various driving situations.

One of my biggest takeaways was how to properly set the rear-view mirrors. I'm sure this was taught in high school driver's training but it really opened my eyes to re-learn that if the mirror is in the correct position, you can see so much more of what is behind you.

The other big point I learned was about airbags. Fortunately, I've never been in a situation where an airbag deployed, so I'm glad to take the instructor's word for it.

Although an airbag can do a tremendous job to prevent you from going through the windshield or smacking into metal parts, you can take a pretty stiff hit from the airbag itself.

Thus, it's advisable to try to position yourself as far away from the steering wheel and airbag as you comfortably can. Each inch farther away works in your favor should an accident occur.

I found this interesting since I tend to sit pretty far back anyway. I'm just a little under average height, but I guess I really like my space because almost every time I drive a different vehicle, the first thing I do is move the seat back, usually as far as it can go.

That's just how I like it. Now I can blame it on the airbags.

All in all, brushing up on what we should know to drive safely is good for all of us.

Enjoy the course – and make sure you get your discount!

Through my grandma's eyes

May 1, 2021 • Senior Connections

When I was growing up, my parents and I lived as part of an extended family with my grandmother Emily Hakel and an uncle.

"Grandma" was the only grandparent of mine remaining alive when I was born, and the living arrangement allowed me to know her well.

We lived on the remnant of an old-time farm about two miles out of town with a barn and several other unused outbuildings. The land was rented to a neighboring farmer.

There still was a functioning hand-pumped well just outside the house, even though we had indoor plumbing by the time I arrived.

There was also an outhouse tucked between some of the outbuildings, but since we had the indoor convenience, I didn't have to deal with how far a trip it would have been several times a day, every day, all year around.

We didn't have any carpeting, so it was our norm to wear shoes in the house all the time. Later in life, it took me quite a while to adjust to the concept of not wearing shoes inside.

Television already existed and we had an old model on which we watched shows in black-and-white. I recall putting away coins at one point to save up for the dream of getting one of those fancy color television sets.

Trips to "the cities" from this area were something you planned a couple weeks ahead. It certainly wasn't a daily commute.

One of my clearest memories of life changing for my grandma was when telephone service came to our area. It was a rural party line, so you could hear others in their conversation and had to wait your turn to make your call.

Mostly, I remember Grandma being so amazed that on that device you could speak and other people who were some-where else could hear you! And vice versa, you could hear them!

When some of our relatives would visit, it was an occasion to wait until dark; then they would set up a projector and show slides of the places they had traveled to.

One uncle was a pretty good photographer, and his interest in pictures filtered down to us.

In those days, we had to buy film, carefully take the pictures we wanted, then take the film to a local store to be sent off for developing, and several days later pick them up to see how they turned out. Not only that, but one had to have some knowledge about shutter speed and exposure, as well as having to make sure the photo was in focus.

Of course, now it's automatic – aim and click, and you can see the results as fast as you can switch apps.

In later years, Grandma got her first airplane ride to visit relatives in California. I wasn't part of that trip but recall it being another important milestone.

Sometimes I wonder what she would think of today's technology and society.

Every once in a while, I chuckle when walking up to a retail store and having the expectation that the door will open when I get close enough.

I can almost hear my grandma laughing at that: "You don't have to open the door, it opens for you!"

That brings me to an idea for the next internet viral video: running as fast as you can to see if you can crash into an automatic door before it can open.

This isn't something for teenagers to try. To be really popular, we need some 60-plussers who can pull it off.

Remember, you're probably on camera so all attempts will be monitored and evaluated. Good luck.

16
Columns for Storytelling

Lobster Country

Part of an enjoyable vacation is being able to tell about it.

How to hit a moose with your car and other Maine stories
Oct. 31, 2005 • Herald Journal newspapers

Linda and I recently enjoyed a trip to Maine for our 25th anniversary.

When we eliminated hurricane country from the choices, it was down to either the backwoods of Maine or the concrete jungle of New York City. Maine won, with the Big Apple still on the list for some other time.

We were sort of adventuresome, at least for us, booking places to stay for only the first three nights and last two, leaving the middle unreserved and open for wherever we might go.

Our stay started at Spencer Pond Camps, well up into the woods.

If you like peaceful, simple outdoors, this is the place for you. There's no electricity or plumbing – just propane and kerosene for the lights and refrigerator. Water is hand-pumped, and each cabin has its own private outhouse.

The nearest neighbor is 14 miles away. Other than loading and unloading, cars are parked in a lot a quarter-mile away, so disruptions are kept to a minimum.

After flying into Bangor four hours later than planned (darn airports!), and getting the groceries we would need for a few days, we drove three hours through rain and darkness, being careful to avoid any moose on the road, to reach Spencer Pond. It was very welcoming to find our hosts had the wood stove fired up so our cabin was warm and comfortable when we arrived.

Being late in the season, we mostly hiked the surrounding woods, in search of Bullwinkle. We figure we put on at least 20 miles through the trails, including getting most of the way to the top of a 3,000-foot mountain.

Surprisingly, our cell phone worked most of the time there. We had warned the kids we would be out of contact range for three days at first. But instead, we were able to call a doctor back in Minnesota and get a prescription refilled while we were halfway up the mountain.

We never did see a moose, though – only droppings.

A tour guide later in the week explained that Maine insurance companies actually teach people how to hit a moose with your car, if necessary.

Moose tend to just come wandering out on the roads, oblivious to traffic, so sometimes an accident is just unavoidable, he said.

If you hit a moose broadside, it will flip up onto your roof and 1,300 pounds will come down right on top of you. Many moose-vehicle accidents are fatal for that very reason.

Therefore, if a collision can't be avoided, you want to try to hit the moose in the hind quarter and spin him around rather than flipping him onto your vehicle.

The same principle applies to hitting deer, he added. Deer won't crush you, but they'll break through the windshield and then kick you to death.

On with the week.

So even though we had no trouble finding Spencer Pond in the rain and dark, we left in broad daylight and got lost. After two attempts to leave and returning to the driveway, I broke down and did something out of character – asked directions.

Turns out we were right the first time, and were within 50 feet of the sign we had been looking for that would tell us we were correctly reversing the route.

From there, we headed to the coast and a day at Acadia National Park and Bar Harbor, and then worked our way down the coast through many of the "drinking villages with a fishing problem," as their T-shirts described them.

At Acadia, we hiked some more, and got our first close-up contact with the ocean at Sand Beach.

Later, Reid State Park offered even better crashing waves along a one-mile beach.

(Autumn travel tip: if the hotel sign says "heated pool," make sure it's an indoor heated pool before you check in.)

Throughout our trip, we were amazed at the courtesy and helpfulness of just about every Maine person we came in contact with.

The best example is when we were stopped alongside the road, looking at a map, and a lady in a van pulled up next to us.

"Where're you headed?"

"Jefferson."

"This is Jefferson (just around the corner) . . . what are you looking for?"

"State park."

"Follow me, I'm going right by there."

And so, she literally drove us to the front gate, flashed her lights, and was on her way.

After checking in at Sea Escape Cottages on Bailey Island for the last two nights, our host told us how to enjoy a great Maine lobster meal.

Our timing was good, because as we were beachcombing that day, we noticed a couple guys still working at the red building along the ocean marked Glen's Lobsters.

We went and asked if they had any lobsters for sale, and a few minutes later, we were on our way with three live ones in a bag.

Getting lobsters direct from the fishermen cost about $8 apiece. At the restaurants, a twin lobster meal was as much as $50 a plate.

To cook lobster, our host explained, you steam them in ocean water.

You know it's an adventure, though, when your supper kicks the cover off the pan while you're cooking it.

And when we were through with an excellent meal, the shells were thrown back to the ocean, as instructed.

We only had part of a day left at the end for Portland, where we saw the major sites by bus tour.

It was especially interesting to learn that the two 9/11 hijackers who flew planes into the World Trade Center towers started in Portland. Our guide mentioned it briefly, and then we looked it up later at home.

Upon leaving, we checked in at the Portland airport at the same place as Atta and Al-Omari before their attacks.

They got on an early-morning flight from Portland to Boston, and then boarded separate flights out of Boston that they hijacked and flew into the towers.

Overall, we found Maine to be much like northern Minnesota, but on a bigger scale.

We commented several times about being reminded of other places we have vacationed. The rocky shorelines often looked a lot like Lake Superior.

But the leaves were larger and of more brilliant colors, and the enormity of the ocean dwarfed even a great lake.

Odds are we probably won't get to go back to Maine again, but if you get the opportunity, we recommend you take it.

To the Summit

When our daughter, Alyssa, graduated from Wartburg College, she received an employment placement with the Urban Servant Corp in Denver. We had visited the Colorado mountains once before but now had a reason for occasional trips.

This column about the joy of reading mentions how I got to know more about mountains:

Reading: My favorite winter activity
Jan. 1, 2020 • Senior Connections

The periods of daylight are finally getting longer again. All the holiday decorations are packed away. And we still have several weeks left before it's comfortable to go outside.

So what do we do in winter?

It's a process of elimination.

I've never developed an interest in typical outdoor winter activities like snowmobiling or ice fishing.

My winter outdoors time pretty much consists of removing snow from the driveway or scurrying between vehicles and buildings.

Staying indoors, even sports don't fill the gap at this time of year.

Over the years, I've soured on football. The Timberwolves have never earned my attention. Hockey is just slippery soccer. Our kids are past high school sports age.

So what's a fella to do?

Go back to the basics: reading.

Winter is a great time to settle in with a good book, and there are millions of choices.

Our libraries offer us the world, no matter what our interests may be. These days, it's just a quick online search to find, and even order, books that we would like to read. In many cases, other similar books are suggested as well.

If a particular book isn't in the local library system, they'll order it from somewhere else.

And it's free!

I can't claim a favorite all-time book, and won't go so far as recommending a reading list. There are so many options, you just have to choose and enjoy for yourself.

I do notice that my reading habits tend to follow a binge pattern – reading multiple similar-topic books in a row. Sometimes I just sort of stumble into finding them.

Growing up, my grandmother enjoyed the Perry Mason series by Erle Stanley Gardner, so that was among my early reading. I can still go back to those books, and if the readings are several years apart, I don't even remember whodunit.

Several years ago while visiting Colorado, I recalled that my second-cousin Galen Rowell was a well-known photographer/mountain climber, so I tracked down some of his books.

That led me on my own expedition in which I was able to survive a couple winters by reading various accounts of mountain climbing on K2, Mount Everest, and others. I developed geographic knowledge of Nepal and the Baltoro Glacier, and could recite safety practices for dealing with altitude.

It became difficult to complain about walking from my work building to my car in 20-below temperatures when the night before I had read about mountain climbers who spent several days in a small tent waiting out a blizzard at 20,000-plus feet.

Another time, and I don't remember the trigger that started it, I tracked down every book I could find written by people who had near-death experiences and their descriptions of what Heaven is like.

That made for many hours of pondering what they wrote and comparing it to the Bible itself.

I've also gone through numerous baseball and running books, and a few autobiographies. The joy of reading is that there is so much available. And there are dozens and dozens of other topics out there that I couldn't care less about – but maybe you do?

If you've made it this far, you must enjoy reading too.

Galen Rowell lived half a continent away in California and was much older than me. As best as I could piece info together, I probably only met him once in person when I would have been about one year old.

Colorado's largest mountains are only about half the height of Mount Everest but are among the highest in the United States. There are a few dozen "14ers," that is, mountains reaching above 14,000 feet in elevation. A number of them require advanced climbing skills while some will let you ascend if you have the willpower to keep hiking in the thin air of high altitude.

On one family trip, six of us set off on Mount Sherman near Fairplay, but as we trudged along at more than 13,000 feet, a dark storm cloud started to form. From my reading, I knew that you do not want to be on the side of a mountain during a lightning storm, and called the journey off. It turned out to be a false alarm but erring on the side of safety probably wasn't such a bad idea.

That fall, after Alyssa and Timothy Montgomery were married in a picturesque mountain setting, I was able to stay on for a couple extra days for some intensive mountain hiking. Alone, I made it to the 14,065-foot summit of Mount Bierstadt near Georgetown.

Reel 'em In

Our son, Rhett, joined the Minnesota National Guard during his junior year at Mayer Lutheran High School.

After he had sustained multiple injuries in the sports of football and basketball that he loved, we made the difficult parental decision to shut him down from further competition. As an alternative, he was able to develop a passion for fishing.

When Rhett's 834th Aviation Support Battalion was completing its pre-deployment training for Kuwait and Iraq at Fort Hood in Killeen, TX, Linda, Chelsea, and I went for a final send-off visit. This was late in 2019, which means that his deployment overlapped the onset of COVID around the world. Because of that, the deployment was extended a few weeks longer than scheduled, the last two as a final quarantine before the soldiers were released back into society.

Rhett continues serving our country as a staff sergeant in the Minnesota National Guard. By the way, for Rhett's wedding to Kassie Solien, our sign department made enlarged vinyl photos of their pet cats and dog and the late Toby Keith so those honorary guests could be part of the celebration, at least in that manner.

As part of our visit before he deployed, we arranged a charter fishing trip. Here's our fish tale:

December fishing on open water
May 1, 2020 • Senior Connections

As we endure through the COVID-19 pandemic, the fishing season appears to be able to go forward. In recognition of the fishing opener coming May 9, here's a look at my most recent fishing outing in December.

First of all, our son Rhett is currently stationed in Iraq with the Minnesota Army National Guard. Before his deployment, he underwent several weeks of training at bases in Texas and Oklahoma.

Our last chance to visit before the deployment was his four-day pass right after Thanksgiving weekend. An avid fisherman, both summer and winter, Rhett found a guide service online and suggested a fishing outing as something we could do while there.

The guide was Bob Maindelle of Holding the Line Guide Service. The outing proved to be the highlight of our weekend.

In Texas, you can open-water fish year around. The approach changes seasonally, based on what is effective, but you still go.

Choices were a four-hour outing starting at sunrise, or four hours leading up to sunset. Those are the times that fish actually bite. A morning outing fit our plans.

Bob sent a very detailed list of what to wear, how to prepare, and an iPhone map point of where to meet.

Everything else was provided. Show up and hop aboard.

It was 40 degrees, but dressed properly, still comfortable. After a run-through of basic safety measures, and even a short prayer, we were off.

Where would we fish?

The starting point was to follow the birds. Wherever seagulls are gathered and diving into the water is the target area. This means there are game fish at the bottom that are driving their prey to the surface. The injured shad are then easy pickings for the seagulls. So follow the birds.

A simple but brilliant, and effective, plan. Compared to what technology can do, understanding nature is better yet.

We stopped in the middle of the seagull activity, and started catching fish immediately. We were fishing for white bass and hybrid bass, with an occasional drum. Some of them were quite small but the activity pace was plenty to keep our interest.

For you hard-core fishermen, we used a stinger-hook equipped 3/8 oz. Hazy Eye Slab in white color. Our technique was dropping the line to the bottom and then a slow, steady lift. As an alternative, if sonar showed the fish were higher in the water, we switched to a slow reeling process which allowed covering just a little more area with the bait. This simple change in method resulted in instant success.

A couple times, someone even caught two fish at once – one on the treble hook and one on the stinger.

When things slowed down, we followed the birds to another location on the lake. Later in the morning, after the birds had their fill, we were back to being reliant on technology, and Bob found us one more spot to keep us busy.

By the time our trip was over, our party had brought in 223 fish, nearly one a minute for the entire time.

No, we weren't over the limit – this was strictly catch-and-release. Besides, we really didn't have any facilities to clean or cook fish anyway. Turns out we even made the honors list as the third highest catch out of Bob's 179 guided trips for the year.

Besides the fishing success, Bob attends to every detail including photos and even a blog summary of the outing.

If you're really interested, go to www.holdingthelineguideservice.com , click on Fishing Reports, and find your way back to Dec. 2, 2019.

Politics

Dr. Scott Jensen and I spent much of our respective careers within 10 miles of each other, but our paths didn't cross until he ran for governor in 2022.

Jensen had gained national notoriety for his public commentary in which he pointed out the errors and inconsistencies in the government's handling of the COVID scenario. For doing so, the 2016 Family Physician of the Year was investigated five times by the weaponized Minnesota Board of Medical Practice, the fifth during the heat of the gubernatorial campaign.

My wife had met Dr. Jensen years earlier through her nursing work and was one of the hundreds of thousands of his online followers. When I started paying attention, I liked his common-sense approach on the big issues. When I met him in person, I saw a sincerity and authenticity that wasn't evident in career politicians over the years. I was all in.

Jensen had awoken thousands of Minnesotans from their political comas, myself included, and energized them to get involved in the political process.

In the newspaper, our coverage was by-the-book fair and balanced. On the viewpoints page, I exercised my editorial voice to support Dr. Jensen several times – loudly.

On the personal side, I managed to become a delegate at our township precinct caucus and went on to the Carver County convention where I placed as the number-seven alternate, making me eligible to attend the state convention.

At a campaign event the week before the state convention, Scott pitched me on taking notes and writing a letter to my grandchildren as a future historical account about what happened in 2022. I latched on to the note-taking idea as it gave me something to do during the many slow moments of the convention, and wrote this column in diary format from the perspective of attending a political convention for the first time:

A citizen's journey into politics
May 20, 2022 • Herald Journal newspapers

You can skip the fishing opener, not watch the Super Bowl, or avoid the State Fair – activities that thousands enjoy – and it doesn't matter.

Politics is different. It is in that intimate relationship of political processes where elected officials are conceived. We can ignore politics, as distasteful and boring as it might be, but there is a consequence.

Those elected officials born from political activities are the ones who make the rules we live by. They determine what we pay in taxes. They make decisions that affect our lives daily, from where light rail lines are built, to funding of police departments, to whether you are supposed to wear a mask when leaving home.

Ignore politics if you choose, but it will come back to affect you.

Even when it comes to voting every couple years, many of us fall short of the intended responsibility. Too often, we vote blindly on party loyalty, based on an acquired perception (accurate or not), or just subconsciously picking a name we recognize in order to feel like we know what we are doing.

Of the approximate 2,200 delegates to the state Republican convention this year, about 56% were there for their first time. For the first time in my life, a week before applying for Medicare, I attended the event as an alternate from Carver County.

But first, let's back up a bit.

Background

Like many people across Minnesota, I was so dissatisfied with how our government was performing that I went from couch to participant faster than a couch-to-5k program.

My hot-button issue was the COVID vaccine mandates that threatened the livelihood of those who declined the jab, and risked serious side effects for those who consented.

A voice of reason in all the madness right from the start was local doctor Scott Jensen, who questioned how the data was being compiled and communicated. He even dared to say so publicly.

And as we know, those who contradict the official narrative get censored, ridiculed, investigated, smeared, attacked, or even labeled as domestic terrorists.

Dr. Jensen seemed like my kind of guy.

He announced his campaign to become governor some 20 months before the election. Once I started paying attention, it didn't take long to jump on his bandwagon. Thus began a venture into politics that is good for any citizen to experience.

Our country was formed on the principle that government is to serve its citizens, not control them. But it's also our responsibility to be involved, to monitor what our government does, and give our feedback to those chosen to represent us.

Over the years, we citizens have gotten too complacent and distracted by activities that are more fun. While we were trying to catch fish, cheering for our favorite teams, or eating corn dogs, look what our government has become! At many levels.

If we are to get involved and there is a particular person we would prefer to be our governor, there is a lengthy detailed process that many of us aren't up to speed on.

It starts with precinct caucuses at which each party chooses delegates to represent them at the county/district level, at which there is another selection process for those who are sent to the state convention where candidates are formally endorsed.

Those who receive delegate status become the targets of every candidate, because it is that group of people that makes the all-important endorsement decisions while the rest of the population watches Netflix.

I was bestowed delegate status in my precinct, and elected an alternate at the county level which provided me the opportunity to go on to the state convention.

The endorsing process is particularly important because it provides a candidate access to the party's resources and lets him/her focus on the general election instead of competing in a primary.

Other candidates still have the legal option to run in a primary, but ethically, the endorsement is meant to end the internal competition and go full speed to November.

Disclaimer

This is not an objective "how to become involved in politics" piece. My favoritism will show, which is part of the point. No one gets involved in politics to be neutral. You are for or against something or someone, most likely on multiple issues.

This is not a news report. It is an account of my experience as a first-time attendee at a state political convention.

Convention diary, day one

I arrived at the Mayo Civic Center in Rochester Friday morning. Despite some rumblings about how difficult the registration process was, I didn't see it. The line into the registration room was long and awkwardly formed, but once in, I was directed to the table for alternates. Without a word, I presented my photo ID and quickly received my credentials.

From there, my first stop was at the Jensen booth to get a copy of Scott's new book "We've Been Played . . . Exposing the Triad of Tyranny."

Next was a wandering tour to get familiar with the venue. From above, I tried to locate where our delegation was placed, should I have the opportunity to be seated on the convention floor. My eyes aren't what they used to be, and from several angles, I still hadn't been certain. Back at the information table, I found a seating map that made it clear. Carver County was in the front middle rows.

Conventions are like going to a Tanya Tucker concert. No matter what the stated starting time is, it won't begin until the main act is ready to go. I knew from the previous county and senate district conventions that a prompt start was unlikely. This was scheduled to start at 10 a.m.; the gavel came down at 11:35.

Organizers were trying to herd 2,200 cats into their proper seats, determining who showed up and going through the list of alternates in order to fill all the chairs. At one point, I got called to meet a lady in a pink Trump hat to be seated, but when I arrived, she informed me that other delegates had been located and I should return to wait in the alternate section. That was as close as I got.

During the wait, I reunited with some people I had not seen for a few years since our kids were in the same activities.

I also had an interesting discussion with another alternate who posed me the question "Why Scott?" The answer, in addition to the above, was that Jensen and running mate Matt Birk have the name recognition that is such a critical asset in an election.

One of the first orders of convention business was the determination of whether to use paper ballots or an electronic voting system. Due to contracts, the convention was to be over by 6 p.m. Saturday as well as not going overnight Friday. Using paper ballots would take at least two hours or more for each voting round, it was estimated. The math was against paper. With multiple rounds of voting expected, there simply wouldn't be enough time.

The argument against electronic voting was a distrust of any electronic system after the 2020 elections. On the drive in, a radio commentator had speculated that the real motivation for paper ballots could be those who wanted to make it take so long that no endorsement resulted.

But convention leaders explained the process and system well enough that electronic voting was approved on a rising vote by what appeared to be a two-thirds to three-quarters majority.

There was a little more jockeying on rules and approving a final agenda, so by a little after 2:30, we were ready to roll.

First up was an uncontested endorsement for Ryan Wilson for state auditor.

Next, Kim Crockett won the secretary of state endorsement in two ballots.

The attorney general was a four-way

contest between Tad Jude, Jim Schultz, Doug Wardlow, and Lynne Torgerson. This one took four ballots with Schultz prevailing.

Each of the candidates had their walk-out music that blared as they entered and exited the stage. Crockett used the repetitious lyrics "Sending out an SOS" which corresponded nicely to the office she is seeking. Schultz positioned himself with "I Won't Back Down." And Jude had the most obvious choice: "Hey Jude."

When there was no activity on stage, the big screens would occasionally fill with a "kiss cam" and "dance cam." The Republicans aren't so stuffy after all.

Later, some of the delegates realized that by dancing with their favored candidate's signage, it increased their odds of being seen throughout the arena.

In the evening, delegates were offered a choice to keep going or call it a day. Then word came that all the governor candidates preferred a fresh start in the morning, and so that was it.

I made a brief visit to Jensen's block party, then opted for some sleep, knowing the job was only half done. In the parking ramp, I stopped to help an elderly couple load a mobility scooter into their vehicle. Noting my t-shirt, the wife beamed: "You're just as nice as Dr. Jensen!"

Convention diary, day two

Saturday morning: I had along some fliers I had made personally to hand out if the opportunity arose, and decided to give it a try. Arriving early, I took up a position in the corridor, offering them to passing delegates: "Good morning, here's why I'm supporting Scott."

After a couple polite "No thanks" responses, I quickly realized this wasn't the right time. Probably 2,198 of the 2,200 coming in already had their minds set, and a piece of paper from me wasn't going to change it. Had it been the other way around, I would have declined in the same manner.

Instead, I milled around a bit and noticed Matt Birk near the arena. I made my way over, introduced myself, offered a message of support, and had a quick photo taken. My wife later commented that I looked "really happy" in the picture. She knows me best.

From there, I made my way back to the upper deck and settled in to what would be my home base for the next nine hours.

It was a pleasant surprise when the convention was called to order only a few minutes past the stated starting time. But there was a different set of cats to herd, some who came just for this day. Then came distribution of the voting devices and repeated demos of how to use them, followed by several speeches from top party members who are currently in office or running for significant positions.

We got to the endorsement process for governor at 10:30. Each candidate was allowed 15 minutes, which generally involved a mix of videos, perhaps some testimonials, and a carefully rehearsed presentation by the candidate himself.

After the first round, there would be 20 minutes for working the floor, followed by a vote.

For further ballots, the process would be three-minute speeches from each remaining candidate followed by voting. Results would be shown privately to the campaigns first to allow for any decision-making, then revealed to the convention. In between would be 10-minute pauses to work the floor. Rinse and repeat until there's a winner or time expires.

At home, I had jotted down a prediction of first-round voting, trying to be realistic. Shortly before the first vote, I became concerned from the vibe of the arena. The intensity of the cheers for Kendall Qualls, likely to be Jensen's greatest challenger, was formidable.

As it turned out, I had predicted the order perfectly, and was also right about

Qualls' support. First round went to Jensen at 26.5% with Qualls right behind at 23.1%, followed by Mike Murphy 18.7%, Neil Shah 15.9%, and Paul Gazelka 15.1%.

Murphy is the mayor of Lexington, a smaller city in Anoka County. Earlier this year, he got Lexington declared a "health freedom sanctuary city," going as far as a city could to enable personal choice over vaccine and mask mandates.

I heard him speak at a health freedom rally last fall and again at our county convention. If not for my allegiance to the Jensen campaign, Murphy would be my pick. He reminds me of a Jesse Ventura without the fame.

Clearly not entrenched with the political brotherhood, Murphy lets you know where he's at with a boldness and sincerity that puts the plastic politicians to shame.

Qualls closed in further on the second ballot, almost within a point, while Shah and Gazelka slipped further back. Before the third round, Shah conceded and threw his support to Murphy, while also taking direct shots at both the front-runners.

That vaulted Murphy into first place on the third ballot, which was something no one would have predicted beforehand.

In the next round, Gazelka dropped out and lobbied for Qualls, joined by Sen. Michelle Benson who had recently left the governor's race. That resulted in a fourth-round ballot of Murphy 31.79%, Jensen 31.45%, and Qualls 30.45%.

At this point, I was convinced there would be a three-way primary. I knew Jensen supporters would hold firm, and assumed the other campaigns were just as dug in.

But over the fifth and sixth ballots, those who had gone to Murphy drifted away, and he was in danger of falling below the 20% level at which a candidate is, by rule, eliminated.

The magic number always focused on was the 60% mark, but at this point I went back and charted the raw vote numbers. I had found four reporters who were live-tweeting the event so I was able to use screen shots of their work to refer to. I was pleased to find that Jensen was gaining votes in each round, but also saw that Qualls was gaining at an even faster pace.

Murphy was forced out on the sixth ballot with 18.59%, essentially right where he started.

Up in the cheap seats, I was thinking "Scott, you need to deal with the gun issue. I've heard you explain it elsewhere, but these delegates need to understand it."

As if on cue, he did, addressing the convention: "Apologies are never easy, but when I was in my first term as a senator, I put myself on the wrong side of the gun issue by thinking I could compel a conversation by putting my name on a bill and removing it six weeks later. That was a mistake, and I'm sorry."

Birk immediately backed him up: "I think what you just saw was character!"

But that significant moment was far overshadowed in the same three-minute segment when Murphy, who had joined them on stage, provided the defining moment of the convention. In his blustery manner, he thundered: "Kendall Qualls offered me the lieutenant governor position, then he took it back . . . Kendall is a sell-out!" And he threw his support to Jensen.

Amidst wild cheers, a Jensen campaign staffer in the next section of seats and I exchanged smiles and fist pumps, knowing this would be a huge swing. But would it be enough?

It wasn't. Not quite. Jensen received 59.02% of the votes on the seventh ballot. It takes 60% to win an endorsement, not 59.02%.

Then the gloves came off.

In the early presentations, Qualls was

composed, speaking calmly and with less fanfare than the others. The vote totals indicated his approach was working.

But now Qualls was visibly rattled. He vehemently defended what he called an attack on his integrity. However, what everyone in the arena knew was that the delegate vote count was what mattered more.

Depending on your point of view, it would be equally plausible to see Qualls as someone who was blatantly backstabbed or a sore crybaby.

The veteran reporters were thoroughly enjoying the fireworks as a welcome departure from conventions that are a two-day coronation ceremony for a predetermined candidate.

Birk brilliantly tried to soothe the situation, drawing on his pro football experience. "There is no harmony in a NFL lockerroom," he said, explaining there are more fist-fights than the public realizes. But it happens between teammates because "we are passionate, we care, and we want to win!"

The Jensen campaign has heavily used a football theme in recognition of Birk's time as a Minnesota Viking and Baltimore Raven. Murphy's move was like an 80-yard interception return for a touchdown, just when the other team was reaching the red zone and threatening to put the game out of comeback reach.

During the next pause for politicking, there was a lot of steam to release. Speakers blasted the "YMCA" song while the dance cam captured the entire convention floor and even those on stage forming letters with their bodies. Yeah, these are Republicans. And the encore was the Macarena.

I was aware that after the initial bump from Shah's delegates, Murphy's support had receded, and feared the same would happen to Jensen. I was right again. On ballot eight, Jensen got only 56.7%, the only time he went backwards in raw votes.

It was now after 5 p.m. and obvious there would be time for only one more round before the imposed six o'clock cutoff.

The last round of speeches included Qualls angrily denying that an offer was made, Murphy displaying his phone with a text message backing up his claim, and Jensen reminding everyone of the overall goal to make an endorsement.

What actually had transpired between Murphy and Qualls, only those men truly know, and they may not agree.

It was announced that the ninth ballot results were being delayed while the candidates conferred. A lady in front of me surmised the results were the same but a concession was being negotiated. A reporter tweeted that Qualls had left the building.

Finally, it was revealed: Scott Jensen received 65.12% and is the party's endorsed candidate.

Coverage

It wouldn't be complete without checking how the state's Big Media spins its coverage. First up was KMSP at 9 p.m., which did a respectable job except for showing a clip of Shah's shot at Jensen without following up with the obvious response.

At 10:00, KSTP had its experienced political reporter Tom Hauser on site and again was credible. WCCO seemed to send a young reporter who got the short straw of weekend duty, and also ran its convention story so far down in the newscast, I was able to see all of it after the other station had completed its coverage.

The night was over, and I adjourned.

More than half of those attending the convention were first-timers. I believe it's reasonable to conclude that a large majority of those rookies were due to Dr. Jensen's efforts of getting people involved.

He had campaigned tirelessly throughout the state and set party records for fundraising. At the same time, incumbent Governor Tim Walz was under fire for his excessive COVID lockdowns, being publicly absent during the George Floyd riots, the Feeding Our Future fraud scandal, and refusing to debate, to name a few.

Yet the certified election results indicated that Minnesota voters desired more of the same as Walz's margin of victory was suspiciously similar to that of 2018, despite the drastic differences in circumstances and opponent.

Thanks Again, Leonard

If you try to extend a vacation, be careful what you ask for.

The Good Samaritan of 2019
Oct. 1, 2019 • Senior Connections

Our week at a cabin up north was over. We had hauled our stuff back, unpacked most of it, and weren't in the mood for vacation to be over yet.

After some quick searching, on a whim we headed off to the Uptown Art Fair in Minneapolis to try to stay in vacation mode.

On the way, Linda used my phone since she wasn't carrying hers. When done, she set it between our seats. Later, it slipped onto the floor. Being a responsible driver (at least then), I didn't try to retrieve it while moving at 55 mph.

We reached the art fair area and had to go a few blocks to find parking, which we did on a street that had cars parked along both sides of it.

Off we went.

Most of the art fair didn't suit my taste (not much art does), but, hey, it was vacation. Somewhere along the way when I put my hand in my pocket, I realized I hadn't picked up my phone from the car floor.

We were over halfway through the displays, coming back on the other side of the street, when suddenly a rain shower popped up.

There were enough awnings and shelters available, but we decided to just keep moving.

With several blocks to go, we started getting pretty wet in the rain, but, hey, it was vacation. We even commented about it being sort of fun to be out in the rain.

We turned the last corner, and there was a tow truck loading up a vehicle . . . it was somebody else's . . . ours was already gone.

It was a pretty quick realization that we had no car, no phone (it was in the car), we were soaking wet in Minneapolis, and there were only a few hours of daylight left.

The gentleman doing the towing confirmed that we would need to find a way to the Minneapolis impound lot. I didn't bother to bore him with the details that we had no phone, no car, were soaking wet, and there was little daylight left, as he seemed to be focused on towing more cars than worrying about the ones that were already gone.

We settled on a plan to head back toward the art fair with the hope that we could come up with a way to hail a taxi.

Along the way (still raining), I noticed a car with a Lyft placard. We don't have Lyft or Uber accounts since we NEVER have use for them, plus we didn't have a phone anyway because it was in the car we didn't have.

I asked the Lyft driver about a ride, but was informed she was waiting to pick someone else up and we would have to call for a ride.

Across the sidewalk, a young man realized our predicament and came to our rescue.

Huddling under an overhang (it was still raining), he called a ride for us, explained how far away the driver was, how long it would take, and the color and license plate of the vehicle to identify it.

A bit later, the driver called back and asked to change the pick-up location as some streets were blocked off because there was an art fair going on.

Our hero negotiated a new spot a couple blocks away, then led us through the rain and a department store, and right up to our ride.

I gave him an overly appreciative handshake and slipped him a $10 bill for his trouble. As we got settled in the vehicle, we made one more eye contact. I mouthed "thank you;" he nodded with the assurance we were on our way.

Having never used a ride service before, I realized en route that not only had our friend obtained the ride for us – he paid for it too!

Had I figured that out soon enough, I would have compensated him way more.

Eventually we reached the impound lot, where everybody else in the line was there for the same reason. A $138 fee later, plus the automatic $45 parking ticket that accompanies a tow, and we were back on the road. My phone was right on the floor where I last saw it.

The impound lot is actually very close to Target Field. Linda declined my suggestion of also taking in the Twins game that night. (Hey, we're on vacation, aren't we?)

Instead, we figured we had dried off enough by then to venture into a restaurant for a hot meal.

From there, we made it home, grateful for no other surprises.

Later, I tried through Lyft's customer service to track the transaction and let us pay for it instead, but the only option allowed would be to get our Good Samaritan a gift card if we knew his email address.

We only knew him as Leonard, with no other contact info available. He only knew us as some old people from way out in Carver County.

So, Leonard, on the remote chance you're reading this or we meet up again, I owe you one!

17
Columns for Life and Death

Special sections are ways that newspapers can give readers more material about certain topics that are not reported on regularly, and give advertisers an opportunity to reach people who are interested in those topics. And the revenue helps the newspaper carry on.

When we were planning such sections for 2016, the idea of a one about end-of-life issues came up. We recognized it was an uncomfortable topic but also saw there are a large number of businesses that provide products and services for those situations.

Offhandedly, salesman Bruce Johnson made a comment about publishing on Feb. 29, but when we looked at the calendar, we would have a newspaper on Feb. 29, 2016.

Thus, our annual Estate, Pre-planning, and Sympathy section was established. The name is awkwardly long but attempts to include both financial and health aspects related to the end of one's life.

That was the formal name. Internally, we simply called it the "death wrap." The term wrap refers to a set of pages that is placed on the outside of a newspaper section, usually due to where color is available in the printing process.

I found this annual section an opportunity to write about a subject that affects us all.

Dying: it's been done before

Feb. 29, 2016 • Herald Journal newspapers

When we were choosing topics for special newspaper sections, the idea of death and dying was awkwardly proposed.

We publish sections on various topics – automotive, farm, health and medical, weddings, baseball, families, home and yard, entertainment, etc.

This one was different. The other subjects are generally viewed positively. This one makes us uncomfortable.

But slowly we realized, despite the discomfort, this topic affects all people.

Everyone gets a turn. One turn.

If you haven't experienced the death of someone close to you yet, you will someday. The only way you won't is if you happen to go first.

After choosing to highlight this topic, we struggled with a name – "Estate and Pre-Planning," "Sympathy and Understanding," "End of Life Issues," or even outright "Death and Dying."

It's a subject that many of us like to avoid, but the issues involving the last stages of life, and death itself, are just as important as any others we face along the way.

Death and dying are an industry – funeral homes, florists, monuments, hospice care, medical care to delay death, estate planning, counseling, life insurance, and many more.

It's a sensitive matter because we know the emotional grief associated with it.

And it's never easy. One day Mom is here and gone the next, or Dad withers away for many months in medical facilities. Whether sudden or prolonged, death is painful.

I'll never forget 20 years ago when my uncle, Ben Hakel, with colon cancer entered hospice care. A nurse asked him how he felt about dying.

His response was: "It's been done before."

We didn't quite know if he was joking or serious, or a combination. But it was a simple, profound statement.

Christians have hope in the knowledge of resurrection and eternal life in a perfect place – Heaven – without pain or problems. All one has to do is accept that gift.

"He will wipe every tear from their eyes, and there will be no more death or sorrow or crying or pain. All these things are gone forever." – Revelation 21:4 (New Living Translation)

An obituary we carried in our newspapers last year included a quote from D. L. Moody which sums it up nicely: "As soon as you read in the newspaper that I am dead, don't believe it for a minute. I will be more alive than ever before."

In the meantime, we have today's newspaper and our "Estate, Pre-Planning, and Sympathy" section. We hope you find it of value.

What is heaven like?

Feb. 27, 2017 • Herald Journal newspapers

What is heaven like?

There are many answers. Correct or not, we don't know – yet.

Quite a few years ago, I heard a reference on tv to Raymond Moody, a psychiatrist who interviewed dozens of people who had near-death experiences. He summarized the common patterns of their descriptions in a book "Life After Life."

Intrigued by that, I later read many books by people who state that they had experiences in which they saw glimpses or spent a short time in heaven, then returned to earthly life.

As Moody saw in his subjects, these independent writings have many overlapping themes and details in their descriptions of heaven.

Of course, we should base our knowledge and hope on God's descriptions of heaven in the Bible, not man's words.

While respecting that position, considering the stories of those who claim "to have been there" offers much to think about. Even reading these books with a healthy dose of skepticism, they are interesting and inspiring stories that can lead a reader to stronger faith.

Many of these authors came to these experiences through serious accidents or illnesses. They underwent severe pain, in some cases lasting months or years.

Once "there," they felt overwhelming peace and love. Some just got glimpses from the outside while others saw more details – the gates of heaven, the Book of Life, even the Throne.

Most of them mentioned brilliant colors, way beyond what we know here, as well as incredible music – sometimes numerous songs simultaneously, yet it all made sense and again was exponentially better than our earthly music. Usually, the writers simply called it "indescribable" with our language.

Communication was often understood but not actually spoken. Messages were thought and received so there was no language barrier.

Many tell of seeing dead relatives, some of whom they had never met on earth. Colton Burpo learned of a sister who died in a miscarriage before he was born, that he had never been told about. He also later identified a youthful photo of a departed grandfather whom he had not met on earth.

Others say they had encounters with people from the Bible – John the Baptist, Peter, and even Jesus himself.

Another common theme in these stories is that those who had a taste of heaven did not want to return, but were told their time had not yet come and were sent back. Often, though they knew what they experienced, they withheld from telling others, realizing they would not be believed.

Marvin Besteman, in "My Journey to Heaven," didn't even tell his wife for five months. Although he remembered it vividly, he had no desire to discuss it at first. Later, he learned that he was sent back to earth for that purpose. "I know that God wants me to tell you what I saw, and trust him with the details," he wrote.

Dale Black didn't write "Flight to Heaven" until 40 years after seeing heaven on advice to keep the experience sacred and live his life accordingly.

On the other hand, "The Boy Who Came Back from Heaven" by Alex Malarkey and his father Kevin, was later recanted and then pulled off the market by the publisher. Alex was severely injured in a car accident at age six. The book was published in 2010 but several years later at age 16, Alex retracted it. His mother, Beth, stated "Alex never concluded he was in heaven. He was a small boy who experienced something extraordinary. The adults made it into what would sell to the masses."

So how should we view these books that have become termed "heavenly tourism" genre?

Are these authors modern-day prophets who were granted a supernatural experience and given the means to tell about it to mass audiences? Or are they greedy pigs who fabricated it all to make a buck?

We cannot know what is in someone else's heart.

John MacArthur in "The Glory of Heaven: The Truth About Heaven, Angels, and Eternal Life" refutes some of these books in detail.

He outright calls them untrue because they do not match visions of heaven in the Bible – especially that they are too self-focused rather than an emphasis on the glory of God.

He writes: " . . . all of them are teeming with false, flawed, and fanciful notions about heaven . . . it elevates human experience to a higher level than the Word of God."

MacArthur warns: "We must reject every anecdotal account that contradicts or goes beyond what Scripture teaches. We must also refuse to get caught up in every kind of speculation, every truth claim, and every supposed new revelation that detracts from or leads people away from simple reliance on the Word of God."

Though I agree, I at least wonder if there is the possibility these authors are telling of real experiences, and what they are describing does not contradict scripture.

If you interviewed a dozen people who went to the state fair, their responses would have much in common but each would provide his or her own details and perceptions of what it was like. Thus, some of the commonalities in these books, written independently at different times by people in different places, are what keep me from dismissing them entirely.

What we can do is be confident that heaven is perfect in the presence of God, and know who will bring us there and how to get there – by trusting in the shed blood of Jesus Christ as the way, the truth, and the life.

Like a wrapped gift, we can tell a little bit about it – size, weight, sound when it's shaken – but we don't know and aren't supposed to know more . . . until the right moment arrives when we're allowed to open it.

Heaven books

• "Heaven is for Real: A Little Boy's Astounding Story of His Trip to Heaven and Back" – 4-year-old Colton Burpo from Nebraska visits heaven during emergency surgery. Also became a movie. Follow-up book is "Heaven Changes Everything."

• "90 Minutes in Heaven: A True Story of Death and Life" – Baptist minister Don Piper from Texas experiences heaven after a car accident. Follow-up book is "Heaven is Real."

• "To Heaven and Back: A Doctor's Extraordinary Account of Her Death, Heaven, Angels, and Life Again" – Mary Neal, an orthopedic surgeon from Michigan, who drowned in a kayak accident.

• "Proof of Heaven: A Neurosurgeon's Journey into the Afterlife" – Eben Alexander, neurosurgeon from Boston, who went into a seven-day coma from bacterial meningitis-encephalitis.

• "23 Minutes in Hell" – Bill Wiese, real estate agent from California. Experienced a visit to hell but was also rescued to heaven.

• "When Will the Heaven Begin?" – Ally Breedlove. The story of her brother who died at 18 from a heart condition, and used videos to share his visions of heaven.

• "My Journey to Heaven: What I Saw and How It Changed My Life" – Marvin Besteman, a retired banker from Michigan. After surgery to remove a pancreatic tumor, he is escorted to heaven by two angels where he is met by Saint Peter.

• "Flight to Heaven" – Dale Black, the lone survivor of a California plane crash at age 19, is healed and strives to live out his life as a reflection of his heavenly visit experience.

• "Waking Up in Heaven: A True Story of Brokenness, Heaven, and Life Again" – Crystal McVea, a child abuse victim from Oklahoma, learns that God has a perfect plan for everyone.

• "Akiane: Her Life, Her Art, Her Poetry" – by Akiane and Foreli Kramarik. A young girl born in Illinois, after a heavenly vision, becomes a prodigy poet and painter, including an image of Jesus she painted that Colton Burpo later identified as "they finally got one right."

• "Heaven" – by Randy Alcorn. Not about an experience, but cites numerous scripture references to show heaven as a physical place.

• "The Glory of Heaven: The Truth About Heaven, Angels, and Eternal Life" – by John MacArthur, a direct refutation of some of the above books, plus scriptural descriptions of heaven.

Where do we go from here?

Feb. 22, 2019 • Herald Journal newspapers

I recall a pastor once saying "Think twice before you tell someone to 'go to hell,' because you need to understand the significance of that."

That's good advice, as often we take hell lightly, or jokingly.

I once told a co-worker "If you go to hell, there will be a ringing telephone and you won't be able to answer it."

I've also described my version of hell as round-the-clock polka music with disco on Thursdays; plus tuna and sauerkraut served at every meal.

Those are embarrassingly shallow comments in contrast to what hell really is.

First, let's consider what happens after one's death.

One school of thought is that existence simply ends. If that's the case, we might as well be as selfish and greedy as possible now, because, hey, we can't take it with us anyway. For those, it will be a rude awakening.

The other option is that life continues in another form.

With that comes the fantasy of reincarnation, where we get to live again as an animal, or perhaps take another try at life as a different person. It's the ultimate recycling. But that's just fictional material for movies.

The actual possibilities are heaven and hell. The Creator of the universe told us so.

The frequency of the word "hell" in the Bible depends on translations, but there are several dozen references to hell. Jesus himself talks about hell often.

Bill Wiese is a former California real estate agent who one night had an out-of-body vision of being in hell. He wrote the book "23 Minutes in Hell," and later followed up with "Hell," a detailed study of what scripture says and what we could expect hell to be like.

Wiese gives some simple explanations to make hell quite understandable, such as:

Suppose you went to the most expensive, fanciest house in the country, knocked on the door, and announced to the owner that you are moving in today. Do you think you'd be cheerfully welcomed? Why not?

Because he doesn't know you. So why would someone expect to go to heaven without a prior relationship?

Wiese answers the question "Why would God create a place like hell?"

God is love. An important attribute of love is free will – love cannot be forced or required; it must be a choice. Everything good is associated with God, and God cannot be part of anything bad. So the other choice is the place of torment, fear, pain, stench – everything bad and evil.

"Why would a loving God send people to hell?"

God doesn't "send" people to hell. It is their choice in free will.

Jesus took on the punishment for all sins in the world, including ours, to make us blameless. If we accept that gift (a prior relationship), we are welcomed into heaven when the time comes.

If we choose to blow it off or outright reject it, then . . .

Do not grieve as those who have no hope

March 1, 2020 • Herald Journal/Senior Connections

Phone calls in the middle of the night are rarely a good thing.

Death of a loved one is difficult to deal with. If it's sudden and unexpected, it's such a shock. If it's from a prolonged disease, there's time to say goodbye, but it's still tragic.

During the past year, our family experienced the sudden variety, on the heels of a premature birth.

When we hosted all our kids and their families together at a cabin last summer, daughter Chelsea and son-in-law Brian used the opportunity to announce that another family member would be added to our ranks.

We were all excited, and everything was going well until one Saturday night in late October.

I had already stayed up way later than usual watching a World Series game. Linda was attending an event with her sisters and returned home even later.

Then the first call came. Chels and Brian were at the hospital, and it was possible labor could begin in the next 24 hours.

About 20 minutes later, another call: a lot was happening and they'd keep us posted.

A few more minutes later: "You better come."

By the time we got there, Peyton was born at 21 weeks, 3 days, being just nine inches long and 13.3 ounces. Within a few minutes, he died in Brian's arms.

Our pastor was able to come comfort everyone and pray with us before Sunday services that morning. Then we went about the unpleasant task of letting other family members know.

Later, it was back to the hospital where everyone gathered again. The Star Legacy Foundation, a support organization for pregnancy loss, sent a representative – a young mom who had experienced the same thing – for an extended photo shoot.

Part of the grieving – and healing – is the acknowledgement and memories of what was, even as short as it was.

My point, for a newspaper section about death, is coping with death.

My go-to verse for death has become 1st Thessalonians 4 which reads in part ". . . do not grieve as others do who have no hope."

So what hope is there?

Jesus not only died for our sins; he took his life back, overcoming death through his resurrection.

Scripture promises he will come for us again, at which point we can spend eternity with him, if we haven't already chosen the other option.

That chapter of Thessalonians also describes how the dead believers will be resurrected, and then those who are left will join them to meet the Lord in the air. The hard part is waiting until then – a daily lesson in patience.

When we lose a loved one, even one we only knew for minutes, that is our hope – our only hope. But as long and far off as it may seem, we also know it is certain.

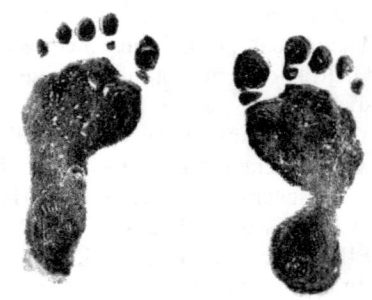

Peyton's footprints, actual size

Cemeteries
Dec. 31, 2021 • Senior Connections

Once in a while, my wife and I will stop and walk through a cemetery.

Besides the local ones where we have loved ones buried, we actually go to other ones, like while we're on vacation, where we don't know anybody.

Linda likes to look for the oldest tombstones she can find, many of which are barely readable. I tend to focus on names, seeing if I can find one that matches a name of someone I know.

There isn't anything more to it than that, just a curious diversion to see what we see.

Did I mention that cemeteries have free admission? Well, at least to visit. If you plan on staying, there is a charge.

Some of the gravesites are well-kept and accessorized with trinkets that others have left in memory. Some of the tombstones are elaborate, others are modest. A few appear quite neglected.

My first experience with cemeteries goes back to when I was a kid and helped my uncle mow the grass at the cemetery where he was caretaker.

Talk about having to go around objects while mowing! I said many times that my tombstone should be a flat, ground-level type that allows a mower to drive right over it. Either that or cemeteries should have artificial turf instead of grass. (Of course, a quick web search shows that there is such a thing.)

One cemetery we visited a few years ago had a couple of driveway marker poles in an area where a roadway was being repaired. I latched on to the idea that such a pole would be an adequate marker for me – stick it in the ground and write my name on some duct tape.

Seriously, I don't see burdening my family with an expensive monument. I'm going to be resurrected anyway, so I don't need deluxe accommodations for my body to rot in while waiting for our Lord's return.

In any case, we all have an invisible expiration date stamped on us. In the scope of things, it is best that we can't foresee when that is.

18
Columns for Freedom

What the federal and state governments did to us in the early 2020s is reprehensible and unacceptable.

You might be able to argue that technically it was legal, but clearly it was wrong – ethically and morally. Worst of all, I blame the complicit corporate media for only promoting the narrative rather than doing its job of investigating all aspects of the issue and reporting both positive and negative factors.

The narratives I speak of are many, including but not limited to, COVID vaccine mandates, injuries from those vaccines, election fraud, climate change – those are the big ones.

With the opportunity to say otherwise in a legitimate, albeit small, newspaper, I took a stand:

Why I'm not getting vaccinated

Aug. 20, 2021 • Herald Journal newspapers

1. Side effects. I already have too many side effects from regular medications and don't want to risk any more variables. Also, we don't know about potential long-term complications that may show up years later.

2. Immunity. I've already had COVID-19, so my natural immunity is broader and better than any artificial attempt.

3. Mistrust. The government, big media, big tech companies, big pharma, and whoever else is part of this don't deserve my compliance.

I acknowledge that COVID-19 is a real thing. A number of people have been gravely ill or died from it.

But, "a number" is a number that can be easily manipulated to advance whatever agenda one wishes.

For example, hospitals received substantial financial incentives for identifying COVID cases regardless of what reason a patient originally came in for.

Also, in the daily brainwashing attempts, the media highlights certain percentage increases of COVID cases like they are drastic, but dismisses the stats of complications from the vaccines as being insignificant.

Those in power have been hugely successful at creating a culture of fear.

First, we were sent to our rooms and locked down in isolation. That was so effective that when allowed out, practically the entire population wore face coverings any time a person went somewhere.

Fear gets people to do things they rather wouldn't.

One citizen made the point that if we were subjected to a "death counter" in the news every day about how many people die and are injured in auto accidents, many of us would be turning in our driver's license and finding other ways to get around.

Beyond masks, our leaders want to inject an authorized but unproven substance into our bodies.

Nearly half the population is unwilling to accept that.

Thus, the government turned to bribes. Step right up to take the vaccine and you'll get gift cards, scholarships, lottery tickets, etc.

That alone is cause for concern when the government is that aggressive to get permission/submission to put something into our bodies.

And when bribes don't work, the next step is to turn us against each other with guilt, blame, and peer pressure.

There are the classes of vaccinated and unvaccinated, and if you don't belong to the right one, you'll be denied admission to events, required to go through elaborate inconveniences of frequent testing, or perhaps even not allowed to work to make a living.

Finally, when we go check character references, I see that the people telling me to get vaccinated (#3 above) are the same ones who said there was no fraud in the last presidential election.

The real enemy to be afraid of is not COVID; it's the power structure trying to get us to surrender our individual freedom.

In response to that, our Delano Herald Journal editor Gabe Licht wrote a dissenting column in the following issue. His piece accomplished several things and did me a favor.

• It provided an example of free speech. That is how it's supposed to be done with controversial issues. Anyone who wishes gets to speak or write. Others can judge the credibility of the content and form their own opinion.

• Gabe's column protected the newspaper by personalizing the debate with me.

• It opened the door for me to follow up with this one the next week:

Vaccines, part 2: one-size needle doesn't fit all
Sept. 3, 2021 • Herald Journal newspapers

As you can imagine, feedback on my previous column about COVID vaccines reached both extremes – positive and negative.

That in itself is important. It shows there are many varying opinions among us.

One function of a local newspaper is to be a forum for public discussion of current issues, aside from social media rants to one's own group of followers or the force-fed monologues on the tv networks.

I didn't say anyone shouldn't get the vaccine. I brought forward reasons why someone might not want it.

I don't believe the vaccine alters DNA or implants tracking devices. Those are just stories made up to paint those who resist as crazy.

Ultimately, it comes down to trust and, most of all, individual freedom of choice.

Pontius Pilate once asked "What is truth?" A couple thousand years later, we still wrestle with that question.

If you're satisfied that the benefits of the vaccine outweigh the risks, and believe the people saying so, by all means, go for it. That is your freedom of choice.

For those who don't, we ask not to be bullied, guilted, or legislated into giving up our right to manage our own health care.

A friend who had COVID described it as "never having been so sick in my life." Another person who tested positive lost his taste and smell; then ran three miles a day during his quarantine period. It affected people differently.

So it is with the side effects reported from the vaccine. It's kept out of the Big Media as much as possible, but listen to people and you'll hear about heart trouble, miscarriages, Guillain-Barre Syndrome, blood clots, and even death.

Certainly, these conditions happen to people all the time, but this would be something for the CDC to study and the media to investigate: why do these complications seem so much more prevalent among the recently vaccinated?

Also, there is no way for anyone to conclusively know potential long-term effects, either from COVID itself or its attempted prevention. This was fast-tracked. We don't even know what we don't know yet.

We'll be told to listen to the science, but the "science" that makes it into the media is way too one-sided to be believable.

When in the history of America has

there been such an overwhelming consensus on any major issue like this is being portrayed to be?

Those who seek to expose it get censored and ridiculed; their work is labeled as "misinformation."

This is the 2021 version of "The Emperor's New Clothes." Just look . . . and see for yourself.

We citizens accepted the stimulus checks without extra encouragement because we judged it to be a good thing.

If the vaccine was also considered a good thing, people would accept it as well, without the incentives or bribes, let alone mandates.

Trust is built in reliable relationships in which you are confident that the other party has your best interests at heart.

Our trust in the media and government is severely broken.

Lucy Media, would you hold the football so we can kick it?

As for choice, the president of the United States wants to give me the option to self-identify as whatever gender I choose. With that thinking, I should be welcome in the women's restroom when nature calls.

Out of the other side of his mouth, that same president wants to take away my option to choose what gets injected into my body, whatever gender it might be.

Mr. President, why wouldn't the "My body, my choice" sentiment of Roe vs. Wade also apply to vaccines?

Emperor Joe, would you hold the football so we can kick it?

Who do we trust? What should we believe?

We all have this little voice deep in our souls that will help guide us to what's right and wrong if we just listen to it.

It's nicer if we live in a country that maintains individual freedoms, or even strives to strengthen them.

We used to live in such a country. I hope we still do, but it's not looking so good right now.

That's what is really at stake here: it isn't even as much about the merit of the vaccine, as the act of having it forced upon us.

Despite the kingdom's narrative, the emperor just isn't wearing any clothes.

The medical industry is being held hostage.

Go ask your doctor to write a vaccine exemption and see what the answer is. I know directly of a case in which a doctor had valid reasons and would have loved to provide an exemption, but had orders from above to withhold it. Why would that be? Answer that one.

Nursing home workers will be mandated to be vaccinated as of this fall. That won't go well.

Nursing homes are already desperately short of staff, so what can we expect when employees who cling to their personal rights either resign or are forced to be fired because of a government dictate? Who will be left to take care of Grandma?

It would be wise for all employers to seriously consider the ramifications of a vaccine mandate.

With "Now Hiring" signs seemingly at every corner, employees can hand in their resignations and go to a vaccine-free work environment.

In fact, a "No Vaccine Required" policy could be a helpful tool in filling those open staff positions. There will be people looking for that. I'm related to at least three of them.

So, what are we to make of this entire situation?

The old adage is to "follow the money." Who profits? What is their motive?

I don't have that answer, at least not yet.

Go ahead and kick the football, Charlie Brown.

Oh, wait! Better look first at who is holding it.

Of course, my expounding didn't solve a national issue. Later, I blew up when Anthony Fauci declared that he had vaccinated Santa Claus, and even worse, the media passed it off as a real news story.

So I quickly organized a press conference with other fictional characters to expose the lies.

Fictional characters come to forefront in political world
Dec. 24, 2021 • Herald Journal newspapers

BREAKING NEWS: In response to recent reports that Big Bird and Santa Claus were vaccinated, two other fictional characters – Tooth Fairy and Paul Bunyan – stepped forward to set the record straight at a press conference earlier this week.

Dr. Anthony Fauci, who is a respected scientist in some circles and despised in many others, asserted that he vaccinated Santa Claus in 2020, and then gave him a booster this year.

Big Bird recently tweeted on his Twitter account that he was vaccinated as well.

The other characters dispute those claims.

"You realize that we're not real, and it's impossible for fictional characters to put themselves into real-life situations," the Tooth Fairy said. "It's especially disturbing that our good names would be used for political purposes."

Paul Bunyan pointed out that in Big Bird's case, it is a copyrighted character so there is a human being behind the Twitter account who actually made the statement about being vaccinated. "That really makes us question what the motive is," he said.

Using popular fictional characters to advance a political point of view is a relatively new occurrence, said a spokesman for the Center for Defamed Cartoons (CDC).

Attempts to contact Santa Claus to verify his vaccination status were unsuccessful because . . . well, why do you think we couldn't reach him?

"I feel bad for Santa's reputation being tainted like that," the Tooth Fairy said. "He only has one chance a year to explain the truth to people. Since I work full-time, I can dispel any rumors as soon as they come up."

"Someone like Fauci should know better," Bunyan added. "He is supposed to represent our national government, but if he makes false statements like that, how are we supposed to believe anything he says?"

Frosty the Snowman was unable to attend the press conference due to other commitments, but voiced support for telling the truth.

Easter Bunny released a separate statement condemning the media's blatant disregard for accuracy, particularly USA Today. "Even if all their fact-checkers called in sick that day, there's no excuse for spreading obvious misinformation. If they present things like that as news, we cannot trust any of their other reports," Easter Bunny stated.

Tooth Fairy and Paul Bunyan closed by urging everyone to think for themselves and sort out the truth from propaganda.

When I go hard on controversial topics like these, the direct responses that reach me are usually about two-thirds positive. However, the people who hate it, REALLY hate it.

Not unexpectedly, some readers demanded that I be fired, while others, choking up with tears, expressed heartfelt appreciation that someone had the courage to say publicly what many people were thinking.

So those were just a primer for my largest narrative buster – an in-depth piece about election fraud that took a full newspaper page. It was so long that the 32 footnotes (see appendix) citing original sources had to run on an adjacent page.

This was the item that exceeded the 1991 April Fools' page in reader reaction.

Election fraud: from 'no evidence' to 'know evidence'
Jan. 13, 2023 • Herald Journal newspapers

Can we agree that fair, secure elections would benefit everyone?

At least, even if we didn't like the results, we wouldn't have to argue with each other if they were valid or not.

Election fraud is a crime. Given human nature, there always has and always will be attempts at election fraud when the stakes are so high.

The Heritage Foundation keeps a database of numerous cases of election fraud in which convictions have been made – not accusations but convicted fraud, judicial findings, and such.[1]

It deeply disturbed me right from the start when the mainstream media insisted there was "no evidence of widespread election fraud" in the 2020 presidential election. After a personal study, I can report: they were irresponsibly wrong or outright lying.

To their discredit, the media's approach was like the little child who covers his/her eyes: if I can't see it, it doesn't exist.

It isn't hard to find dozens – even hundreds – of credible sources that, even when not directly proving fraud, provide more evidence to raise even the most skeptical eyebrow.

As Peter Navarro points out, election fraud is accomplished not by a single "silver bullet" but by "a thousand cuts" on a wide scale.[2]

With a little effort, I found that yes, Virginia, there is widespread evidence of fraud! Yes, including Virginia, as well as Georgia, Pennsylvania, Michigan, Wisconsin, Arizona, and unsurprisingly, Minnesota.

The problem

All things considered, there are four major areas of concern:

• sloppy voter rolls that make it practical for illegitimate votes

• mail-in and expanded absentee voting rules – perhaps the easiest way to cheat

• the vulnerability of electronic voting equipment to manipulation (even easier?)

• worst of all: too many people in positions of power who won't act to correct the problems, or will even enable further abuse

Of course, proving election fraud is more difficult than suspecting it. Like any crime, the goal is to get away with it. To prevent it, we need to understand how it happens.

There are many forms and places in which it can take place including false registrations, impersonation at the polls, illegal assistance or intimidation, ineligible voting, duplicate voting, fraudulent use of absentee or mail-in voting, and buying or selling votes.[3]

In a pre-election debate on KSTP-TV, Minnesota Secretary of State Steve Simon boasted about 16 individual cases of voter fraud that were prosecuted. He was called out on that, since it was akin to celebrating that 16 people were arrested for DUI on a given night while everyone knows those are only the ones who got caught. It's unrealistic that every crime of intoxicated driving – or voter fraud – was identified and dealt with.

Proof

Mainstream media has been grossly negligent, both in what is presented as "reporting" and what is ignored. Instead of asking direct, hard questions like Dan Rather and Mike Wallace used to do, Big Media now functions as a promotional arm of government rather than a watchdog.

However, Dinesh D'Souza's "2,000 Mules," with research by Catherine Engelbrecht and Gregg Phillips of True the Vote, by itself has shown the 2020 presidential election was stolen.

Before ranting that "Mules" was debunked, one needs to read the book version which lays out in careful detail the method and math of how illegal ballots were used to flip the election in five key states. The book, which followed the original documentary film release, also shoots holes in the debunking attempts.

In case you're not familiar, the term "mule" comes from drug trafficking in which someone is paid to deliver an illegal product on behalf of someone else.

True the Vote used cell phone tracking data to identify the activity of people in Georgia, Arizona, Wisconsin, Michigan, and Pennsylvania who made numerous visits to ballot drop boxes after having also visited "stash houses" to apparently pick up ballots. Many of the multiple drop box visits occurred in the middle of the night.

Right off the bat, the question arises why someone with a valid vote, even if he/she delivered it at 3 a.m., would have a purpose to go to several other drop boxes. This pattern of overnight drop box visits by the mules with handfuls of ballots was backed up by video confirmation where it was available. States were required to have video surveillance of the drop boxes, but it was sporadic at best.

The number 2,000 comes from the most active offenders; widening the criteria a bit identified at least 54,651 mules.

You need to read the book and view the film to appreciate the full details and impact.

Separately, Seth Keshel, a former Army captain of military intelligence, provides his own analysis identifying 74 mule rings, including two in Minnesota.[4]

All of that is before we get to the censorship and financial influence of social media and Big Tech companies, which is another long, detailed story. The recently released "Twitter Files" showed everyone how the government and Big Tech conspired to influence the election, among other things. Mark Zuckerberg put millions into tainting the election process, and his Facebook/Meta manipulated search results and censored so-called "misinformation."[5] Other tech companies appear just as complicit.

There are so many weaknesses in our election process that come into view when one pays attention.

"Ballot harvesting" is when someone collects absentee or mail-in ballots from others and delivers them. This is legal in some states, including Minnesota where an agent is allowed to handle ballots for up to three other people, although that limit isn't enforced.[6]

"Ballot trafficking" is when there is

payment involved, either for someone to vote for a specific candidate, or make deliveries of valid or phony ballots for a fee. It is NEVER allowed that any kind of payment can be involved in the voting process.

In many ballot trafficking situations, fraudsters prey on the most vulnerable: the poor, elderly, those whose primary language is not English, the homeless. Often some aid or assistance may be provided to them in exchange for a "Sign here, and we'll take care of your ballot for you."

Voting at home

The largest hole in election security is the early voting and mail-in methods. Across the nation, states used the cover of COVID fear to invoke emergency powers and turn our election processes into something never seen before.

When you vote in person at your precinct, there is a formal supervised process. You check in (even without ID), receive your ballot, proceed to a private booth and mark your choices, then turn in your completed ballot, and receive a red "I Voted" sticker. In this environment, there is little opportunity to be unduly influenced or do something illegal.

Contrast that with letting people vote in their homes in the name of making it "easy."

This is like a teacher assigning a take-home test, but allowing anyone to return it for multiple students. Do you think there might be some cheating?

Even the witness signature requirement is weak. How valid is the signature verification process when hundreds of thousands of ballots must be processed on the receiving end?

In Michigan, Secretary of State Jocelyn Benson directed that deviations in signatures should be overlooked, with doubts resolved in favor of inclusion and counting the ballots. That was later ruled invalid by a judge, but too late to affect the election results.[7]

It's also important to note, as Sebastian Gorka points out, that once phony or illegally handled ballots are placed into the stream with legitimate votes, there is no longer any way to identify or remove them. The outer envelopes carry confirming information, but ballots are anonymous.

Voter rolls

Cheaters are skilled at identifying people who are on the voter rolls but unlikely to vote (possibly dead) and request absentee ballots on their behalf.

There are cases where people in nursing homes or dementia units had nearly 100 percent turnout, due to someone who "helped" them by making sure they were registered, received their ballot, and of course, voted.

Another tactic is "cloning" in which an additional voter registration is created at someone's second property address. If you own a cabin, was a vote cast there in your name without you knowing it?

Even worse is when ballots are mailed to everyone on the list. For those who know where to look, such as college campuses where students have long moved away but their names and addresses remain on the rolls, collecting those ballots is easy picking.

Seth Keshel nicely describes the need for clean, accurate voter rolls in another piece.[8]

To do it right would take starting over and having legal voters re-register. It would be a major undertaking, but how else can we remove the dead, illegal aliens, duplicates, and phantoms from being part of our election process?

You have to make an appointment to see a doctor, a reservation to eat at certain restaurants, and buy a ticket to go to a ball game or concert. Why not confirm your intention for something as crucial as voting with validated registration?

Is this making it easy to vote? No.

Is it voter suppression? Heck, no!

Everyone who is eligible is encouraged to vote, but is also expected to put some effort into it.

Government doesn't go out of its way to make any other tasks "easy." Try getting a permit for something. So why should the all-important act of voting be sacrificed?

Remember that voting is a right but also a responsibility. The people we elect are given the power to make the rules we live by, to determine what we pay in taxes, and to operate (or abuse) the system our country runs on.

In American Thinker, Jay Valentine describes how an election manager can change the zip codes on thousands of voter records before mailing out ballots, which then are returned as undeliverable.[9]

After they're collected, the zip codes are restored. The National Change of Address Database doesn't pick up the switch that quickly, and the affected citizens continued to receive all their other mail without knowing the difference.

Consider this: if you move even a few miles, you're likely in a new precinct, but your name remains in the previous voter roll until corrected. If a ballot is mailed to your old address, it's potentially available for someone to hijack.

Just in our family, I can think of a couple situations where it would have been simple to vote in two locations – previous and current addresses. They didn't, of course, but if they had, would anyone have bothered or been able to figure it out?

Machines

There's an argument about who originally said something to the effect of "Whoever counts the votes is who wins." Regardless of who said it first, the truth of it stings.

Writing on Substack, Erik van Mechelen of Midwest Seeds goes into brilliant detail on the vulnerability of electronic voting equipment. His book "[S]elections in Minnesota" is a must-

read.[10]

It boils down to two gaping holes of concern when we feed our ballot into a machine: Internet connectivity and the programming of the tabulator.

It's only common sense that any equipment that can be accessed remotely is vulnerable in these days of hacking. Such hacking could be by the big bad Russians, or more likely, it's an intentional back door for those in the fraud business.

We'll start in the hot spot of Antrim County, Michigan, where a 4G wireless modem was found in a vote tabulator.[11]

By the way, van Mechelen reports that 65 Minnesota counties use that same model.

Antrim County is also famous for confirmed errors by the voting equipment[12] as well as being the example engineer Jeff Lenberg used in demonstrating on video how easy it is for a programmer to flip votes from one candidate to another while making the machine's vote reports match, even though the original paper ballots intended something else.[13]

Next we go to Mesa County, Colorado, the center of the documentary "[S] election Code."[14] This film highlights Elections Clerk and Recorder Tina Peters, who was certain she was running a flawless election process until . . .

the Grand Junction city council election of April 2021.

Grand Junction historically has been a two-thirds conservative community, so it was surprising, to say the least, when four challengers all were victorious over the conservative candidates.

The stunning moment of truth for Peters was when she realized that those underdogs knew they had won and even knew the margin of victory half an hour BEFORE the election officials had completed their work and announced results!

This began the exposing of how the machines are programmed. See the three

Mesa County Reports.[15]

As required by law, Peters had backed up election records, although she had to go beyond help from her own county IT department to do so. After a vendor installed a software update that was termed a "trusted build," a comparison of the before and after records revealed the changes and deletions that the update made.

It's naive to think that could be the only place suspicious programming was used in electronic voting equipment. It's just the best-known one.

van Mechelen writes in depth about Cast Vote Records (CVR). Simply, these are image captures of each ballot that goes through a machine, which "allow the machines to tell on themselves," he says. Of course, it would also allow them to prove their legitimacy, if used transparently.

That leads to several more curious questions.

First, he notes that machines have an on/off setting for recording the Cast Vote Records, as documented in an operator's manual. Why would it ever be turned off, since that's the function that can provide validation?

Next, try asking for the Cast Vote Records from your county elections department through a Freedom of Information (FOI) request. The typical responses, he explains, are: "we don't have them, we don't have to create them, and/or we don't have to give them to you."[16]

This is consistent with the response to my FOI request for CVRs in Hennepin County for the November 2022 election: "Hennepin County did not produce a Cast Vote Record for the 2022 election. Ballots and therefore ballot images are not available for public inspection per Minnesota Statute 204B.40."

Only a minuscule amount of CVRs have been publicly obtained in Minnesota so far, however, Rhode Island was able to produce CVRs for its entire state.[17]

In a letter to Crow Wing County in early 2022, Steve Simon stated the system "worked as it was designed" while in effect advising the county not to follow through on requests for CVRs.[18] Thus, in context, his message appears to be that the system is designed to keep details hidden from citizens. Why?

Poor leadership

That leads to the fourth, and largest problem of all: those in positions of authority who refuse to act to clean up the system, or intentionally find ways to make it weaker.

This includes elected officials, appointed workers, judges, and law enforcement – who use their power to advance their political leanings through actions or by not acting. Not everyone, of course, but enough to keep the systemic fraud going.

As shown in Mesa County, election workers can follow the book and unknowingly perpetuate fraud. Others may smell a rat but stay silent out of fear of retaliation.

Hans vans Spakovsky, former commissioner at the Federal Election Commission, explained the strategy of an activist group suing a complicit state official. Instead of defending the laws in place, the official agrees to a settlement waiving or changing election law requirements.

That certainly looks to be the situation in 2020 when Steve Simon settled two cases that removed witness requirements and extended deadlines.[19]

Statistics

If you're not shaking your head in disgust yet, let's look at some more statistical data.

• Wisconsin: in Madison, there were 341 registered voters at a 15-unit apartment building; 385 registered voters at a 184-bed care center; and 323 registered voters at an address at which the building was demolished in 2018.[20]

• Colorado: 5,500 dead people and

25,000 non-residents voted.[21]

• Michigan: census data shows 7.6 million residents of legal voting age, but the state has 8.1 million registered voters.[22]

• Florida: a resident received three voter registration cards in the mail with names of people he didn't know, two of whom were dead.[23]

• Pennsylvania: the number of ballots cast was 202,377 higher than the number of people who voted.[24]

• Arizona: the cities of Topawa and Sells had ratios of voters to voting age population of 158% and 200% respectively.[25]

• Arizona, 2022: from April to October, a net 225,171 "inactive" voters were added to the voter registration records.[26]

• In the documentary "Standing in the Gap," Joe Oltmann points out there were 166 million registered voters in 2020 and 155 million votes cast, a 93% turnout which he describes as a "probability next to zero." For comparison, the last Super Bowl had 112 million viewers. Are that many people more interested in elections than football?

It goes on and on and . . .

The website www.2020electionirregularities.com describes many more cases of statistical anomalies, suspicious conduct, reports on voting machines and mail-in ballots, etc. Go see for yourself, but allow plenty of time.

Let's highlight a Minnesota reference: in 2020, about 700,000 absentee ballots were not connected to a voter in the statewide voter registration system (SVRS) 25 days after the election, and five days AFTER the state canvassing board certified the results.[27]

And in 2022, it happened again: two weeks after the election, only 317,372 of 657,575 accepted absentee ballots, 48%, were aligned with a voter in the SVRS.[28]

Further, a citizen volunteer group of mathematicians, scientists, IT veterans, and engineers compiled a statistical vote analysis of the 2020 presidential election in 14 states, including Minnesota, specifically looking at the "vote dumps" – instances in which one candidate received an abnormally large amount of votes in a short period.[29]

In every case, the dumps favored Biden. Minnesota's recorded a net advantage 113,755 votes for Biden, which they assessed to be a probability of 1 in 10-to-the-81st-power.

All 14 states studied had something similar, some of them multiple dumps. For reference, they determined a probability of 1 in 10,000,000,000,000,000, 000,000,000,000,000,000,000,000 ,000,000,000,000,000 (10-to-the-58th-power) is equivalent to being dealt 10 royal flushes in a row.

Their report does not attempt to uncover the why or how these vote spikes occurred, but simply documents that they did.

Solutions?

Seth Keshel provides a 10-point plan for restoring true election integrity:[30]

1. clean out the voter rolls

2. ban all electronic election equipment

3. voter ID with paper ballots only

4. ban mail-in voting (exception for overseas military and disabled)

5. ban early voting

6. drastically smaller precincts

7. ban ballot harvesting

8. election day is a holiday

9. new reporting requirements for transparency

10. heavy prison sentences for all who commit fraud

Keshel points out that a key piece is that four of them can realistically be dealt with at the county level. Given who is in charge in state offices and the unlikelihood of them making any meaningful improvements, citizens need to take up the fight at the COUNTY level, he advises.

Counties are responsible for certifying their election results, and have some say in how elections are conducted to make certain their results are valid.

The four tasks for counties are making the voter registration rolls accurate, eliminating machines, refusing drop boxes for harvesting, and opening the system for public inspection.[31] For its 2022 primary election, Otero County, NM, removed drop boxes and machines and went to hand-counting ballots.[32]

Keshel is developing an organization of citizens to work on restoring election integrity from the ground up. For more information to become involved, see the link in footnote 31.

Quoted in "[S]elections in Minnesota," Jeffrey O'Donnell nails it: "If Americans' votes are to be recorded and counted by machines, every aspect of those machines' operation, configuration, and data must be recorded, immediately available at no cost or administrative burden to citizens and their independent examiners, and confirmed 100% accurate through that independent verification. The absence or shortfall of any of those three imperatives (recorded, available, and independently verified) should immediately cause the public to distrust both the purported results from those machines, and also anyone who insists that they accept those results."

I support that standard for those in charge of elections: provide all the data, easily and promptly, and if it's verifiable, all the "election deniers" will be quickly silenced. Anything less invites – no, requires – suspicion, deservedly so.

So much for "no evidence."

Footnotes in are in Appendix 1 on page 188. The original publication at bit.ly/knowevidence contains live links.

Over the next winter, I took a different angle on the crisis issue of election fraud. Having obtained Capt. Seth Keshel's Precinct Mapping Project reports for our local counties, I spent numerous hours on my own time researching population and voting history, and compiling it into tables for each of the local precincts that Keshel identified as problem areas.

From there, I sought responses from election officials in the counties, precincts that were affected, and the secretary of state's office.

I put together an extensive news story including all the data and responses. It was excellent journalism, if I say so myself – very well balanced so readers could judge for themselves. It didn't make it into the printed newspaper. Other leaders in our company were afraid there would be too much negative reaction.

I understood and had my own concern. It would be similar to discussing sensitive topics like domestic abuse, addiction, infidelity, etc.; it's one thing to speak generally, but if it is occurring in your family, the subject becomes taboo.

We negotiated to publish it online only to get a feel for responses first. There was very little reaction, which I attribute to a combination of being only online and the fair balance of the article – each point of view was so well-represented, it would have been difficult to complain. It also went to a level of detail that perhaps many people were unwilling to study.

After that, we had so many other things needing immediate attention that exposing election fraud got pushed down on the to-do list.

The piece would have taken about two and a half newspaper pages in its entirety. To boil it down to a single statistical example, Keshel estimated 7,930 of Wright County's votes in the 2020 presidential election were likely fraudulent. His determination considered registered voters, incumbent vote comparisons, and historical voting patterns and trends.

Keshel's calculation was not based on voter turnout, but a look at turnout helped validate his conclusion. In the previous three elections, Wright County's turnout was 71%, 70%, and 69%. In 2020, it jumped to 76% but if you removed 7,930 votes, turnout would have been 69% – right in line with normal patterns.

It takes a deep dive into the data to fully appreciate the significance of election fraud. The original story is online at **bit.ly/electionWCM** (case sensitive). I had an accompanying column, which is much shorter and gives a good taste of the flavor, reprinted here:

Commentary: follow-up questions from election fraud story

March 15, 2024 • West Carver News

If someone says he sees smoke near your house, do you want to check if there's a fire?

This week, we present an extensive report about the topic of election fraud reaching into our local counties.

Let's get right to the big question: why would you publish such a thing?

We understand some of you are unhappy, even offended, that we give so much attention to the topic of election fraud. It is an unpopular subject, one that we'd prefer didn't exist.

But does election fraud exist? Is there illegal drug trade in our area? How about financial scams? Less likely but not impossible are human trafficking, child porn exchanges, counterfeiting, money laundering, and fencing stolen goods.

All of those involve a coordinated interaction for some type of personal benefit, while sharing a common trait of preferring not to be noticed. Can we honestly say "That doesn't happen here."?

We have the rare opportunity to take a serious national issue and incorporate it with local data so you as citizens can see for yourselves and make your own judgment.

Reporting this is a daunting task, one that many media outlets seem to avoid, for whatever reason. But society is best served when there can be open, public discussions about the difficult topics. We need to think about them and talk about them if there is to be any hope of making things better.

Based on historical patterns, a national organization is stating that there seem to be parts of our local area that have been affected by election fraud. Like a medical lab test that gives results outside of an expected normal range, it is a signal that, hmmmm, we probably ought to look closer.

We strove to present a balanced report in good old "he said, she said" fashion.

There's a national organization, the Precinct Mapping Project (PMP), that says election fraud probably occurred in our area. Local election officials vouch that their results and procedures are true and valid.

Might they both be right, at least to some degree? All along, we did not and do not claim any wrongdoing locally. PMP says it appears ballot harvesting activity in Hennepin County spilled into areas of our counties.

Is it possible, or even probable, that fraud can be accomplished within the framework of the current election system, even when local officials follow the laws and procedures flawlessly?

We compiled data tables of population and voting history for each of the local precincts that were called into question. It's a grueling amount of information, but it allows you to focus right on your home area to see if you agree or disagree with what they're talking about.

We ask that you don't just swallow the idea of fraud, but also don't just dismiss it. Please take the time to examine the concept and data to form your own opinion about its accuracy and impact.

Then let's have that open, public discussion – preferably in a respectful manner aimed at finding solutions, not making further enemies.

Here are a few more questions:

• How can elections be improved so everyone can be confident in the validity and trust the reported results?

• How can voting be reasonably accessible to those eligible to vote, yet tightly restricted to only those?

• What are the costs?

• What can be done in time for this year's election cycle?

• What actions can be taken at the county level to protect our votes from potential outside manipulation?

• And the most important question of all: what do YOU think?

19
Columns for Fun

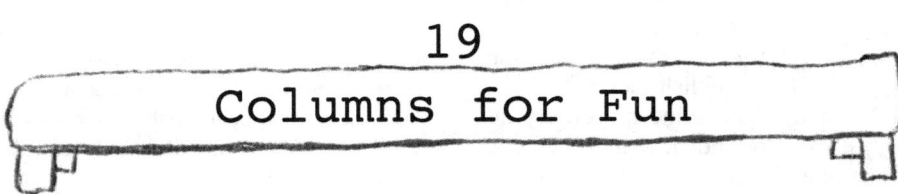

Okay, enough of the heavy stuff, so let's wrap this up with a few columns on lighter topics. These are some of my favorites.

The perils of watermelon selection
Aug. 19, 2022 • Herald Journal newspapers

On a recent routine shopping trip, we came across one of those large cardboard boxes full of watermelons that are put in place with a forklift. A melon seemed like a nice summertime treat, so we decided to get one.

I waited patiently while my wife studiously did the knock test on several melons to identify which was the ripest, most delicious one to choose.

She settled on one at the bottom of the front corner of the partially full container. Then it was my turn to do the lifting.

I had to move one other watermelon out of the way to clear the path.

Then I suddenly burst out laughing as I realized what was happening: the distance over the side of the cardboard box and the weight of the chosen melon combined to reach the point where my balance was in jeopardy.

I almost – emphasis on almost – fell into the watermelon box.

I stopped to regroup, both physically and mentally; then successfully retrieved the object of our desire, and we were on our way.

On the way home, though, we enjoyed even bigger laughs, recalling what might have been, had I actually fallen in.

We would have wanted to track down the store manager and ask to see the surveillance video, and even get a copy of it to post on social media. It would have been a viral hit.

I also knew that beyond the falling in, the process of getting out would have been even more hilarious.

We wondered about what other shoppers and store employees might have thought. Would it have been something unique, or do old people tumble into the watermelon bins a couple times a week? "Oh, it's just another one."

By the way, the melon was delicious. It would have been worth it.

Camping revisited

Sept. 1, 2023 • Herald Journal newspapers

Last fall on a whim, we decided to pull our tent out of storage and see what shape it was in.

It had been, as best as we could figure, at least 15 years since we had used it. Maybe it was even 20 or 25 years.

We used to camp quite a bit. Then children entered the picture. Then there were more of them. Then they got bigger. Eventually camping fell by the wayside as there were plenty of other activities to do, both optional and required.

Now with an empty nest, we can revisit some memories from the past.

I'm talking about real camping – in a tent. Not driving a living room on wheels into the woods and claiming to be outdoors.

The enjoyment of tent camping is very much dependent on weather conditions. I concede that motor home camping offers insurance against crappy weather. Unless you're willing to wait until the last minute and take whatever campsite might be left, reserving a camping spot ahead of time is a gamble with the weather.

Since our tent passed inspection, we decided to give it a go for a one-night outing to Crow Wing State Park before we had to be back home for another obligation.

The weather was perfect. There were no bugs. This was fun!

We were hooked again, so the next weekend we tried to dodge the rain forecasts by heading to Camden State Park in southwestern Minnesota. Although we probably got less rain than the rest of the state, it was far from dry.

Still, we vowed to do it again this year when spring rolled around.

Of course, this spring was tardy, and every weekend was lousy weather until there was finally one with a good forecast – but we had other commitments.

By the time we did get to camp, in June, the mosquitoes at St. Croix State Park were fully grown and angry. Three weeks later, we tried again at Lake Shetek, only to be awakened by early morning thunderstorms and wind gusts.

For an August trip, we booked three weeknights at Sibley State Park well in advance (see gamble above). As we packed in light rain and left in drizzle, two weather apps and Ken Barlow all assured us that clearing was just a couple hours away.

We hit the weather jackpot: not another drop of rain, plus moderate temperatures for what could very well have been the dog days of summer.

Often, days go disappointingly slow for me, but these flew by quickly as we hiked, kayaked, chopped kindling, prepared and ate meals, peacefully stared at campfires, and simply enjoyed the camping lifestyle. Again, a special thanks to whoever controls the weather.

The only thing left undone was making a reservation for the next outing.

One thing about camping is that it forces you to live at a slower pace, which is the beauty of it.

Even morning coffee involves a process of building a small fire to heat water. I had joked about getting a campsite with electricity and taking our microwave and coffee maker along, but we didn't do that (yet).

We wouldn't have room anyway. I was reintroduced to how many supplies and how much equipment is needed, just for two people for a couple days. That may have something to do with why we gave it up previously.

Several times while gathering and packing all the items, I reminded myself that those steps are part of the experience as well, and that made it more enjoyable.

It's not supposed to be quick and easy. You don't hurry up and rush into the wilderness to slow down and relax.

I recall some gorgeous fall weekends from years ago with sunny days and cool evenings, the kind that drew us back to try again.

We're in the mode of getting out there while we're still physically able to. No sense in saving retirement money for years and years so that someday . . . well, we can't any more.

Fall is here and it's time to go. See you in the woods?

Camping tips

Those of you who are experienced or hard-core campers probably know this already, but here are a few things we've learned recently:

• A tripod grill is a valuable tool that's easy to transport and flexible for various types of cooking. Lesson: spend the money to get a good one that is adjustable both with the legs and the chain.

• A few years ago, we stayed at a resort that provided a "Kindling Cracker." When we resumed camping, this quickly went on my Fathers' Day/birthday wish list. It's a sturdy metal splitter in which you pound the wood down to make pieces as small as you want instead of attacking it with a hatchet. Much easier and safer! See more at kindlingcracker.com

• If you're a fan of state parks, especially trails, the Avenza Maps app is a great tool. Download the state park map you're visiting; then the app uses your phone's location services to keep track of where you are. It's especially handy to use on a trail. If you're not sure which way to go at a crossing, move about 50 feet and the app will show if that's the direction you really wanted. More info at mndnr.gov/geopdf

Everyone likes a good recipe

July 2023 • Herald Journal/Senior Connections

In a recent conversation, I was asked if I'm a good cook.

After thoughtful consideration, the answer was that I'm not "good," but I certainly could survive.

I don't mind working in the kitchen once in a while. The payoff is that, except for the worst failures, the reward for the effort is having something to eat.

My style of cooking is to take an easy approach.

For example, my favorite cheesy potatoes recipe needs just five ingredients: frozen hashbrowns, chopped onion, cream of mushroom soup, sour cream, and grated cheese. Mix together and then bake until heated through but not burnt. The original recipe prescribes exact proportions but sometimes I wing it.

I have success with the no-measure method in some cases, like egg salad. Combine chopped celery, green onions, some mustard, relish, lemon juice, pepper, celery seed, mayo, and of course, hard-boiled eggs.

It also works great for potato salad. Just add boiled, cubed potatoes to the above.

Similarly, I used to make what I called "Informal Meatloaf." There's no recipe. Just use the ingredients you think belong in it in whatever proportion seems adequate. Even more surprising, that turned out pretty good too.

I'm also a sucker for trying to imitate foods either from an experience or ones I hear about.

Several years ago, Denny's restaurants advertised an ice cream sundae topped with maple syrup and bacon. I never had theirs, but made it at home, and it was great! I also found that maple syrup makes a very nice topping for ice cream without the bacon. Give it a try if you haven't.

A little more extreme, there was a minor league baseball park that once served cheeseburgers on Krispy Kreme doughnuts. Again, I didn't taste the original, only my copycat attempt. The first few bites were sort of good, but it didn't qualify for the make-again list.

Continuing with baseball references, a couple years ago at the Field of Dreams game, there was a concession based on the "baseball, hot dogs, apple pie, and Chevrolet" theme. At its core, it was a hot dog served in an elaborate apple pie dish. For my home version, I cheated and just stuck a hot dog into one of those single-serving apple snack pies from the grocery store. It was worth a try to find out, but not to repeat.

Getting to more formal recipes, there are a couple of traditional family favorites.

For years, my in-laws would gather for chive dumplings on Mothers' Day, an occasion that fit nicely both for a visit and when chives would be ready in spring. It was a large-scale production that took all afternoon to prepare in order to serve a few dozen people. Here it is, multiply as necessary:

Chive Dumplings
Chives
1/2 to 11/2 stick butter
Dried loaf of bread
13 eggs
8 Tblsp. water
1/2 tsp. baking powder
1/2 tsp. salt
6 C. flour
Brown chives in butter or margarine; add diced bread, then 5 eggs. Mix dough (remaining eggs, water, dry ingredients). Divide into 4 portions and roll flat, cut into triangles. Add filling and pinch shut. Boil in water, add butter or margarine, season to taste.

From my side of the family, one of my favorites was my grandma's crullers.

This was simply dough rolled out thin, then deep fried and covered with sugar. I still like to binge on this once every year or two. They are best going from pan to sugar to mouth in quick succession.

Crullers
2 eggs or 4 egg yolks
1/2 tsp. salt
1 eggshell water
flour
Make dough quite stiff like for noodles. If you use 4 yolks, use 2 shells of water. Roll out dough, cut in pieces, and deep fry. Sprinkle with sugar immediately.

A few years ago, I stumbled across a homemade salad dressing in an old-time recipe book, and of course, I had to give it a try. It was good enough that I merged it with another recipe, and then through several more attempts, refined it further into what has become a staple in our house.

For this one, I do follow specific proportions. Warning: it has a bit of kick, so if you don't prefer hot stuff, you might want to back off on the cayenne pepper.

Homemade Salad Dressing
1 can tomato soup
1/4 C. sugar
1/2 C. veg oil
2/3 C. vinegar
1/2 tsp. garlic powder
1/2 tsp. onion powder
1/2 tsp. cayenne
1 1/2 tsp. celery seed
Mix all together and shake well.

Finally, there is my all-time favorite self-made recipe.

When we were first married, my wife was in a bowling league every other week. The girls would usually get their food during that outing. That meant that if I desired to eat, I was left to fend for myself. Thus, "Bowling Hotdish" was born out of sheer necessity.

As you would expect, it was based on an imitation of something else. At the time, Campbell's had a soup called Noodles and Ground Beef, which is just what it sounds like, with a tomato-based sauce. Through a few trials, I came up with something better.

And so, dear readers, I share with you the absolute very best hotdish you will ever find anytime, anywhere. You never know, maybe they will serve it at my funeral luncheon.

Bowling Hotdish®
2 lb. elbow macaroni
2 lb. hamburger
1 onion, chopped
2 28-oz. cans tomatoes
1 can tomato soup
1 to 2 C. ketchup
1/2 C. oregano (yes, that much)
Salt
Pepper
Cook macaroni according to package directions. Brown hamburger with onion and drain. Combine all ingredients including juice from canned tomatoes. Use enough ketchup to give it a good consistency. Salt and pepper to taste. Heat through, and this can be served immediately, but the flavor is even better from simmering. Makes quite a few servings plus some great leftovers.

It's about time

Dec. 31, 2021 • Herald Journal/Senior Connections

The intricacies of the calendar often amaze me.

As we know, the calendar is a tool to try to measure time in relation to the earth's daily rotation, its revolution around the sun, and the moon's revolution around the earth.

Also as we know, there are 365 days in a year, split into 52 weeks.

But wait: 52 x 7 is only 364 days! There is one more day slipped in there somewhere, two in leap year.

I first became aware of this long ago in budgeting for a weekly newspaper when, lo and behold, one year we had 53 publication days.

For example, for a newspaper published on Fridays, we know there are four months every year that contain five Fridays. This matters on both the revenue and expense sides.

But once in a while that extra day falls on Friday, making 53. However, it's not once every seven years. Leap year changes when the days fall, so it's a very unusual pattern of how often it occurs.

I've never put the effort into figuring out what the pattern is; I just know to watch for it.

Then there are payday cycles.

If you get paid every other week, you know there are 26 periods in a year. That makes for some interesting withholding calculations on things like insurance that are monthly amounts divided into two-week periods.

Some companies make that calculation. Others simply withhold twice a month and skip the two instances a year when there are three paydays in a month.

A few years ago, our company switched to a twice-a-month pay cycle instead of every two weeks. This brought to light some other calendar quirks.

Most pay periods contain 11 working days, but a few are 10 days and a few are 12 days.

Offhand, that doesn't seem like a big deal, but when you translate a 9 percent variance down to take-home pay, it becomes quite noticeable. We learned to point this out to new employees to avoid unhappiness later.

It is even more important when the second half of February ends up with only nine working days.

That brings together two cycles conspiring against an individual: your March payments are due after the shortest month of the year at the same time you're getting the smallest paycheck of the year.

Lenders have accommodated for these variances by charging interest on a daily basis. To my knowledge, they haven't yet gotten to the point of adjusting for Daylight Saving Time changes when certain days are 23 or 25 hours.

As for months, according to my research (everything on the internet is true, right?), the original concept was that each quarter would have two 30-day months and one 31-day month. Then politicians got involved, and you can imagine where things went from there.

Reportedly, Julius Caeser took a day from February and placed it in the month of July he named after himself. Then Augustus Caeser did the same thing with his namesake month. Sorry, February, you can't beat the Roman empire.

In my studies, the piece of trivia that I was most surprised to learn is how the leap year formula really works.

It's not just every four years. If the year can be evenly divided by 100, it is not a leap year, unless it can be evenly divided by 400.

Thus, year 2000 was a leap year. (And the toilets still flushed properly.)

Since we missed 1900 and most of us won't make it to 2100, this fun fact becomes sort of irrelevant, at least for the time being.

Throughout history, there have been a number of calendar adjustments in consideration of equinoxes, politics, and general accuracy, not to mention Joshua 10:12-14.

Currently, our calendar is deemed accurate to within one day for every 3,236 years, so we should be good for a while yet.

20
Conclusion

Well, folks, we've reached the point that is best described in one of my favorite lines I heard in a movie and is attributed to Richard Paul Evans:

"A story is never over. The author just quits telling it."

Appendix 1

Footnotes for 'Know Evidence' column, page 171

1. Peter Navarro, "The Immaculate Deception: Six Key Dimensions of Election Irregularities:" 3. https://www.scribd.com/document/488495896/Navarro-Report#

2. https://www.heritage.org/voterfraud

3. Dinesh D'Souza, 2,000 Mules (book version): 35-36

4. Seth Keshel, "74 Harvesting and Mule Rings: Where They Were, How They Did It, And The Impact - Our Work is Now Corroborated," https://skeshel.substack.com/p/74-harvesting-and-mule-rings-where

5. 2,000 Mules: 10, 114

6. Newsweek, "What Project Veritas Is Claiming About Ilhan Omar and Illegal Ballot Harvesting," https://www.newsweek.com/project-veritas-ilhan-omar-illegal-ballot-harvesting-1534555

7. 2,000 Mules: 94

8. Keshel, "Point One To True Election Integrity: Clean Out the Voter Rolls," https://skeshel.substack.com/p/point-one-to-true-election-integrity

9. Jay Valentine, American Thinker, "Here's How They Did it: Real-time Election Fraud," https://www.americanthinker.com/articles/2022/11/heres_how_they_did_it_realtime_election_fraud.html

10. Erik van Mechelen, [S]elections in Minnesota: an Introduction to How Machines Controlled 2020 and Why We Must Return to Hand Counting Paper Ballots, https://leanpub.com/sim2020/

11. [S]elections in Minnesota: 31

12. "Antrim Michigan Forensics Report," https://www.depernolaw.com/uploads/2/7/0/2/27029178/antrim_michigan_forensics_report_%5B121320%5D_v2_%5Bredacted%5D.pdf

13. "Hacking Democracy – Antrim County, MI Edition," https://rumble.com/vgi89t-hacking-democracy-antrim-county-mi-edition.html

14. [S]election Code, https://selectioncode.com/

15. "Mesa County Reports 1, 2, and 3," https://frankspeech.com/article/mesa-county-voting-system-forensic-examination-and-analysis-reports-1-2-and-3

16. van Mechelen, "How to Use Public Data Requests to Access Public Records for Better Decision Making (And to Help Government Where Current Processes Do Not Account for Fundamental Weaknesses in Overall Transparency)," https://erikvanmechelen.substack.com/p/how-to-use-public-data-requests-to

17. [S]elections in Minnesota: 73

18. van Mechelen, "Cast Vote Record Cover Up in Minnesota - Part 1," https://erikvan-mechelen.substack.com/p/cast-vote-record-cover-up-in-minnesota

19. Peter Callaghan on MinnPost, "Secretary of state agrees to deal on absentee ballots; Republicans cry foul," https://www.minnpost.com/state-government/2020/06/secretary-of-state-agrees-to-deal-on-absentee-ballots-republicans-cry-foul/; and Willis Krumholz on Alpha News, "Steve Simon is attempting to turn Minnesota's absentee ballots into mail in ballots," https://alphanews.org/steve-simon-is-attempting-to-turn-minnesotas-absentee-ballots-into-mail-in-ballots/

20. Keshel, "Clean Out the Voter Rolls"

21. [S]election Code

*22. "Suspicious Voter Registration Data," https://2020electionirregularities.com/suspicious-conduct/suspicious-voter-registration-data/

23. Miami Herald, "Voter Fraud: Dead Republicans come back as Democrats," https://www.gopusa.com/voter-fraud-dead-republicans-come-back-as-democrats/

*24. State Lawmakers: "Pennsylvania Has 202,377 More Ballots Cast Than Voters Who Voted," https://2020electionirregularities.com/statistical-anomalies/state-lawmakers-pennsylvania-has-202377-more-ballots-cast-than-voters-who-voted/

*25. Palmieri Report, "Highlights From PIMA County Election Integrity Hearing," https://thepalmierireport.com/highlights-from-pima-county-election-integrity-hearing/

26. World Tribune, "Maricopa lawsuit reveals injection of 225,171 'inactive' voters just before midterms," https://www.worldtribune.com/maricopa-lawsuit-reveals-injection-of-225171-inactive-voters-just-before-midterms/

27. [S]elections in Minnesota: 67

28. van Mechelen, "2022 MN Absentee Data Absent," https://erikvanmechelen.substack.com/p/2022-mn-absentee-data-absent

29. The Thinking Conservative, "2020 Presidential Election Startling Vote Spikes," https://www.thethinkingconservative.com/wp-content/uploads/2021/01/Vote_Dumps_Report_1-6.pdf

30. Keshel, "The Ten Points to True Election Integrity: An Epilogue," https://skeshel.substack.com/p/the-ten-points-to-true-election-integrity

31. Keshel, "Four for the Election Integrity Core: Phase I," https://skeshel.substack.com/p/four-for-the-election-integrity-core

32. The Paper (ABQ News), "Otero County Commission Votes to Remove Voting Machines and Ballot Boxes," https://abq.news/2022/06/otero-county-commission-votes-to-remove-voting-machines-and-ballot-boxes/

*Although valid at publication of the column, certain links referenced are now inoperable.

Appendix 2

What makes a good newspaper?
Press ethics handout by J. Brent Norlem, St. Cloud State University

The following are excerpts from a published preliminary report (Editor and Publisher magazine, June 9, 1962) by a Code of Ethics Criteria Committee of the Associated Press Managing Editors Association. After considerable study over an 18-month period, this committee of managing editors reports that integrity, accuracy, responsibility, and leadership are the criteria of a good newspaper.

Integrity
• Maintain vigorous standards of honesty and fair play in the selection and editing of its content as well as in all relations with news sources and the public.
• Deal dispassionately with controversial subjects and treat disputed issues with impartiality.
• Practice humility and tolerance in the face of honest conflicting opinions and disagreement.
• Provide a forum for the exchange of pertinent comment and criticism, especially if it is in conflict with the newspaper's editorial point of view.
• Label its own editorial view or expressions of opinion.

Accuracy
• Exert maximum effort to print the truth in all news situations.
• Strive for completeness and objectivity.
• Guard against carelessness, bias, or distortion by either emphasis or omission.
• Correct promptly errors of fact for which the newspaper is responsible.

Responsibility
• Use mature and considered judgment in the public interest at all times.
• Select, edit, and display news on the basis of its significance and its genuine usefulness to the public.
• Edit news affecting public morals with candor and good taste and avoid an imbalance of sensational, preponderantly negative, or merely trivial news.
• Accent when possible a reasonable amount of news which illustrates the values of compassion, self-sacrifice, heroism, good citizenship, and patriotism.
• Clearly define sources of news, and tell the reader when competent sources cannot be identified.
• Respect rights of privacy.
• Instruct its staff members to conduct themselves with dignity and decorum.

Leadership
• Act with courage in serving the public.
• Stimulate and vigorously support public officials, private groups, and individuals in crusades and campaigns to increase the good works and eliminate the bad in the community.
• Help to protect all rights and privileges guaranteed by law.
• Serve as a constructive critic of government at all levels, providing leadership for necessary reforms or innovations, and exposing any misfeasance in office or any misuse of public power.
• Oppose demagogues and other selfish and unwholesome interests regardless of their size or influence.

Guide for a good newspaper
• A good newspaper should be guided in the publication of all material by a concern for the truth, the hallmark of freedom; by a concern for human decency and human betterment; and by a respect for the accepted standards of its own community.

Appendix 3

Recommended videos

Now that you're done reading, here are some key documentary videos that the corporate media avoids, thus validating their importance:

INJURIES FROM COVID VACCINES

Died Suddenly
https://rumble.com/v1wac7i-world-premier-died-suddenly.html
or search for "Died Suddenly" on Rumble.com

Anecdotals
https://www.anecdotalsmovie.com/

DOCUMENTATION OF ELECTION FRAUD

(S)election Code
https://selectioncode.com/

Let My People Go
https://rumble.com/v4l6byc-let-my-people-go-by-dr.-david-clements.html
or search for "Let My People Go" by David Clements on Rumble.com

GOVERNMENT AND MEDIA OUTRIGHT LIE TO PUSH A NARRATIVE

The Fall of Minneapolis
https://www.thefallofminneapolis.com/
(The George Floyd case)

About the Author

Winsted, 1978

- Silver Lake Leader, sports column, 1975-76, started while in high school
- Part-time at West Central Tribune, Willmar, sports dept., 1976-77
- Temporary reporter at Hutchinson Leader, 1976
- Redwood Gazette, Redwood Falls, regional reporter and girls sports, 1977-78
- Winsted Journal, reporter, 1978-1982
- Lake County News-Chronicle, Two Harbors, editor, 1982-1983
- Winsted Journal and Lester Prairie Journal, editor, 1983-1986
- Winsted Publishing (Winsted/Lester Prairie/ Howard Lake), general manager, 1986-2001
- Herald Journal Publishing, based in Winsted, general manager/minority owner, 2001-2021
- Herald Journal Publishing, no longer owner, continue as general manager, 2022-2024
- Continuing with Herald Journal Publishing in transition to new general manager

A few blocks west, 2024

Name Index

Revelation 21:1–4